Red Dwarf: Discovering the TV Series

Volume I: 1988–1993

Also by Tom Salinsky

Books

The Improv Handbook
with Deborah Frances-White, 2008

Best Pick: A Journey through Film History and the Academy Awards
with John Dorney and Jessica Regan, 2022

Star Trek: Discovering the TV Series
The Original Series, The Animated Series and The Next Generation
White Owl, 2024

Plays

Coalition
with Robert Khan, 2013

Brexit
with Robert Khan, 2018

Red Dwarf: Discovering the TV Series

Volume I: 1988–1993

A Complete and Unauthorised Guide to the Classic Comedy Show Onscreen and Behind the Scenes

Tom Salinsky

WHITE OWL

First published in Great Britain in 2024 by
White Owl
An imprint of Pen & Sword Books Limited
Yorkshire – Philadelphia

Copyright © Tom Salinsky 2024

ISBN 978 1 39903 494 4

The right of Tom Salinsky to be identified as Author of this Work has been asserted by him in accordance with the Copyright, Designs and Patents Act 1988.

A CIP catalogue record for this book is available from the British Library

All rights reserved. No part of this book may be reproduced or transmitted in any form or by any means, electronic or mechanical including photocopying, recording or by any information storage and retrieval system, without permission from the Publisher in writing.

Typeset by Mac Style
Printed in the UK by CPI Group (UK) Ltd, Croydon, CR0 4YY.

Pen & Sword Books Limited incorporates the imprints of After the Battle, Atlas, Archaeology, Aviation, Discovery, Family History, Fiction, History, Maritime, Military, Military Classics, Politics, Select, Transport, True Crime, Air World, Frontline Publishing, Leo Cooper, Remember When, Seaforth Publishing, The Praetorian Press, Wharncliffe Local History, Wharncliffe Transport, Wharncliffe True Crime and White Owl.

For a complete list of Pen & Sword titles please contact

PEN & SWORD BOOKS LIMITED
47 Church Street, Barnsley, South Yorkshire, S70 2AS, England
E-mail: enquiries@pen-and-sword.co.uk
Website: www.pen-and-sword.co.uk
or
PEN AND SWORD BOOKS
1950 Lawrence Rd, Havertown, PA 19083, USA
E-mail: uspen-and-sword@casematepublishers.com
Website: www.penandswordbooks.com

For Rob and Doug. Please don't be cross with me.
And, as ever, for Deborah, who puts up with so much smeg.

Disclaimer

This book is not authorised or endorsed by the BBC, UK TV, Grant Naylor Productions, or anyone else associated with the production of Red Dwarf. No infringement of any copyrights is intended.

Contents

Acknowledgements — viii
Notes — ix
Introduction — x

Part Zero: Shipwrecked and Comatose — 1

Part One: Steptoe in Space — 13
  Series I — 15
    The Making of Series I — 15
    Impressions of Series I — 23
  Series II — 37
    The Making of Series II — 37
    Impressions of Series II — 45
  Series III — 58
    The Making of Series III — 58
    Impressions of Series III — 71

Part Two: Boys from the Dwarf — 89
  Series IV — 91
    The Making of Series IV — 91
    Impressions of Series IV — 100
  Series V — 112
    The Making of Series V — 112
    Impressions of Series V — 121
  Series VI — 132
    The Making of Series VI — 132
    Impressions of Series VI — 140

Afterword — 154
Appendix: Series I–VI Rankings — 155
Index — 157

Acknowledgements

The author would like to thank…

Marc, Jonathan, Charlotte and everyone at Pen & Sword.

Victoria, Jessica and everyone at AM Heath.

Peter Ridsdale-Scott.

Louise North and everyone at the BBC Written Archive.

Everyone at the British Library.

Kate Hinckley, who tried and failed to find accurate ratings data for me.

Andy Holland for the pictures.

Notes

When referring to the television series, the words **Red Dwarf** are shown in **bold**. The words *Red Dwarf* are shown in italics when referring to the spaceship, as are the names of other spacecraft.

Titles of individual episodes are shown in *italics*, as are the names of other shows, movies, franchises and publications.

Statement about sources

Sources consulted include www.reddwarf.co.uk, www.ganymede.tv, www.robgrant.co.uk, www.dirtyfeed.org, *Stasis Leak* by Jane Killick, *The Red Dwarf Programme Guide* by Chris Howarth and Steve Lyons, *The Red Dwarf Smegazine*, Robert Llewellyn's *The Man in the Rubber Mask*, the script books *Primordial Soup* and *Son of Soup*, *The Garbage Pod*, the short-lived *Drive Room* online fanzine, as well as IMDb of course, and various back issues of *Broadcast*, *The Times* and *The Listener*. Episodes were watched on the official Blu-rays and DVDs, where commentaries and documentaries provided a wealth of useful information, and I viewed various discussions, watch-parties, convention appearances and interviews on YouTube, including Robert Llewellyn's *Carpool* and the *Red Dwarf Quarantine* series.

Author's note

Has any piece of television ever been made available to the public in more versions than *The End*? For my research on this project, I watched the transmitted version, the transmitted version with cast commentary, the transmitted version with commentary from Doug Naylor and Ed Bye, the remastered version, the remastered version with commentary from Ed Bye and colleagues, the first edit, the first edit with commentary from Rob and Doug, and the YouTube lockdown commentary with Rob, Ed Bye and Paul Jackson. You could probably read this whole book in the time that took me. The same material is also covered in comic strip form and in the first **Red Dwarf** novel. A Japanese dub is included on one of the releases, but I didn't think I would benefit greatly from watching that as well.

Introduction

I was there at the beginning. February 1988.

Aged 16, I was already well on my way to becoming a *Doctor Who* nerd. I'd devoured *The Hitchhiker's Guide to the Galaxy*, first on TV, then as a book, then as the radio series. I watched as *Star Cops* came and went. I'd been forbidden to watch *Blake's 7* by my parents because it was too violent. I was also completely obsessed with *Fawlty Towers*, Monty Python and the films of Mel Brooks and the Marx Brothers. *Red Dwarf* could have been made for me.

I taped the first three series off-air. I stuck with them when I was at university – writing and performing in my own comedy sketch shows – and was disappointed when a seventh series didn't tick round like clockwork sometime in 1994. I grew up, got married, and began my own career, which now includes writing comedy plays and researching and talking about movies on my podcast *Best Pick*. Doing that, I've discovered that the stories behind the stories are sometimes as interesting – and can be more interesting – than the stories themselves.

Red Dwarf came back, went away, and came back again on Dave. *Back to Earth* had its faults, but it was nice to see the lads get together for one last hurrah. Except it wasn't. Three years later, there was another set of six half hours. A tenth series, almost a quarter of a century after the first! And another after that. And another after that. At the time of writing, the ninety-minute special *The Promised Land* is the last we've seen of Lister, Rimmer, Cat and Kryten, but that was already over three years ago, and if researching this book has taught me anything, it's that you can never count out **Red Dwarf**.

So, with a *Star Trek* watch ongoing, and with – apparently! – time in my schedule, I idly wondered if I'd definitely seen every episode of **Red Dwarf**, and whether they'd still hold up if I watched them again. As the idea lodged in my brain, the opportunity to work with the lovely people at Pen & Sword came up, and the result is currently in your hands.

My approach with projects like this is to write the kind of book I want to read. I'm interested in how things got made, and I'm interested in other people's reactions to those things. Luckily, there are scores of incredible stories to tell about the making of **Red Dwarf**. Most of them have been told in various documentaries, commentaries, interviews, articles and special features, but I've checked as many details as I could, going back to primary sources, and where possible by conducting some new interviews. And then I've tried to streamline everything into a coherent narrative, without – I hope – misrepresenting anyone. Where recollections differ, I've either acknowledged that, or resolved the contradiction with my own research. As usual, any mistakes are my own.

I'm also fascinated by other people's critical analysis, so when we're done with how each series got made, we'll go through the show episode by episode and I'll tell you what I think. I come to praise **Red Dwarf**, not to bury it, and I'm never watching these episodes in order to find fault. I'm writing this book because I love this show and I want to pay tribute to the talented people whose hard work made it a reality. But, like many of them, I'm not blind to its faults, and I have my own preferences, biases and predilections. So I'll give you my thoughts on these episodes as I rewatched them, not in order that you swallow my opinions wholesale, but in order to contribute to an ongoing conversation about the programme that we all adore.

For each episode, I'll give you some basic facts. You'll get the key creative team for the series and then the transmission date, viewing figures (and the episode's placing in the weekly charts for that channel) and the main guest cast. Each episode gets a star rating out of five: one is dreadful, two is disappointing, three is fine, four is very good and five is faultless (and half stars are the subtle gradations in between). I'll give my impressions of the episode, and then I'll check off some regular features.

Under **The one with**, I'll just briefly jog your memory about which episode this even is. **That Rimmer's a solid guy** is where I'll point out some issues with having a holographic (or as the writers put it, *hologrammatic*) character among your leads. Some episodes of **Red Dwarf** have dated, either because technology has moved on or because social mores have – or simply because it's funnier or more relatable to have characters from the future refer to things in our present. I'll discuss those under **There's a time and a place**. Like all writers, the **Red Dwarf** team steal liberally from other media. I'll list such appropriations under **Influences, references and rip-offs**. Of course, I don't claim any special insights into the writers' creative processes. I'm just noticing things that seem familiar to me – so I also don't claim that this section (or any section) is comprehensive. Next, for each episode I'll nominate a **Best gag** and a **Worst visual effect**. And lastly, there's **Continuity is for smegheads**, which is where I'll discuss aspects of the show that cross from episode to episode, or inconsistencies within the same episode. The first three series were remastered in 1997 and so I'll point out any interesting changes that crop up there.

This text grew somewhat in the writing. Intended as a single book, the sheer quantity of facts, stories, opinions, observations, references and memories eventually overwhelmed the good people at Pen & Sword and so we've decided to issue this work in two volumes. I've also broken **Red Dwarf**'s history into four main chunks. The first three series, during which everybody figured out what this show was and how to make it, I've called 'Steptoe in Space' for reasons that will become clear shortly (if they aren't already). The next three series, where **Red Dwarf** became a well-oiled machine, I've called 'Boys from the Dwarf'. The final two sections you'll find in *Volume II*.

Oh, and this is a book for fans. There will be spoilers.

So, if you're ready, let's begin at the beginning. Just how did **Red Dwarf** ever get on the air?

Part Zero

Shipwrecked and Comatose

> 'Three million years from Earth, the mining ship *Red Dwarf*.
> Its crew: Dave Lister, the last human being alive,
> Arnold Rimmer, a hologram of his dead bunkmate,
> and a creature who evolved from the ship's cat. Message ends.'

You've got to admit, it's one hell of a pitch.

Red Dwarf first aired on BBC2 on 15 February 1988, in the era of four mainstream UK television stations, when Filofaxes were in every yuppie's briefcase and mobile phones were luxury items the size of small house bricks. Its most recent, 74th, episode was broadcast in 2020 in the era of iPhones, Disney+, YouTube, podcasts and TikTok. And yet, for a long time it was the show nobody wanted to make, and for a while it seemed like a cursed project that would never get off the ground, let alone into orbit. Today there are fan clubs, regular conventions, and books, like this one. But the story of **Red Dwarf** doesn't start in 1988. It doesn't even start in 1983, when the first script was written. It arguably starts in 1970.

That was when John Carpenter and Dan O'Bannon wrote *Dark Star* while studying film together at the University of Southern California. Over a couple of years, they gradually patched together enough material to make a comedy science fiction feature, shot entirely on 16mm film, with Carpenter himself redubbing some of the dialogue. They found a producer who was prepared to distribute it, but more reshoots, this time on 35mm film, were deemed necessary before it could be released, which it eventually was in March 1974. According to O'Bannon, 'We had what would have been the world's most impressive student film and it became the world's least impressive professional film.' And indeed, almost nobody took any notice when it was first shown, but *Dark Star* went on to be very influential and a cult success.

O'Bannon took the basic idea of 'blue collar workers in space' and melded it with a haunted house to create *Alien*, which was noticed by rather more people, rather more quickly. Carpenter continued down the straight horror road and had a huge success with *Halloween*, which more or less defined his career. But at some point in the early 1980s, two young comedy writers from Manchester named Rob Grant and Doug Naylor saw *Dark Star* and thought to themselves: somebody should do a sitcom like that.

Rob and Doug met at Chetham's Hospital School in Manchester and joined forces as a comedy writing team when they left Liverpool University. After making connections at BBC Radio Manchester, and getting some sketches on the air, they were offered a year's contract to work for BBC Radio Comedy, and the result of that was a sketch show of their own. Six episodes of *Cliché* aired in 1981, followed by the sitcom *Wrinkles* about an old people's home, which, Rob recalls, achieved the second worst audience appreciation score in the history of radio. Despite this, it was granted a second series, and their career as comedy writers was off and running. Moving down to London, they began contributing material to TV shows like *A Kick up the Eighties*, *Three of a Kind* and *Cannon & Ball*.

It was a fascinating time to be starting a comedy career because the whole industry was approaching a turning point. At the same time as well-established shows like *The Two Ronnies*, *The Morecambe and Wise Show*, *Terry and June* and *The Benny Hill Show* were regularly topping the ratings, something new, called 'alternative comedy', was already beginning to invade the schedules.

Depending on who you ask, alternative comedy began in London in either May 1979 with Alexei Sayle hosting at the Comedy Store, or October 1980, when Rik Mayall, Adrian Edmondson, French & Saunders, Nigel Planer and Peter Richardson made their debuts as The Comic Strip at the Boulevard Theatre in Soho. Newly created Channel 4 snatched up The Comic Strip for their opening night's programming and the Enid Blyton spoof *Five Go Mad in Dorset* aired in November 1982. Not to be outdone, the BBC commissioned anarchic flat-share comedy *The Young Ones*, which first went out on BBC2 the same week. *Not the Nine O'Clock News*, which made stars of Rowan Atkinson, Mel Smith and Griff Rhys Jones, and was produced by John Lloyd, had started in 1979. *Spitting Image*, the savagely satirical puppet show also produced by Lloyd, began in 1984. Comedy was changing.

One person navigating that change was a young producer named Paul Jackson. He had comedy in his blood, being the son of a light entertainment producer named T. Leslie Jackson, who had worked on shows like *This is Your Life* and *What's My Line*. The younger Jackson worked his way up from assistant floor manager and eventually produced shows like *The Two Ronnies* and *Blankety Blank*, as well as the sketch show *Three of a Kind* starring Lenny Henry and Tracey Ullman, which actively sought out new comedy writing talent, including (as noted) Rob Grant and Doug Naylor.

Jackson also worked with comedian Jasper Carrott. Carrott, along with Dave Allen, had been doing something rather like alternative comedy for about ten years before the term had even been coined. Both men's relaxed, personal, storytelling styles contrasted sharply with the cartoon characters on most sketch shows, and the mother-in-law jokes still filling the airwaves from comedians like Bernard Manning and Frank Carson. It's easy to see why an ambitious producer like Paul Jackson wanted to work with a comedian like Carrott, who was anything but cosy.

The show they worked on together was called *Carrott's Lib*. The cast included a versatile performer named Chris Barrie, and the writing team once again included Grant and Naylor. As alternative comedy continued its assault on the mainstream, Jackson became the go-to man at the BBC – someone who could tame wild performers like Rik Mayall, Ben Elton, Lenny Henry and French & Saunders, but who knew how not to neuter them entirely. The shows he produced and/or directed, including *The Young Ones* and *Saturday Live*, still captured some of the punk energy of those thrilling live performances, but without the whole structure collapsing.

As Paul Jackson built his career, Rob Grant and Doug Naylor kept writing, and cemented their reputation as dependable creators of solid comedy sketches. *Cliché* returned to BBC Radio 4 as *Son of Cliché* in 1983, and thereafter, the pair became head writers on *Spitting Image*, including creating the lyrics to the chart-topping spoof novelty record 'The Chicken Song', whose infuriatingly catchy melody was composed by Philip Pope.

But, frustrated at not being given the creative freedom they expected, they walked away from *Spitting Image* and realised that what they really wanted was their own television sitcom. Various ideas were considered, including several from *Son of Cliché*, such as the superhero parody *Captain Invisible and the See-Thru Kid* (the joke being that neither hero could see the other), or *The Spanish Detective* who kept injuring people with his enormous flares. A Mike Hammer spoof called *Lance Bland News Hound* even got as far as a pilot script. But their thoughts kept turning to science fiction, and especially *Dark Star*.

Another recurring character from *Son of Cliché* was 'Dave Hollins, Space Cadet'. Played by cast member Nick Wilton, Hollins was an astronaut who had been in suspended animation for 300 years and was now the last surviving member of the human race. With only his computer Hab (Chris Barrie) for company, loneliness was driving him slowly insane. Gingerly, they pitched the idea to Paul Jackson – what about a science fiction sitcom? Jackson told them very firmly: anything but science fiction. Nobody at the BBC gets it. But ideas kept coming...

If their lead character was going to be the last human alive, what about pairing him with a computer simulation of his dead bunkmate? That would give them a traditional sitcom shape: two men who get on each other's nerves but who are forced to live together. This wasn't going to be *Star Trek* with jokes, it was going to be *Porridge* in the stars or *Steptoe and Son* in space. Grant and Naylor even had lunch with legendary *Steptoe* writers Ray Galton and Alan Simpson, who impressed upon them the importance of clearly defining this central relationship, so that two characters just walking down the street could be funny because of how they related to each other. Indeed, the very first scene of the very first episode of **Red Dwarf** is Lister and Rimmer walking down a corridor. To further insulate themselves from accusations of being 'too sci-fi' they imposed additional rules on themselves: no cute robots and no aliens.

'Dave Hollins' being the name of a real-life footballer, their lone human survivor became Dave Lister. His reanimated bunkmate became Arnold Rimmer. Hab the computer became Holly. A race of sentient biros in the radio show inspired a creature who evolved from Lister's cat. And, following a trip to the library to consult some books about astronomy, the *Melissa V* became a mining ship named *Red Dwarf* (the initials reflecting the first names of the writers). At first, both were nervous that the Cat was a surreal step too far, but a couple of early readers were hugely enthusiastic about the character, particularly Rob Grant's brother. Rob went out and bought a cat for research purposes and carried on writing.

To create a believable set of names for their characters, Rob and Doug thought back to their schooldays, where they'd known a Lister, a Todhunter, even a Rimmer – although the first names were changed to protect the innocent. Years later, the real Rimmer got in touch with Rob and revealed that he'd become a pilot with the RAF and had flown the Royal Family out of Kuwait at the start of the Gulf War. In essence, he had become Ace Rimmer! Hollister's name looks like a combination of 'Holly' and 'Lister', but this doesn't appear to have been deliberate. In the first **Red Dwarf** novel, it's a different character entirely: 'a short, dumpy American woman who'd had the misfortune to be born with the surname "Kirk"'. In the abandoned US pilot, the equivalent part is Captain Tau played by Lorraine Toussaint.

The first draft of the script was written in 1983 in a holiday cottage in Wales, donated by Doug's father. This getaway, which seemed the perfect place for some creative isolation, nearly doomed the project when the two men had a near-fatal car accident halfway up the mountain. For Doug, who lost a leg in a car accident when he was just 7 years old, this must have been doubly traumatic.

Who knows what expletives they might have let out as they lost control of their vehicle, but they probably wouldn't have been broadcastable. That created a problem because the very thing that had drawn them to *Dark Star*, and the very thing that would differentiate **Red Dwarf** from almost every other science fiction show on television, was class. Recalling jobs they'd had in their younger years, including working the night shift at a mail order company, Rob and Doug conceived of their heroes as sitting at the bottom of the hierarchy – unlike so much American science fiction which was only concerned with the captain and the senior officers, or fantasy wizards like Obi-Wan Kenobi.

There was less to choose from on British television, but the heroes of *Blake's 7* all sounded like they went to RADA and most incarnations of *Doctor Who* so far had been erudite bohemians or eccentrically dressed establishment figures. Everyone in science fiction, it seemed, was either professional, upper middle class, or classless.

The closest thing the BBC had ever done to **Red Dwarf** was Douglas Adams's famed *Hitchhiker's Guide to the Galaxy*, which had only lasted six episodes on television in 1981, partly because it was so difficult to produce. But the key joke of that series, in any medium, is that Arthur Dent is comfortably upper middle class and out of place. He's essentially walked off the set of *The Good Life* or *Yes Minister* and onto the bridge of a starship – that's what makes him funny. Rob and Doug wanted something much more, well, down-to-earth. They wanted a relatable, working-class hero, like Harold Steptoe or Fletcher from *Porridge*. But how can you write a relatable working-class hero who can't swear? *The Young Ones* pushed the boundaries of good taste with cries of 'bastard' but that was about as far as they could go, and it wasn't enough.

On *Porridge*, writers Dick Clement and Ian La Frenais had solved the problem of BBC teatime profanity by repurposing the Polari word 'naff' as a general-purpose swearword that would offend no one. After a short while playing around with various vowels and consonants, Rob and Doug came up with 'smeg', which they claim has nothing to do with either male genital hygiene or high-end Italian home appliances (although Rob also recalls learning the word 'smegma' from Tracey Ullman at a post *Three of a Kind* Chinese meal). Today, **Red Dwarf** fans proudly proclaim their own status as 'smegheads', testament to the success of this linguistic innovation. Although, this santisation didn't stop nineteen viewers from calling the BBC complaint line, following a feature about the show on an edition of *Points of View* in October 1988, to object to the word on the grounds that it had 'sexual connotations'.

Several more revisions later, the script was sent to the two most powerful men in British comedy: John Lloyd and Paul Jackson. Both read it and liked it enormously, and for a while, there was talk of a co-production, even of the show being made by the *Spitting Image* production team, but in the end, it was under the aegis of Paul Jackson Productions that the script was sent to the BBC. From the beginning, Rob and Doug had wanted this to be a BBC show. Almost all their professional work had been on the BBC, save for *Spitting Image*, where they still felt they had been poorly treated. And – crucially – being on a publicly funded channel meant they had a full thirty minutes to play with, instead of having to make time for commercials.

BBC Head of Light Entertainment Gareth Gwenlan rejected the project. Paul Jackson was both offended and surprised. This was a good script, it was exciting and different, and surely, he had proven himself to be a safe pair of hands? With support from Rob and Doug's agent, the script was submitted again and rejected even faster. Just as Jackson had suspected, there was a deep-seated suspicion about science fiction at the BBC.

Rob says he would have given up at this point, but Doug was tenacious. They asked for and got a meeting at BBC Light Entertainment and prepared a long speech about how everybody loved science fiction, how the most successful movies of all time had been science fiction, how shows like *Star Trek* had enormous fan bases, but this was all waved away by Gwenlan as 'our cousins across the pond' as if no British person had ever gone to see *Alien* or enjoyed *Close Encounters*. Eventually, Gwenlan proposed a compromise that would lure a conservative BBC audience into watching a television sitcom set anywhere other than suburban England. What if, he proposed, the series opened with a shot of a sofa in front of a pair of French windows, but then we keep pulling back to reveal that it's a sofa and French windows on board a spaceship? Rob and Doug's response is not recorded.

As the meeting wore on, Gwenlan began to realise that he was losing the argument. Okay, he conceded, maybe the BBC should do a science fiction sitcom, and if you want to write it, I'll give you a commission. With balls of steel, Doug Naylor pulled out the script for **Red Dwarf** and dropped it on the desk like Eddie Murphy dropping a microphone. 'Here it is. We've written it.' And so it was that the BBC rejected **Red Dwarf** for a third time. Along with 'smeg' and its various derivatives, other terms of abuse created by Rob and Doug include 'gimboid', 'goit' and, in one episode, 'gwenlan'.

Unwilling to take it to commercial television (even though Channel 4 offered to make it as a one-off TV movie), Rob and Doug began looking for other projects. Meanwhile, Paul Jackson went to BBC Manchester to film a very ambitious Ben Elton-scripted series called *Happy Families*, a story that consciously echoed the classic Ealing Studios movie *Kind Hearts and Coronets*, including casting Jennifer Saunders in multiple roles. This was something of a departure for BBC Manchester, which had previously done shows like *A Question of Sport* for the most part. But going outside London, shooting the series on location, and being away from executives' prying eyes, had all suited Elton and Jackson, who knew they were doing something risky.

Despite its excellent comedy pedigree, *Happy Families* didn't attract a huge audience and wasn't particularly influential, but due to the way BBC accounting worked in the 1980s, as budgets were being drawn up for the next year's shows, an allocation was automatically made for *Happy Families Series 2*. Neither Ben Elton nor Paul Jackson had any intention of making a second series of *Happy Families*, but suddenly, there was a little pot of money at BBC Manchester for Paul Jackson to do whatever he wanted with. In fact, it wasn't so little, because *Happy Families* had been shot entirely on location and on

16mm film rather than the cheaper videotape. Unable to believe his luck, Paul Jackson's next move was to call Rob Grant and Doug Naylor.

In charge of Light Entertainment at BBC Manchester was a man named Peter Ridsdale-Scott who was keen to expand the output of his corner of the corporation. He had been reading a lot of comedy scripts from hopeful writers, often on his commute between Manchester and London, but he felt many of them were nothing new. Aware that BBC Manchester wasn't thought of as much of a creative powerhouse, he wanted to spend his budget on something fresh, something dangerous. And then, on one train journey he recalls letting out a laugh so loud 'it could have been heard in Carlisle'. He had just got to the part of the **Red Dwarf** pilot script where the Cat makes his first entrance. Ridsdale-Scott told his boss Hugh Williams this was what he wanted BBC Manchester to produce, and Williams told him, 'I trust you.' The science fiction sitcom about bringing people back from the dead was itself back from the dead. Ridsdale-Scott called Paul Jackson and told him to get to work.

Suddenly, **Red Dwarf** was turning from some words on pieces of paper into a television show. Jackson's first appointment was producer/director Ed Bye. Bye had worked with Jackson on *Girls on Top* with Ruby Wax (to whom he is now married) and *Filthy Rich and Catflap*, which had reunited *Young Ones* stars Rik Mayall, Nigel Planer and Adrian Edmondson. He was hugely enthusiastic about the project and Rob and Doug were happy to accept Jackson's recommendation. Ed Bye went on to direct forty out of the first fifty-two episodes of **Red Dwarf**. Now it was time to find a cast. John Lloyd impressed upon them the importance of not hiring the usual Oxbridge faces. Given that he was working on *Blackadder* at the time, Doug Naylor thinks he was only worried that Paul Jackson would try to steal his cast (and indeed, Hugh Laurie is said to have been among those who auditioned).

For the two crucial characters of Dave Lister and Arnold Rimmer, both Rob and Doug were keen to find really good actors, rather than comedians who could act – and this was also the advice they'd received from Galton and Simpson. One of the first people they spoke to was a RADA-trained theatre actor who had received Tony and Drama Desk nominations for his performance as Valmont in *Les Liaisons Dangereuses* at the Royal Shakespeare Company. This was Alan Rickman, who liked the script enormously, but was unsure about whether he should play Lister or Rimmer – or both. He was also unhappy about auditioning for these TV people, but he did agree to have a drink with Ed Bye and the writers, during which they managed to get him to do an impromptu reading. Eventually, he decided he didn't want to do it if there was a live studio audience.

Paul Jackson meanwhile had remembered working with Chris Barrie on *Carrott's Lib*. Barrie had also been a core part of the *Spitting Image* team, providing the voices of David Coleman and Ronald Reagan among many others, so he knew Rob and Doug, and he'd hosted an episode of *Saturday Live* where he'd seemed very comfortable in front of a crowd. Jackson also recalled that he came from a military family, which might give him an insight into the uptight, career-oriented Arnold Rimmer – although he ended up auditioning for Lister too. Barrie's version of Rimmer went down well, but there was some disquiet about giving such an important role to an untrained impressionist. A far better choice, everyone agreed, was Alfred Molina, who'd made his mark as Sergei in *Letter to Brezhnev* and who loved the script. Okay, great, Alfred Molina will play Rimmer. Sorry, Chris, another time.

While this was being decided, Jackson was also faintly nervous about the possible racist overtones of the Cat, described in the script as 'an incredibly smooth looking black guy wearing a grey silk suit'. Keen to make sure that his pet project wasn't going to become a hate crime, Jackson sent the script to right-on performance poet Craig Charles, whose mother was Irish and whose father was from Guyana. Charles had also appeared on *Saturday Live* and had been slowly building up a following which even extended to him appearing on the incredibly conservative three-times-a-week BBC1 chat show *Wogan*. Charles read the script and saw nothing racist in the Cat character, but when he reported back to Jackson, he mentioned that he'd like to audition for the part of Lister.

At this stage, Rob and Doug still had in their heads Dave Hollins being driven mad by isolation. They were imagining Lister as a British version of Christopher Lloyd's Reverend Jim character from *Taxi*, and elements of this can still be seen in the broadcast version of *The End*, especially when Lister is talking to Captain Hollister about the fate of his pet cat, and arguably during the famous 'everybody is dead, Dave' sequence. This angry young beatnik wasn't anything like they'd imagined and – to make matters worse – he was a Scouser. There was no way that two Manchester lads were going to cast a scally from Liverpool as the lead in their career-defining sitcom.

But Jackson was intrigued by the idea and insisted that Charles meet the writers and audition. Charles, who had literally zero acting experience, recalls his then partner sending him off to the meeting with cheerful words of encouragement to the effect that he couldn't act, and he wasn't funny. But on meeting him, Rob and Doug found themselves bowled over by this cheeky, charming guy who was not at all like the spiky, combative character they'd seen on TV. And his reading was the best they'd heard yet. Could they really cast a performance poet with no acting experience as Lister?

With a degree of prescience, Jackson was also considering the possibility that up-and-coming actors like Molina and Rickman would shortly have plenty of offers of stage and television work – maybe even movies – which might make it difficult to reunite the cast for a second series, should they get that far. Casting unknowns would give them a lot more flexibility. With Galton and Simpson's advice still in their heads, Rob and Doug were uncertain – but now so was Alfred Molina. He was full of ideas for how the character of Rimmer should develop. When, Molina wanted to know, would he stop being a hologram? Ideally before the end of the first series, right? Worrying that he didn't really connect with the material, and unsure how he would pair with Craig Charles, the team eventually came back to Chris Barrie, who had already been told that he didn't have the part, but was delighted to learn that he now, in fact, did.

The other two regular parts – Cat and Holly – were much easier to cast. Holly, who was only going to be a voice-over in any case, was comedian Norman Lovett, who everyone thought had just the right wry quality to lift what was, at this stage, a fairly straight part (and female, in the original draft script). Jackson had seen him on, yet again, *Saturday Live*, and everyone knew him from the stand-up comedy circuit – in fact, he originally auditioned to play Rimmer. And although they saw dozens of actors, dancers and singers, West End performer Danny John-Jules was the first person to read for the Cat, and everybody's favourite. In part, Ed Bye and Paul Jackson were very impressed by the insouciant, catlike way in which he swaggered in half an hour late. John-Jules now recalls that he hadn't been aware that he'd got the time wrong. His dad's old wedding gear, a genuine Zoot suit, provided an impromptu costume.

And so, far from assembling a top-flight line-up of serious theatrical types, the main roles had ended up going to a poet, an impressionist, a dancer and a stand-up comedian. But there was a chemistry between the four of them that just felt right. Craig Charles and Chris Barrie even disliked each other for real, which was convenient for Charles, who was still nervous about making his professional acting debut at prime time on BBC2. Now, many years later, they've become much closer.

Given that a lot of other actors were needed for episode one, but all their characters were going to be killed off, Rob and Doug idly wondered if they could get some really big stars to play these parts. Their fantasy casting included John Cleese, Ronnie Barker, Leonard Rossiter and even Sean Connery as the captain. They imagined the fun as the BBC2 audience watched all these familiar faces fall by the wayside, leaving only Craig 'Who's He?' Charles left standing. It's not clear whether this idea got any further than off-hand remarks in the pub, but in any case, the other people actually cast included London-based American actor Mac McDonald as Captain Hollister, Alfred Molina's castmate from *Letter to Brezhnev* Alexandra Pigg as Lister's love interest Kristine Kochanski, and former Footlights president Robert Bathurst as Todhunter – rather than any of the megastars they'd contemplated.

While casting continued and Ed Bye started his pre-production, Rob and Doug had to write more scripts. When a new TV show is being developed, it's usual to produce an initial 'pilot' episode which may or may not form part of an eventual series. This gives everyone involved a chance to see what's working and what's not and sometimes major changes can take place between pilot and series, as can be seen by looking at the unbroadcast pilots of *Blackadder* or *Seinfeld* or *The Big Bang Theory* (to name just three examples).

But such was the confidence of Peter Ridsdale-Scott, and such was the eccentric way in which the show had been commissioned, that a full series of six shows was going before the cameras, and Rob and Doug had to come up with five more scripts before seeing anything resembling a finished episode. Eventually, they produced the remaining stories, which covered Rimmer trying to construct a new body for himself, Lister aiming for promotion, the crew seeing echoes of their future lives, cat religion, and finally, an episode that would see Lister's symptoms come to life. This would end with Lister bringing Kochanski back as a hologram, with the hope that she would become a regular character in the second series, giving them more stories to tell.

Now, all they had to do was film it. The traditional method of recording sitcoms was in front of a live studio audience. Today, only a handful of comedy shows are shot this way, but in 1987 it was absolutely standard (Douglas Adams had to fight like mad to stop a laugh track from being added to the television version of *Hitchhiker's*). So, that meant that the cast would rehearse the material during the week – in this case at the BBC rehearsal rooms in Acton. And then, this being a BBC Manchester production, the whole team would travel up to Manchester to record the show in front of an audience, almost as if they were performing a play. During these rehearsals, while Ed Bye lined up shots, Paul Jackson was on hand to make sure that these young lads, many of whom liked a good time, were showing up to work promptly, were doing what was required of them and were learning their lines.

Jackson became infamous for insisting on speed runs, the actors racing through the dialogue without pausing for breath – and going back to the start if anyone made a mistake. Rob Grant was worried that this would provoke resentment and hostility against the actors who were less sharp on the words, but most of the cast look back now and recognise the armour-plating which that gave them once they got in front of the audience. Nothing could throw them. The lines had been chiselled into their memories.

The plan was to record the six episodes of the first series in early 1987 for transmission later that year. Sets had been designed. Studios had been allocated at the BBC's Oxford Road facility in Manchester. Tickets had been sent out to audience members and the first episode was taking shape at Acton. Then – disaster struck. With rehearsals for the first episode well underway, negotiations between the BBC and the Electrical, Electronic, Telecommunication and Plumbing Union broke down and 500 electricians walked out on strike. This meant that it would be impossible to record the first episode of **Red Dwarf** as planned. Peter Ridsdale-Scott attended the last rehearsal to break the bad news personally. It was a shattering moment for all concerned. There would be no opening night. There would be no actual performance of 'The End', as the first episode was ironically titled. They would have to regroup and rethink.

Undeterred, Paul Jackson decided that rather than waste time re-rehearsing the first episode, which would likely teach them nothing new, they should use the second week to rehearse episode two, record that as originally proposed, and try to find some time and money to come back and pick up episode one later, even if that meant losing an episode along the way. Scarred, but unbowed, the cast and crew reassembled and found all the best ways of delivering the dialogue and blocking the action for the second episode, *Bodysnatcher*. Again, the studio was made ready, the sets were assembled and transport to Manchester was booked.

And again, the ongoing industrial action meant that no recording could take place.

It's not clear how many times this happened. Some of the cast and crew recall that they went through this appalling process for all six episodes of the first series. Surviving paperwork uncovered by John Hoare indicates that recording dates were booked in Manchester for five shows, but that doesn't necessarily imply that the sixth show was never rehearsed. What is clear is that by March 1987, virtually all of the £1.2 million allocated to **Red Dwarf** had been spent and the BBC had nothing whatever to show for it. Once again, the sitcom that nobody wanted to make had crashed and burned and – the BBC's top brass were certain – would be missed by nobody.

By this stage, Rob and Doug were ready to give up. The cast certainly felt that a lovely opportunity had fallen through their fingers, but for the writers, this was exquisitely painful. They'd got so close to seeing the things they'd imagined in a Welsh cottage four years ago actually come to life, and yet now it was exactly as if they'd never even typed the words 'Red Dwarf' in the first place. However, Paul Jackson, sensing that he was going to have to go back and argue for more money, had begun inviting BBC executives to some of the rehearsals so they could see for themselves just how incredibly well this cast was coming together. And once the non-series finally ground to a halt, Peter Ridsdale-Scott made sure that the sets were preserved (even if that meant storing them privately).

Eventually, the industrial action was settled, and Jackson and Ridsdale-Scott began a bureaucratic battle to once more resurrect the series. BBC accountants can't have been happy that a million quid had been spent and they had nothing to put on the air. On the other hand, with scripts written, sets designed and built, casting having taken place and heads of department ready to go – where were they now going to get six shows any cheaper? It took around another six months of bargaining, pleading, memo writing and arm-twisting but eventually, the word came from on high. **Red Dwarf** could be remounted.

And so, the cast emerged from stasis and began the process all over again. And here's where our story really begins.

Part One

Steptoe in Space

Series I

The Making of Series I

The first thing that happened was that episode two was scrapped. Rob and Doug later said that, with hindsight, they would have scrapped *Waiting for God* as well, but they were too busy squabbling with the producers of *Spitting Image* to focus on rewriting a series they both assumed was dead.

The original episode two, *Bodysnatcher*, was recreated with cartoon illustrations and the voice talents of Chris Barrie for one of the DVD releases and is dealt with in more depth in the Apocrypha section of *Volume II*. As planned, the series ended with *Confidence and Paranoia*, and the return of Kochanski in hologram form. The writers' new idea was to have Rimmer put a copy of *his* hologram data onto the disc marked 'Kochanski' and so when Lister tries to resurrect the love of his life, he actually has a second Rimmer to deal with. Thus, the episode *Me²* was born, and became the season finale. Since *Bodysnatcher*, which would have been the second instalment, had included two Listers, it was the obvious one to drop, as they now had an episode about two Rimmers.

Once again, episodes were rehearsed in Acton and then the company were taken up to Manchester for the recording. This time, they actually got there and even found sets and costumes waiting for them. Various ideas had been discussed for how to visually signify Rimmer's hologram nature. Ed Bye had originally considered having him, and only him, in black and white, but this would mean either painting the actor blue or never having him on the same set as everyone else – and neither of these was deemed plausible. Rob and Doug wondered why they didn't just dress him in grey clothes and put grey make-up on him, but in the end, a big silver H was glued to his forehead instead. Great care was taken to make sure that the H didn't come unstuck – with the result, so Chris Barrie says, that removing it at the end of a night's filming tended to remove great chunks of his flesh as well.

Of course, if Chris Barrie had been painted grey, he might have disappeared altogether. Keen to get everyone on the same page, Rob and Doug had talked to Ed Bye and the heads of department about the ship being like a submarine, and referenced films like *Dark Star* and *Alien*. Experienced BBC designer Paul Montague remembered being at boarding school during the Second World War and knew exactly the kind of oppressive, sombre atmosphere they had in mind. Or, as Rob Grant later speculated, he had shares in a grey paint factory, which is why there wasn't a splash of colour to be seen anywhere. Even the beer cans were military grey (or is it ocean grey?).

Rob does, rather sweetly, remember coming to the first prerecord and seeing the sets and – far from thinking 'Why is this all so grey?' – he became a little overwhelmed that the spaceships and people and props that he and Doug had imagined had now been made real. Sharing a lift with two extras in costume, he looked at them and quietly thought to himself, 'I made you up.'

On these early shows, Rob and Doug had very little actual power. Their opinion wasn't often asked for and when it was, they weren't often listened to. But they despaired at the relentless monochrome set and knew that their comedy show needed a bit more visual interest. Unable to get their voices heard through traditional channels, they resorted to colluding with assistant floor manager Dona DiStefano, who would run secret errands to local shops to buy coloured props to leave around the set. On one occasion, she even remembers grabbing red and green folding chairs from the BBC canteen as the studio audience was being admitted.

Doug Naylor recalls being in the studio and complaining about there not being enough detail on the set. Fortuitously, someone from the art department asked what he meant, and he began speculating that maybe there should be a mirror on that wall, or some shelves, or something. He quickly excused himself and went back to the gallery, only to hear director Ed Bye angrily demanding to know what was causing the hold-up on the floor. Doug peered at the monitor, only to see that shelves were now being added to the set, on his orders. For the next couple of years, he learned to keep his mouth shut.

Once a show is up and running, there will be a built-in army of fans who will clamour to get tickets to recordings and who will whoop and cheer when their favourite characters appear. **Red Dwarf** was brand new, unseen by anyone and recording in BBC Manchester, which, as noted, produced very few similar programmes. So, as the time to call 'action' approached, Rob and Doug were horrified to realise that the seats were less than half full. With warm-up man Tony Hawks trying to generate some enthusiasm (himself doing this job for the first time, having been recruited in the London comedy club Jongleurs by Ed Bye), the writers headed over the road to the pub and managed to drag in a couple of dozen extra punters. Nevertheless, the reaction to the first episode was muted. About the only thing that made them really laugh was 'proper actor' Robert Bathurst being unable to get through his long, convoluted speech about stasis. 'I got what I wanted out of that,' a cheerful Ed Bye told a shaken cast and writers at the end of the recording, while privately thinking, 'I really haven't got what I wanted out of that.'

Looking at the first edit a few days later, it was clear that further work would be needed. 'I've got one note for you,' said Paul Jackson to the writers. 'More jokes?' asked Doug Naylor. 'More jokes,' responded Jackson. So, as they prepared to put episode two before the cameras, Rob and Doug started rewriting episode one. Ever the canny producer, Jackson had told BBC Manchester that the problems created by the strikes would mean that they needed seven studio days to record six episodes. In fact, the strikes were almost a year ago, but aware that there could be some fairly significant teething problems, he wanted a spare recording day in his back pocket. This proved very useful, as the extra day was used to pick up new material for several episodes, not just *The End*.

One other beneficiary of this extra recording was Norman Lovett. As arguably the most well known of all the cast (Chris Barrie's most high-profile show was *Spitting Image*, on which he was heard but never seen), he was understandably annoyed that his role as Holly was limited to just a voice. Not only did this mean that his pay was drastically reduced, but he felt that he would be able to give a much funnier, more complete performance if the audience could see as well as hear him. 'Get me boat race in the shot,' he began telling anyone who would listen. 'This is where the money is.'

Around episode three, Ed Bye relented, and a corner of the studio was hurriedly found where Lovett could sit against black drapes, neck concealed with more black material, and then his image piped into practical monitors on the set. To make him look more computer-y, various 1980s image processing techniques were tried, with the result that Holly's appearance varies wildly across the first six episodes, but these were gradually toned down to nearly nothing. Ed Bye reportedly wanted to put his voice through something like a ring modulator as well – the machine used for Dalek voices on *Doctor Who* – but Lovett insisted that he was funniest as himself. That was the joke, right? Holly's supposed to be a super-intelligent computer but he looks and sounds like Norman Lovett.

Another change that took place during the enforced hiatus was some of the casting. The actor originally selected to play the hologram George McIntyre had to drop out and was replaced, and Alexandra Pigg was no longer available to play Kochanski, so Ed Bye picked another young performer, one who'd made a big impression in *Gregory's Girl*, Clare Grogan. Grogan was also in a band, which was cool, and she seemed perfect as Lister's ideal woman. Checking the actor's directory *Spotlight*, Ed Bye found her contact details and invited her for a meeting. But he shortly realised that – very unusually – *Spotlight* included details of two different Clare Grogans. Bye peered at the two very smudgy photos. He had *definitely* invited the right one to the meeting in Manchester, hadn't he? Better give the agent a quick call to make sure.

Minutes later, a squad of assistants were despatched to the station in London to stop the wrong Clare Grogan from getting on the train. The real *Gregory's Girl* was contacted, was happy to come and meet the team, and got the part – although, her namesake continued to haunt her, as when she arrived for make-up, she was disconcerted to see a photograph of the other Clare Grogan pinned to the mirror. 'That photo doesn't look much like you,' commented the make-up artist. 'No, because it isn't me!' retorted Grogan. Credited as 'C.P. Grogan' (short for Clare Patricia), she appears in three episodes across the first two series.

Someone else who was grateful for the hiatus was effects designer Andy Bowman, who had been given two weeks to build three radio-controlled 'skutters', as the voiceless service bots were called. (They aren't cute robots if they don't talk.) Bowman recalled that getting skutters that functioned at all took him the better part of three months and that if the recordings had gone ahead as scheduled then they would definitely not have been ready. They were made of heavy iron, to give them some stability, and to house the massive batteries that they needed, but the metal casing interfered with the radio controls, which meant that sometimes they would start moving and never stop, creating chaos in the studio. A glove puppet version was also made for close-ups of them doing anything even slightly dextrous. For the pedantic, both 'scutter' and 'skutter' can be found in official **Red Dwarf** material, but 'skutter' is used far more frequently, and so is my choice here.

Next to go before the cameras was *Balance of Power*, which ended up going out as show three. This was intended to test what could be done within the show's framework without any new science fiction elements, so the story is just about Lister and Rimmer. There are no crises threatening the ship, no murderous lifeforms on board and none of the crew is transformed in any way. There is a flashback scene, so we do get a return appearance of Chen, Peterson and Selby. At this stage, Rob and Doug thought that this was something they would do quite a lot – a way of filling out the cast without selling out their concept. In fact, apart from a brief appearance from Mac McDonald as Captain Hollister in Me^2 (filmed in the same studio session as *The End*), it never happens again, at least not in this way.

Waiting for God, which dealt with the legacy of the evolution of the Cat race, saw a high-profile guest star booked on the show for the first time. Noel Coleman had been acting in film and television since the early 1950s and had appeared in *Z Cars*, *Dixon of Dock Green*, *The Avengers* and *Doctor Who*, and was the narrator of beloved children's animated series *Pugwash*. When he turned up in Manchester, he was nearly 70 and the outtakes make it clear that he barely understood the script, couldn't remember the last-minute rewrites he'd been given, and found the costume very uncomfortable – and that was before he had to collapse back into his chair, resulting in the heavy hat he was wearing slipping down and cracking the bridge of his nose. Ouch. Future guest stars would have a rather easier time of it.

Not for the first time, or the last, Rob in particular was frustrated at the limitations that shooting in a smallish television studio in Manchester imposed on the production. He and Doug had imagined a great cathedral in which the Cat Priest would be found, but all the set designer could come up with was more military grey walls (or were they ocean grey?) and some cobwebs. This episode also saw the debut of John Lenahan as the Talkie Toaster. Lenahan, an American magician well known on the London comedy circuit, had been approached to do the warm-up for the first (abandoned) recordings and had read for Talkie Toaster then, but he wasn't keen on doing warm-up work. When Tony Hawks got the warm-up job, somewhat to his surprise, Lenahan was still invited to provide the voice of the Toaster (Hawks is also heard, in the first of his various supporting roles, as the voice of a dispensing machine).

Audiences would first hear Lenahan in *Future Echoes*, which would test Ed Bye's ability to marshal his limited resources to near breaking point, as well as the actors' powers of concentration. As the ship breaks the light barrier, time starts behaving in odd ways, so Chris Barrie, for example, had to play the same scene twice, once with Craig Charles in the wrong place, saying words Rimmer can't hear, and then again as an actual conversation with Lister. With the video effects needed to get two Rimmers in shot at the same time, it was a complex undertaking for all concerned, but everyone felt like this was a much stronger, funnier, more interesting episode than the previous two and so it was moved up to second in the running order.

Doug says this was where they really started to feel free to write the show they wanted to write. Even in the studio, watching the episodes being recorded, they had felt as if they were getting away with something. They were acutely aware that this was a show that the BBC had rejected three times (as Rob put it: you weren't anyone at the BBC if you hadn't rejected **Red Dwarf**) and now it was going before the cameras. According to Doug, he constantly expected the BBC Comedy Police to come in and arrest them: 'Why are you up in Manchester secretly making this show? You know we don't like it.'

This episode also introduced Lister's electric bike. Rather than build something entirely from scratch, effects designer Andy Bowman bought a Sinclair C5, stripped off most of the white plastic and added the raised handlebars. Clive Sinclair, who had invented the slimline pocket calculator in the 1970s, and brought affordable home computing to Britain in the early 1980s, launched this ludicrous electric tricycle in 1985, and for a while, it was a perpetual punchline on UK comedy shows. Costing about £400 (over £1,000 in 2022, allowing for inflation), it had a top speed of 15mph, a battery that lasted about two hours and handlebars for steering, conveniently located under the seat. Possibly, being a chassis for futuristic vehicles, filmed in television studios with perfectly flat floors, was the ideal application of this very niche vehicle.

The last two episodes are where Rob and Doug really started to explore the possibilities of a science fiction sitcom. Much of *Confidence and Paranoia* is about further power plays between Lister and Rimmer, and other effects of Lister's mutated virus (such as live fish and exploding dignitaries). But when Craig Ferguson and Lee Cornes appear as aspects of Lister's personality, the show roars into demented life. Ferguson was another familiar face on the comedy circuit, often in the guise of his alter ego Bing Hitler, but – uniquely among **Red Dwarf** guest stars – in 2004 he became the host of a late night American talk show, taking over from Craig Kilborn on CBS's *The Late Late Show*, a job he held for the next ten years. Lee Cornes would also have been familiar to British eighties comedy fans, being one-third of The Wow Show alongside Mark Arden and Steve Frost. Paul Jackson knew him because he'd done the warm-up for *The Young Ones* – and he was yet another actor who had auditioned for Rimmer.

Much-criticised set designer Paul Montague cleverly built the outside of *Red Dwarf* to include elements of the studio structure, including the wall and stairs, and the BBC special effects team supplied a satisfying bang to blow up a dummy of Ferguson, substituted for the actor during a momentary recording break. Rob and Doug are both scientifically literate and often used real science as a jumping-off point for **Red Dwarf** scripts, but here they erred, because exposure to a vacuum would not cause a person to explode (but then again, Confidence isn't a person).

If *Future Echoes* was ambitious, then early drafts of *Me^2* – in which two holographic Rimmers interact with each other – were pretty much suicidally insane. Paul Jackson told Rob and Doug to cut the number of Rimmer/Rimmer scenes in half if they were going to have any hope of recording the episode in the time allowed. As with many sitcoms, **Red Dwarf** would prerecord a few scenes here and there, even though at this stage there was no location work. Sometimes this was just to get tighter camera angles, such as in *The End*, where Rimmer's exam scene needed to be filmed shot by shot. But so much of *Me^2* was effects-driven, requiring multiple takes to get the desired effect, that around half of it was prerecorded and just played to the audience as they sat and watched it on monitor screens.

For the theme music, Paul Jackson tapped Howard Goodall, who'd written songs for *Not the Nine O'Clock News* and composed the theme tunes for *Blackadder* and *Mr Bean*. Goodall deliberately avoided both a current and a 'futuristic' sound, instead opting for something he hoped would be timeless, evoking Phil Spector and the Wall of Sound. The closing titles featured his jaunty song 'Fun Fun Fun in the Sun Sun Sun', with the vocals provided by Jenna Russell – a singer and actor now more famous as the second Michelle Fowler on the BBC's *EastEnders*. The same recording has been used on almost every episode since.

The opening titles used an arrangement of the same basic melody, but in a more sombre minor key to provide a whiff of 'proper' science fiction, like Stanley Kubrick's *2001: A Space Odyssey* (as well as a bit of Mahler's Fifth Symphony). Goodall recorded the opening theme at Angel Studios, once a Methodist Church, in which stood an enormous old pipe organ gathering dust. **Red Dwarf** became one of the first productions actually to use the thing in many years, and it had to be specially retuned for the purpose.

The first thing that had ever been shot for **Red Dwarf** was the title sequence that would accompany this music. It was devised by the writers and the director over some pints, and shown to Howard Goodall in an early form before he began writing his music. Model supremo Derek Meddings built an enormous miniature of the *Red Dwarf* spaceship, about 8 feet long, incorporating an asteroid embedded in its side – the idea being that this was what was being 'mined' – and a ramscoop at the front for fuel. He supplied this behemoth to Peter Wragg's effects team, who shot it using motion control cameras in January 1987. Ten years earlier, this technique had caused *Star Wars* fans to lose their minds, but by now the equipment and processes needed were well within the grasp of the BBC, given even a modest amount of time and money. The stunning opening shot of *Doctor Who*'s 1986 season, showing the TARDIS being drawn into a space station, was evidence of that.

For once during the production of early episodes of their show, Rob and Doug were delighted with what they saw – except for one thing. The beautifully photographed and intricately detailed model spaceship was bright red, the last thing they had expected. They were imagining something industrial and battered, like the *Nostromo* from *Alien*, but I don't think it had occurred to anyone in the effects team that the ship would be anything other than red in colour. It's called *Red Dwarf*, for pity's sake.

As impressive as the model work was, the opening credits didn't quite live up to the storyboards. The intention had been to pull out from Lister painting the outside all the way back to a wide shot of the ship in space – and for a while, because of the electricians strikes, the only material for **Red Dwarf** that Craig Charles had actually shot was silent footage of him holding a paintbrush and wearing a spacesuit repurposed from the Sean Connery film *Outland*. Only when trying to assemble the finished product did the effects team realise that they also needed an intermediate-sized model, which they now had no time or money to build or shoot, so there's an obvious dissolve from a medium shot to a wide shot instead of the single smooth pull-back originally envisaged.

Nevertheless, this sequence still got this new show off to a very classy start. Having missed out on producing the series, John Lloyd couldn't resist ringing up the writers to tell them what he thought. 'I loved the opening titles,' he explained, 'but then the show started...' Peter Ridsdale-Scott was much more cheerful. He remembers getting the train down from Manchester to attend the BBC weekly programme review meeting in London and turning to the back page of *The Times* to discover that the first episode of **Red Dwarf** was BBC2's third-most watched show of the week. Lift off.

Impressions of Series I

Written by Rob Grant and Doug Naylor. Designed by Paul Montague. Costumes by Jackie Pinks. Executive producer: Paul Jackson. Produced and directed by Ed Bye. Starring: Craig Charles, Chris Barrie, Danny John-Jules, Norman Lovett.

S01E01 The End ★★★☆☆

TX: 15 February 1988 on BBC2. Ratings: 4.75m (3rd for the week). Featuring: Mac McDonald, C.P. Grogan, Robert Bathurst, Mark Williams, Paul Bradley, David Gillespie, Robert McCulley.

It can't be denied that Series I of **Red Dwarf** is grey. But there's also a benefit to the sheer anonymity of the set design and the general (forgive me) *mise-en-scène*. The interplay between Lister and Rimmer isn't what you'd call sophisticated. Exchanges like 'Is that a cigarette?' 'No, it's a chicken' feel like placeholders for better ideas, or early drafts from writers still getting to know their characters – and this is after five years of script development, a double rehearsal process, and a series of reshoots. This stuff is hard. As the writers themselves point out, watching the first assembly of *The End*, the rewritten, reshot version does at least include some jokes, whereas the earlier version, although it has some good character work, is pretty much joke free, and that meant – for an audience meeting these characters for the first time – laugh free.

But, right from the beginning, Rob and Doug knew that if we didn't key into who these two men are, where they sit in the hierarchy, and how they see themselves and each other, then nothing else about this series was going to work. Remember: this was conceived as *Steptoe* in space. You can't appreciate what it's like to be Harold and Albert if you keep being distracted by the computer-generated rags and bones dancing around in the background.

It's instructive to compare this with the US pilot (see the Apocrypha section in *Volume II* for a more detailed analysis). This is far, far more interested in who Kryten is, whether or not Lister will get off with Kochanski, how Holly works, and all kinds of other things that are nice to have but not essential, especially when you're trying to tell the same story in two-thirds the time. Here, Lister and Rimmer are front and centre, where they should be.

What kills the pace slightly, and is cut down a little in the *Remastered* version, is the death and resurrection of George, the flight co-ordinator who is the first hologram in the series. An attempt seems to have been made to paint him a deathly shade of grey – Yes, grey! Even the smegging cake is grey, for pity's sake! – but he doesn't look quite like a reanimated corpse, and why should he? The trouble is that this is a very laborious way of walking us through the concept of holographic reincarnation. Why not just have a hologram crewmember at the start of the episode? Then we don't have to deal with the bewildering fact that George seems positively delighted by his change in status – more than can be said for Rimmer, who is rather more understandably upset. (And anyway, what happened to George? Is a radiation leak fatal to holograms too?)

Gone in the reshoots and re-edits is a truly terrible scene of Lister conducting an impromptu funeral for the ship's deceased crew, many of whom he didn't know. This concludes with a toe-curling eulogy for Rimmer, which he delivers himself, and which prominently features his enthusiasm for mild sexual assaults. Ugh. What isn't a waste of time is the material with Chen, Petersen and the gang. Not only do we get a bit of Mark Williams – and who doesn't want that? – it also means that when Lister is revived from stasis, we feel the loss. We see the same (grey) sets that once teemed with (some) people now empty and lifeless. We liked hanging out with Lister and his mates and we won't get to do that anymore.

Hacked together from two different recording sessions, and with everybody feeling their way, in many ways it's astonishing that this works as well as it does. For a first-time actor, Craig Charles is freakishly good, lounging about the sets with a completely natural insouciance. And Chris Barrie manages to be uptight, ridiculous, and yet vulnerable at the same time – having him faint in the exam room is *so* important (something Rob says actually happened, not to him but to another boy at his school).

It's been said before that typical American sitcom episodes begin with a problem and end with a solution, whereas typical British sitcom episodes begin with aspirations and end with dashed hopes. That second formulation doesn't describe *The End* entirely accurately, but it is important to note that – like many of their legendary predecessors and descendants – Lister and Rimmer are both losers. The vital difference is that Lister is a happy loser and Rimmer is a frustrated loser. Lister may have idle fantasies of raising horses on Fiji, but he's completely contented doing silly bar bets with his mates and eating curry. He likes himself. Rimmer is never satisfied with whatever he has, and always believes he's capable of more – which he almost certainly isn't. You need two very able and very likeable actors to make these two specimens appealing, and that's what you get here. The pacing and the plotting all need work, but this relationship succeeds from the very beginning and that's what continues to power the series today.

Norman Lovett is tremendous as Holly, and let's spare a thought for the Cat too. While hologram characters were a pretty new idea, the notion of the Cat is totally out there. It takes a while for the series to figure out how to integrate him into the storylines (in early drafts of these scripts he never spoke to the other characters at all, and in most of the first batch of episodes, he generally just comments from the sidelines) but the concept is easily graspable, instantly funny and – once again – the production team found the ideal actor to bring him to life. Danny John-Jules read Desmond Morris's book *Catwatching* for inspiration (and the BBC listings magazine *Radio Times* kept the secret of his identity by just putting 'Danny John-Jules as ?'). Add to this some highly respectable model work, a dancing skutter, and nice moments for Robert Bathurst and Mac McDonald, and you have a very decent introduction to the world of **Red Dwarf** – with sure, some clunky moments here and there and a few stumbles, but nothing I'd be desperate to change.

The one with: 'Everybody is dead, Dave.'

That Rimmer's a solid guy: Ghost rules apply for the most part. Floors support holograms but walls and other objects can be walked through like they're not even there. George is able to sit on a folding rec room chair for some reason, while Rimmer is unable to lean on the big table in the middle of the drive room without falling through it.

There's a time and a place: Amusingly (and not for the last time in early **Red Dwarf** episodes) even in the era of instantly replayable videotape, it hasn't occurred to the writers that one day photos won't need to be developed. Lister's cat is discovered only because he sends negatives to the ship's lab for processing. Invigilator's instructions before Rimmer's exam include 'No modems, no speaking slide rules.' Rimmer is as dead as a can of Spam (and death is like being on holiday with a group of Germans). Everything is written down on pieces of paper, sometimes in notebooks, sometimes held in place on clipboards. Chen is waiting for Rimmer's arm to come out in paperback.

Influences, references and rip-offs: As noted, *Alien* and *Dark Star* are heavy influences. Some of the exam material is drawn from *Cliché* and *Son of Cliché*. Frankenstein the cat is named after the novel by Mary Shelley about reanimating dead matter (appropriately enough).

Best gag: After 3 million years in stasis, Lister responds to Rimmer, who is aghast at him smoking: 'I gave them up for quite a while, but I'm back on them now.'

Worst visual effect: The model work is exemplary, but there's some pretty egregious chromakey fringing whenever Rimmer's hologram nature is represented visually.

Continuity is for smegheads: There are 169 people on board *Red Dwarf*. Rimmer will later be able to ask Holly for props such as a notebook, but here he complains that he can't touch anything and so can't write up Lister's insubordination (maybe he hasn't read his hologram orientation manual thoroughly). Lister's goal at this stage is to start a farm on Fiji. This is gradually downplayed and is never referred to again after Series I, although it does form the inspiration for Howard Goodall's lyrics, which close this and almost every other episode. Why is a chicken soup machine repairman working on the ship's drive plate in the first place? It's asking for trouble, really, isn't it?

Remastered: On all these episodes, there's a new title sequence, starting with the pull-out from Lister painting the ship – done as originally envisaged in a single shot – and then going into a Series III style quick-cut montage. All the material has been reframed to a slightly wider aspect ratio, it's been 'filmised' and the colour grade has been pushed (you can almost hear the 1-inch video tape scream out in pain). In static shots, you can see more convincing stars out of the ship's windows (but not when the camera moves). The model spaceships have been redone as CGI and sometimes this is an improvement (the CGI *Red Dwarf* looks great, if skinny), other times, less so. For Series I, much of Holly's material has been reshot with a less intrusive video effect and in some cases, some new gags. There is a more immersive soundscape with more ship background effects and more individual bleeps and bloops when buttons are hit.

In this episode, cuts have been made to a few scenes to improve the pacing and the score has been both added to and subtracted from. There's a series of shots of the CGI *Red Dwarf* after Lister goes into stasis and a new bit of music, but there's no score under 'Everybody is dead, Dave.' Unconvincing skutters and unconvincing extras crowd the foreground during the first Lister/Rimmer scene and George's funeral respectively – but a fairly smooth video effect hides the swing bin lid that George's ashes are placed in. There's also a new bit of music for the Cat's first entrance. Due to music clearance issues, on Netflix the track 'See You Later Alligator' was replaced with a recording of the popular football chant 'Here We Go', although the original soundtrack is retained on the home video and NOW TV versions. Holly gets a couple of extra gags. Maddeningly, after insubstantial Rimmer attacks and passes straight through the Cat, the sound of crashing pots and pans is heard. How? Why?

S01E02 Future Echoes ★★☆☆☆

TX: 22 February 1988 on BBC2. Ratings: 3.4m (13th for the week).
Featuring: John Lenahan, Tony Hawks.

I find it hard to believe that the production team got so excited about this one. Is it better than *Balance of Power* and *Waiting for God*? Yes, a bit, but it's still very far off what the show is capable of, as it will demonstrate in just a few weeks' time. Meanwhile, we have this, which feels unfocused and disjointed, isn't really about anything, and is only sporadically amusing. There's barely any narrative momentum, and the early material with Rimmer's haircut feels like faintly misogynistic padding. (His refusal to look in a mirror is hopelessly contrived. Would he really not even run his hands through his newly shorn hair? We know he can touch himself...)

This and the next nine episodes start with Holly giving us the story so far (*Parallel Universe* has a different opening entirely). Insofar as this is needed at all, the Series I version is a bit wordy. All ten of these introductions include one-off gags, very few of which raise more than a weary chuckle from either me, or the studio audience. When she took over as Holly, Hattie Hayridge recorded a few of these, but they weren't used. By Series III, it was clear that even newcomers were happy to accept the premise of the show without further explanation: he's the last human, he's a hologram, he's a cat. Let's go.

Juggling the running order means we're left wondering for another week why on earth Holly chose to resurrect Rimmer as a hologram. There's a perfectly reasonable, fairly convincing explanation for this, which probably ought to have been in episode one, but was written into what was episode two, which then became episode three. Briefly, Rimmer was the person Lister talked to the most and knew best and therefore the one most likely to keep him sane. (In the US pilot, Rimmer's personality disc is the only one that survived the accident, which is simpler, but not as rich.)

The rearrangement of episodes also means that here's where we first meet Talkie Toaster, a fun character to be sure, but one whose Genuine People Personality owes much more to *The Hitchhiker's Guide to the Galaxy* and much less to Rob and Doug's own style, which they are starting to flex here, both in the characters and in the construction. The scene where Rimmer has the same dialogue twice is brilliantly worked out and played with precision by Chris Barrie and Craig Charles, who confessed that the time travel intricacies were beyond them, but who nodded obligingly as Rob and/or Doug gamely tried to explain it for the third or fourth time.

So, on the one hand, there's some satisfyingly complicated plotting here; but on the other hand, the tone is all over the place. Rimmer goes from aghast at the horrible sight of Lister's death to crowing about how painful it will be for him, in about ten seconds. His dismay at being left alone on the ship also seems to evaporate without explanation. Craig Charles, on only his fourth day as an actor in a television studio, admirably goes for broke when heading back into the drive room, he thinks to meet his doom, but even his talents can't knit together the disparate pieces of this fragmented episode.

We leave our heroes with a glimpse of the future: a 171-year-old Lister with a metal hand tells them to go to the drive room, where they see an image of Lister holding two baby boys ('Stop crying and say cheese' was Craig Charles's ad-lib, because the infants supplied would not be silent). This was an ambitious attempt to create some multi-year arcs, the intent being to pick up these threads and develop them over several series. Eventually, the two writers conclude that funny is more important than consistent for this show (and they're bang on the money) and most of these ideas are quietly abandoned.

There are lapses of taste here too. Lister, learning of his own son's death – which is treated as a whew-nothing-bad-has-happened-after-all moment – is profoundly ick and when the same events are dealt with in the novel *Infinity Welcomes Careful Drivers* it becomes his grandson, which I suppose is slightly less upsetting, but still no reason to start celebrating. Also ick – Rimmer's dad took his own life, it seems.

The one with: Lister's kids.

That Rimmer's a solid guy: Doing exercise seems a bit of a waste of time for a being made of light, but it's not completely out of character for Rimmer. Holograms need haircuts.

There's a time and a place: Rimmer refers to Holly as a 'jumped-up Filofax'. Polaroid cameras are still in use. References are made to Moss Bros., Hell's Angels and famous Soho hairdresser Teasie Weasie Raymond – on which subject, Rimmer's haircut reminds him of 1960s pop star Helen Shapiro. Talkie Toaster sings Bart Howard's song 'Fly Me to the Moon', first recorded in 1954 by Kaye Ballard but now most associated with Frank Sinatra.

Influences, references and rip-offs: Any number of time travel stories, movies and TV shows have played around with time in similar ways. This particular implementation calls to my mind the 1972 *Doctor Who* story 'Day of the Daleks', which features a brief appearance from future versions of the Doctor and companion Jo Grant in episode one.

Best gag: Holly, trying to steer the ship: 'Look, we're travelling faster than the speed of light. That means by the time we see something, we've already passed through it. Even with an IQ of 6,000 it's still brown trousers time.'

Worst visual effect: The split-screen stuff is relatively smooth – good practice for *Me²*, which is coming soon – but Craig Charles's old-age make-up is terrible.

Continuity is for smegheads: Lister's plan at this stage is to go back to Earth and remain in stasis for the duration of the trip. After this episode, going back into stasis is barely ever referred to again, and the idea of going back to Earth seems progressively less important as the series progresses. At this stage, Lister's sandwich of choice is bacon with French mustard. We get another rendition of the 'Lunar City 7' song. Doug was very fond of messing with the closing titles. This time they roll over a slowly developing Polaroid of Lister and his sons.

Remastered: New exterior shots of the ship breaking the light barrier. Dialogue trims including Rimmer complaining about his ears. Heroic music plays as Lister races to the drive room – and then peters out as the dialogue starts. There's another new music cue as Lister goes to his 'death'. Robert Bathurst's name has gained an extra H in the middle in the closing credits.

S01E03 Balance of Power ★★☆☆☆

TX: 29 February 1988 on BBC2. Ratings: 4.25m (9th for the week).
Featuring: C.P. Grogan, Paul Bradley, David Gillespie, Mark Williams.

Part of the pitch to the BBC, as discussed, was that this wouldn't be effects-heavy, off-puttingly complicated, nerd-only science fiction nonsense. It would be a good old-fashioned two-men-who-don't-like-each-other sitcom, which happened to take place on a spaceship 3 million years in the future. They could just as easily be in a suburban living room, or a junkshop or a prison cell. This episode was designed to test just how well that would work, and it's... a bit dull.

As noted, it does tackle some of the awkward questions raised in episode one – such as why Holly brought back Rimmer and what the chain of command looks like on board the ship. We get some further explorations of how holograms work, some of which are fun – Petersen's arm going full *Evil Dead* on Rimmer; some of which are ick – Rimmer peering down Kochanski's shirt. We also get to see Lister with his mates again, which is nice. But neither the writers nor the cast are quite on top of the characters enough for this to really work. They will be soon. In just ten episodes time, we'll get *Marooned*, which is virtually all Lister and Rimmer trapped in a room together talking, and it's brilliant, but here it's just all a bit too thin and underplotted.

For all their insistence on having thirty luxurious minutes to play with each week, Series I episodes in particular often feel as if there isn't enough story to sustain a full half hour, and whole scenes go by in which characters just chat about nothing much. That's fine if there are razor-sharp jokes coming at you every twenty seconds, or if we know the characters so well that we can just watch them bounce off each other for a bit. But at this stage the writing isn't strong enough and – remembering this was written and shot as the second episode – the characters aren't defined enough. So, a rollicking story with the ship in danger, the cast transmuted, a crazy high concept, or a brilliant guest star would all have helped. Instead, we have Lister competing in The Great Dwarfish Bake-Off, while the Cat just sort of hangs around the place, and it's... a bit dull.

The one with: Lister passing his officer's exam (seemingly).

That Rimmer's a solid guy: Holograms need a shower in the morning. If a hologram gets someone else's body part, that body part is controlled by that personality, for some reason (or maybe this was Holly screwing around). In this (and pretty much every) episode, when Rimmer lies down in his bunk, the weight of his body moves the sheets and pillows. This is basically unavoidable, so I won't go on about it. On the other hand, Lister does walk straight through Rimmer, which is very rare.

There's a time and a place: Rimmer wants Lister to put on something classical like Mozart, Mendelssohn or Motörhead. The skutters are supposedly watching John Wayne. Holly brings up Jean-Paul Sartre's *Huis Clos*, of all things. Lister refers to head of the Nazi armed forces Hermann Göring as a 'drug-crazed transvestite' (and I thought Rimmer was the fascist dictator enthusiast). In the flashback, Lister is at a 1990s nostalgia night.

Influences, references and rip-offs: As noted, this is virtually an episode of *Porridge*.

Best gag: 'I'm taking learning drugs and all I'm memorising is this conversation. Where's my revision timetable, Lister? It's Saturday night, no one works Saturday night...'

Worst visual effect: Although it's nice to see Lister walk through Rimmer's hologram, it's weird that Chris Barrie briefly goes see-through when it happens.

Continuity is for smegheads: Lister can't remember how many irradiated haggises are left even after Rimmer gives him the count four times. Far from having had a relationship with her, Lister exchanged only 173 words with Kochanski during his time on board the ship. This compares with 14 million words exchanged with Rimmer, and given that Lister has only been with the company for eight months (according to the next episode) that makes him *very* chatty. Second appearance of C.P. Grogan, although this time she isn't who she appears to be, which means – rather weirdly – that in Series I Grogan has more lines as Rimmer than she does as Kochanski (four as herself, twelve as Arnie – a further handful from each episode hit the cutting room floor). At this stage, Lister is already searching for Kochanski's hologram disc, which he will eventually find (he thinks) at the end of *Confidence and Paranoia*.

Remastered: There's a new piece of music when 'Kochanski' enters while Lister is taking his exam, and new sound effects when Rimmer is beating himself up. The 'black card' conversation and its call-backs have been removed. Something a bit closer to actual John Wayne is shown in the ship's cinema.

S01E04 Waiting for God ★☆☆☆☆

TX: 7 March 1988 on BBC2. Ratings: 3.75m (8th for the week).
Featuring: Noel Coleman, John Lenahan, Tony Hawks.

Well, look, this is nobody's favourite episode, but some of the problems here could have been avoided. At this stage, Rob and Doug still thought that new viewers would benefit from some general life-on-board-*Red Dwarf* material at the beginning of each episode to ease them in. That runs the risk of getting us off to a slow start, and as time goes on, this approach will give way to a different method of arranging an A-plot and a B-plot which is, if not unique to **Red Dwarf**, then at least unusual (*Bodyswap* is the first clear example, so jump to that episode if you want to know what I'm talking about). But the two strands of this story don't affect each other at all, and they don't resonate in any interesting ways. That would be fine if even one of them was interesting or funny, but they're both flawed in conception, and neither is particularly well executed.

This version of Rimmer is obsessed with aliens – evidently, he didn't read the pitch in which aliens were explicitly ruled out. So when a mysterious object is brought on board, he thinks it must be of alien origin and even invents a name for the alien race that created it. Lister can see easily that it's a garbage pod, and we find that out too. That means we get to laugh at Rimmer – ha ha, what a doofus – but it means we *know* that this plotline isn't going anywhere, and indeed, the punchline is: just as we were told, it's a garbage pod. But also, the Rimmer I know isn't a doofus. He's petty, small-minded, childish, selfish, arrogant, smug and error-prone – but he's not a dummy. Except here, and it's pretty frustrating to watch.

Meanwhile, anyone who watched *The End* three weeks ago will remember that the Cat identified the last surviving human as Cloister the Stupid and presumably will be less than riveted as Craig Charles and Danny John-Jules proceed to have that exact same conversation again, following which they immediately have it a third time, just in case anyone wasn't paying attention at the back. Even in an episode that seemingly centres him, the Cat continues to be underused: Rimmer and the Cat's conversation about the Cat's shiny thing (a yo-yo) is pure filler.

It all builds up to the revelation of one more very elderly cat, somewhere in the bowels of the ship, where Holly – who controls every single aspect of *Red Dwarf*'s operation – can't detect him. By now, we're stuck repeating the same jokes, and even Noel Coleman's committed performance can't elevate the material. This would like to be devastating satire, but it's just an old actor in silly clothes raving about mustard stains, alas. Lister and the Cat remain remarkably unaffected by the entire interaction, which also does much to rob it of any real power.

It's probably not unfair to say that **Red Dwarf**'s early reputation rests on episodes one, five and six of Series I. Luckily, episodes five and six are both crackers, and Series II is much smoother sailing.

The one with: The weird old cat dude.

That Rimmer's a solid guy: Holograms don't need clothes, so why does Rimmer mind if Lister wears his? Also, wouldn't they have fallen apart after 3 million years? (In fact, so many things seem incredibly well preserved after all this time that it would be tiresome to keep pointing them out, so I won't, but try not to think of this when you see Lister's guitar or Rimmer's diary or the Cat's yo-yo.)

There's a time and a place: John Wayne, Victor Hugo, *Casablanca* and Motörhead are well remembered, but Shakespeare of all things is fading from the shared cultural consciousness. Barry Manilow's 1981 hit 'Bermuda Triangle' is right at the forefront of Lister's mind, however. People still eat cinema hot dogs and wear unconvincing toupées. Cat hasn't heard of Columbo – Rimmer thinks he discovered America wearing a dirty Mac. Lister reassures the Cat Priest that his place in Fushal will include 'Cork floors, your own barbecue on the patio, double glazing, a phone, everything!'

Influences, references and rip-offs: There are elements of things like *Life of Brian* but as Rob Grant himself points out, here they're only knocking down their own icons, so it doesn't have much impact ('Aunt Sally satire'). Getting a 'squiggly slimy thing stuck to your face' recalls *Alien*, of course. The holy war over the colours of hats echoes the conflict between the big-enders and little-enders in *Gulliver's Travels*. The name of the episode is a play on Samuel Beckett's *Waiting for Godot* in which the titular character never appears.

Best gag: Craig Charles sliding down that glass panel lips-first is a sight to behold.

Worst visual effect: Hardly any call for them in this ship-bound episode.

Continuity is for smegheads: The upset of the status quo that ends the previous episode on such a thrilling note is discarded at the very beginning of this one, in Holly's catch-up for new viewers, which is a pretty devastating betrayal. Eighteen weeks have passed since Lister came out of stasis. Rimmer is obsessed with finding aliens who can give him a real body – but this fixation doesn't last very long. In *Future Echoes*, Rimmer was said to have failed the astro-navigation exam ten times. Here it's the engineering exam eleven times. It's implied that he has to imagine making love to a woman. Holly reads out Lister and Rimmer's crew evaluations (a similar scene occurs much later in the Series XII episode *Skipper*). The closing titles are interrupted once more – they literally stop dead – for Rimmer to vocalise his despair at the true nature of the pod they intercepted.

Remastered: New music cues for the Cat's investigations. New pictures of Cloister. Lister's journey to the Cat Priest has been reorganised and some of this scene has been cut down. A new shot of the Priest's ashes being shot into space has been added, and there's new music here too.

S01E05 Confidence and Paranoia ★★★★☆

TX: 14 March 1988 on BBC2. Ratings: 3.8m (17th for the week).
Featuring: Craig Ferguson, Lee Cornes.

The issue of quarantine is clearly one that bothers Rob and Doug. This time around, Rimmer (much more sensible than last week's doofus version) is appalled that Lister has been poking around the officers' quarters before these have been decontaminated. Lister promptly contracts space pneumonia, which gives him solid hallucinations. That's the beauty of a science fiction comedy. You can just say 'solid hallucinations' and make that the story. Because it's a science fiction show, you aren't stuck with two people who hate each other – anything can happen. And because it's a comedy, nobody expects you to take half a page of sciencey-sounding gibberish to explain it. Imagine this plotline on *Star Trek: The Next Generation*! Geordi La Forge would have been spouting technobabble for about a week.

The early incarnations of this idea are neither visually striking nor of much plot significance – the big problem with this episode is pacing. But when Lee Cornes and Craig Ferguson show up, the entertainment quotient goes through the roof. Splitting Lister's personality into two opposing forces is a quite brilliant idea, and this proves to be a very, very rich seam, which Rob and Doug will return to again and again with episodes like *Back to Reality*, *Polymorph* and *Demons & Angels*.

This combination of science fiction absurdity, but rooted in the character relationships, is not only a wonderful joke-generation mechanism but makes for strong plotting too. It's just frustrating that Ferguson and Cornes don't show up until the episode is past the halfway point and then they only stick around for eleven minutes. It's a pretty perfect eleven minutes, though, and a brilliant cliffhanger ending.

The one with: *The Late Late Show*'s Craig Ferguson.

That Rimmer's a solid guy: Holograms needs teeth-cleaning and shaving. Rimmer puts out his hand to detect raining fish (although none of them hit him).

There's a time and a place: According to Holly, the worst book ever written is *Football, It's a Funny Old Game* by Kevin Keegan (Keegan's actual autobiography, published in 2018, is called *My Life in Football*). Confidence quotes the tagline from *Alien*, of all films. There is much talk of Agatha Christie, including Holly delivering a massive spoiler for *Murder on the Orient Express*.

Influences, references and rip-offs: Confidence and Paranoia are possibly a development of the angel and devil personas that feature in many Looney Tunes and Disney cartoons, among other places.

Best gag: Cat pretending to get up and follow Rimmer is brilliantly done by Danny John-Jules.

Worst visual effect: The exploding Mayor of Warsaw is pretty feeble – although the demise of Confidence is spectacular. And the dust storm looks very nice too.

Continuity is for smegheads: Last episode, Rimmer was clear that staying in quarantine is a stupid waste of everyone's time. This episode, it's a wise precaution that Lister should have been aware of. Wait till we get to Series V. During her date with Rimmer, Yvonne McGruder may have been concussed. Yikes. Lister's beer milkshakes, seen last episode, are celebrated by Confidence as one of several great ideas. The much-sought-after personality disc is labelled 'CZ Kochanski', but every other source gives her first name as 'Kristine' with a K. It is reiterated that there were 169 people on board *Red Dwarf*. Note that sustaining a hologram is vastly power-intensive. As more and more stories take place off the ship, this will more often than not be quietly forgotten about.

Remastered: New opening gag from Holly. New music cue for Confidence and Paranoia. The excellent dust storm effects created practically have been replaced with crummy looking CGI.

S01E06 Me^2 ★★★★☆

TX: 21 March 1988 on BBC2. Ratings: 3.8m (12th for the week).
Featuring: Mac McDonald, Tony Hawks.

The final moments of *Confidence and Paranoia* promise major changes, and this time – unlike with *Balance of Power* and *Waiting for God* – the writers keep their promise. There really are two holographic Rimmers on board the ship and they can't wait to start making Lister's life a misery. If last week's episode used a comedy science fiction plot device to dig into Lister's personality, here we're doing the same thing with Rimmer, possibly to even greater effect. Starting this story in the closing seconds of last week's instalment means we aren't hanging around for the plot to kick in, and the revelation that the two Rimmers get on each other's nerves, while not exactly unexpected, is nonetheless deliciously satisfying.

But this is really about what makes Rimmer such a loser, and – to be honest – that's a question that's going to be asked and answered a lot over the next seventy or so episodes. Here, it seems as if the only thing that drives him is a chilled-soup-based social catastrophe from his younger years, and while the story is great (and works even better in the later novelisation) it's a little hard to take that those would genuinely be his dying words.

So, there are definitely still some rough edges here – and in later series, the writers would take a strong concept like this and give it one more twist. But the sight of the two warring Rimmers is a very beguiling one, both Craig Charles and Chris Barrie seem to be completely inhabiting the characters now, and that last exchange is absolute perfection.

After some fairly major uncertainties in the middle of the series, these last two episodes managed to turn the whole thing around, with strong plots, excellent characterisation, a cast getting more comfortable every minute and no shortage of good jokes. Bring on Series II.

The one with: Gazpacho soup.

That Rimmer's a solid guy: More need for light to exercise its muscles, for some reason. Unlike the various other props, and indeed foodstuffs, that Holly provides Rimmer with from time to time, his whisky (straight, with ice and lemonade, a cherry and a slice of lemon) just invisibly hits the inside of his mouth.

There's a time and a place: Rimmer's death is stored on a video, complete with VHS fast-forward effect. The onboard cinema, with smoking and non-smoking section, includes an advert for the local Indian restaurant.

Influences, references and rip-offs: Meeting oneself (and finding oneself annoying) is a familiar device, from 'The Three Doctors' in *Doctor Who*, to the eighties TV movie *The Giftie* with John Wells and Richard O'Sullivan, to fairy stories like some of the books in the *Wizard of Oz* series. There are also echoes of this idea in John Wyndham's 1961 short story 'Random Quest'. There's an explicit hat-tip to *Citizen Kane*, which also made much of its hero's dying words. Rimmer's dialogue about being a nothing parallels Brando's famous speech in the 1954 film *On the Waterfront*.

Best gag: Holly's elaborate practical joke, recycled and buffed-up from 'Dave Hollins: Space Cadet', is Norman Lovett at his deadpan finest.

Worst visual effect: Rimmer's death scene is smothered under 1980s video effects, but never seems all that fatal. Craig Charles awkwardly leaning, so as to keep his body clear of the split screen between the two Rimmers, is a bit unfortunate.

Continuity is for smegheads: Lister treats us to a particularly boisterous rendition of 'Lunar City 7'. Rimmer complains that Lister irritated him by humming for two years, but in *Waiting for God*, Lister had only been with the company for eight months before the accident. Sustaining two holograms appears to be highly possible with absolutely no other ill effects whatsoever. Despite this, it is never tried again. Rimmer 1 says of Rimmer 2, 'What a guy!' This will later be said of Ace Rimmer by everybody (except, to her chagrin, Hattie Hayridge, whose 'What a guy' mysteriously ended up on the cutting room floor). Arnold Rimmer gains a middle initial, J., and adds 'BSC, SSC' after his name – standing for 'Bronze Swimming Certificate' and 'Silver Swimming Certificate'.

Remastered: Some of Rimmer's less inclusive language has been snipped out. Rimmer's video has new music. An attempt has been made to beef up his death scene but it's still not all that convincing.

Series II

The Making of Series II

Typically, a new sitcom shown in the spring, which had gone down moderately well, would be repeated in the autumn and then a second series commissioned, which would go out in roughly the same slot the following year. But Series II was commissioned while Series I was still on the air – very unusual for a new show. Various theories have been advanced as to why this happened so quickly, ranging from a hole in the schedule, to a desire from an outgoing executive to throw his successor under the bus by committing another million plus quid to an obvious turkey – but regardless, Rob Grant, Doug Naylor, Ed Bye and Paul Jackson were soon back into the swing of things.

Given the opportunity to make six new episodes, Rob and Doug did their best to correct what they felt were mistakes in Series I – both in the production and the writing. And in fact, far from welcoming a repeat viewing of the show they'd worked so tirelessly to create, when it was offered, they successfully blocked it, confident the next batch would be better and not wanting to remind viewers of what they felt was a shaky start. The first **Red Dwarf** episodes to be repeated were those from Series II, which were rerun immediately before Series III was shown in the autumn of 1989 and Series III was itself repeated in late 1990. Series I wasn't seen again until 1994. (For a full list of BBC transmission dates, see *Volume II*.)

And the two men were still adjusting to the fact that they had been effectively demoted from shot-callers and taste-makers on *Spitting Image* – a show whose creation they had nothing to do with – to 'just the writers' on **Red Dwarf** – a show they had invented from the ground up. Doug recalls that he had to limit his interventions, whether in the rehearsal room or during recordings, to three per day and he had to be right every single time. Once the scripts were delivered, Paul Jackson and Ed Bye were the ones in charge.

Before writing the second series, they did spend some time talking to their collaborators about what was possible and what wasn't. Say they wanted to do an entire episode underwater, for example. Could that be done? Barely able to speak, Ed Bye was just about able to croak out 'Probably not…' Could they do a beach in paradise? Oh yeah, they might even be able to afford some foreign location filming with the increased budget they were expecting. Great, we'll do that story, then. And so this new set of stories was written with a much clearer idea of what was working, what was achievable, and what they should steer clear of.

Sadly, BBC accountants had a different idea of how Series II was going to pull off more location filming and more guest actors. Their view was that with sets already built, casting having taken place, and model shots already in the can, the second series need not cost as much as the first and so they allocated slightly less money the second time around. Nonetheless, Rob and Doug felt freer to let their creative impulses off the leash. They understood the characters and the people playing them. It was clear that episodes like *Confidence and Paranoia*, with a bit of extra conceptual fizz, worked much better than purely character-driven stories like *Balance of Power*, and so they continued to explore different tropes, ideas, and concepts, getting inspiration from popular science books and articles as well as science fiction movies and their own imaginations.

Where Doug at least agreed with the BBC brass was the need for additional characters. With their self-imposed *no other humans, no aliens and no cute robots* rules in place, that was going to be difficult. But Doug eventually managed to persuade Rob to allow him one robot in one episode. As they developed the character of Kryten, the prissy mechanoid butler who hasn't noticed that his charges have become desiccated skeletons over thousands of years, they knew just who should play him. Rob and Doug's early sitcom *Wrinkles* had included an actor named David Ross and both writers had been absolutely delighted by his facility with their dialogue and his charm in front of an audience. Ross was very happy to play the part, but his claustrophobia was somewhat triggered by the need to have his entire head encased in alginate to create the form-fitting Kryten mask, and he insisted on holding someone's hand for the twenty minutes it took the stuff to set hard.

Worse was to come, because on the day of recording, he was called to the set at 5:00 a.m. and the costume and mask-fitting took the next eight or nine hours, barely getting him ready for the afternoon camera rehearsal, and then his head had to remain encased in rubber for the evening recording. Although he may regret not being able to attend the many lucrative science fiction conventions that Robert Llewellyn has graced with his presence, David Ross may not have wanted to go through that experience more than once.

The fact that the three women aboard the crashed ship have been reduced to mere bones is the big surprise in the middle of this episode, and – ever the showman – Paul Jackson was determined to not let the studio audience get ahead. On his orders, the *Nova 5* set was carefully prepared and then a large black drape was hung in front of it so that no one watching could tell what was behind. Only then was the audience admitted, the quick close-ups of Kryten on the set having been filmed earlier in the day and played in during the recording. The plan was to whip away the black cloth moments before the first shot of the set was needed, and so capture the audience's authentic reaction to seeing the skeletal crew for the first time. Alas for Jackson, during a scene change earlier in the evening, the drapes were taken down prematurely. The producer got something of the response he was hoping for, but no cameras or sound equipment were recording anything.

Paul Jackson's reputation for unbridled fury and intolerance of anything less than perfection is legendary, and production manager Mike Agnew recalls that following this, he was yelled at by Jackson for nearly a minute, their faces only inches apart. Watching the final episode though, we're still waiting for the moment when *Lister and Rimmer* see the skeletons, and that gets the big laugh that everyone was hoping for – from the audience at home as well as in the studio. So often, comedy is in the reactions, not the actions, and it helps that Ed Bye shoots this brilliantly, cutting to a close-up of Chris Barrie at exactly the right moment.

On recording days, Doug Naylor liked to watch from the gallery (where the director sits, observing the outputs of all the different cameras, and relaying instructions via headphones to the studio floor) and on this occasion, Ed Bye's wife Ruby Wax had dropped by. When the female astronauts were revealed to be lifeless skeletons, she couldn't resist leaning over to Doug and whispering to him, 'And they said you couldn't write for women.'

Doug also had the opportunity to see the very top of the studio, where great steel cages supported the lights and cabling. Remembering how effective it had been using the studio steps for the exterior of *Red Dwarf* in *Confidence and Paranoia*, he thought that this would make a marvellous location for some more industrial-looking parts of the ship and suggested it to Ed Bye. A few meetings later, it was made clear that filming anything in that part of the studio would be a complete health and safety nightmare and there was no way it was going to be allowed. So, they went ahead and did it anyway, and shots taken there can be seen in various episodes, including *Kryten* and *Queeg*.

At this time, there was no thought of Kryten playing any future role in the series, and the scheduling certainly wouldn't have permitted them to write him into any subsequent episodes of Series II (several of which were already in the can by this point), but Doug in particular saw great potential in him and loved the interplay between the human, the hologram and the mechanoid. As transmitted, the episode ends with a freeze-frame of Kryten in his Marlon Brando biker gear – it's not established that he ever leaves *Red Dwarf*. That gave them a thread to pull on for Series III.

Next to be transmitted, but first before the cameras, was *Better Than Life*, which saw our heroes enter a virtual reality video game where their every wish could come true. While talk of foreign locations had emboldened the writers, when the time actually came to plan the filming, the production team quickly realised that their search needed to be within a two-hour drive of their Manchester base, and that led them to a beach in Rhyl, North Wales. But Rhyl in May isn't anyone's idea of paradise, and when they arrived it wasn't only windy and cold, it was also raining. Hard. Shots of Lister and Cat relaxing in deckchairs, sipping cocktails and wearing shorts and Hawaiian shirts, had to be abandoned because the actors were turning blue, and their teeth were chattering so much they couldn't speak. Some of this material was eventually recorded on a later, sunnier day, and at a different location.

Some thought had been given to moving the shoot inside the nearby leisure centre, but although happy to accommodate the BBC cameras, Sun Centre in Rhyl made it clear that they weren't going to close the facility and send everybody home at this short notice, and nobody thought they could get the shots they needed while surrounded by screaming kids dive-bombing each other in the pool.

Vehicles also caused problems for the production. An E-type Jaguar and a motorbike were borrowed for use during the shoot, but the owners were carefully not told that these would both be driven across a beach. In fact, sand was a menace in general. During a shot of the Jag speeding away, one of the cameras was sprayed with the stuff, scratching the lens and messing up the electronics. Then the tide came in faster than anyone was expecting, and the E-type had to be towed out of the silt, as its tyres had lost all traction. History does not record the owner's response when reunited with the car.

Someone else visiting the beach from hell was Norman Lovett. Resourceful effects designer Andy Bowman had built a caterpillar trolley to hold a television monitor so that Holly could trundle about, and so he is seen in various locations during this episode. Bowman's plan had been to stack a VHS player in the lower portions of his machine so that Holly's lines could be prerecorded, but the technicians at BBC Manchester had other ideas, and insisted that for the sake of image quality, the monitor needed to display a live picture. And so, the Hollymobile constantly trails a large cable behind it, including in these scenes, for which Lovett was – very gratefully – in the back of the Outside Broadcast van, wrapped in warm blankets.

As the dream turns to a nightmare, Rimmer, Lister and the Cat find themselves buried up to their necks in sand. This was achieved by digging a pit about 3 feet deep, in which the actors gamely knelt. The hole was then covered by wooden boards and sand poured on top. The illusion is moderately convincing, but the boards can be seen to move a few times. Given the howling gale and constant drizzle that is evident in shot after shot, though, this is a minor quibble.

Thanks for the Memory is a bit of a return to the style of Series I. It's almost entirely shipbound, apart from a few quick shots of Lister with Lise Yates, and some hijinks on a pair of suspiciously similar planetoids (one with an atmosphere and one without) and there are no guest cast members, except for the briefly glimpsed Sabra Williams. What little location work there was, was largely done on a reclaimed landfill site outside Manchester. This looked suitably barren and alien, but it stank to high heaven, and turned many of the cast into lifelong hypochondriacs, perpetually blaming every subsequent ache, twinge and illness on their time spent in that toxic environment.

As the evening location work for this episode dragged on, Craig Charles became increasingly aware that some miles away his then-wife was about to give birth to their first child. As soon as his dialogue scenes were finished, he jumped into the waiting car and sped off to the hospital, where his son was placed into his arms. He'd missed the birth by about twenty minutes. Back at the landfill, floor manager Mike Agnew donned Craig Charles's spacesuit and leg cast and stood in for him, but having larger feet than the real Lister, he found the cast in particular very painful. The result is very poor continuity for both Lister and the Cat, with casts appearing on different feet in different scenes and being absent altogether in several shots.

For this and the previous story, a new set was used – the Observation Dome, which combined a Peter Wragg miniature with colour separation stars and some physical pieces designed by Paul Montague. It was intended as an alternative to the bunk beds, and Rob and Doug referred to it as the 'pathos set' but it was never used again after these two episodes. Part of it was recycled as the dream machine seen in *Parallel Universe*.

Picking up on some of the themes of *Future Echoes* from Series I, *Stasis Leak* was another time travel episode, forming the second part of a loose thematic trilogy with *Timeslides* from Series III. Once again, the cast were largely baffled by the intricacies of the plotting, but a short-tempered Paul Jackson told them to get their heads down, learn the lines and be funny, and leave the temporal problem solving to Rob and Doug.

Filming for the Ganymede Holiday Inn, where Lister and the Cat track down Kochanski, took place at the Midland Hotel in Manchester, where the cast was also staying, which meant they all got a lie-in. Ed Bye judged that the lobby was big enough that they didn't need to close it, and so they grabbed their shots – including Cat spraying a woman's fur with seltzer water – during ordinary business hours. The following year, the hotel declined to accept their booking and the team had to find another Manchester hotel.

Returning for this story were Mac McDonald, who got a noseful of green paint for his trouble, Mark Williams as Petersen, and C.P. Grogan as Kochanski. Weirdly, despite some shuffling of recording dates vs transmission dates for these episodes, nobody seemed fazed when Grogan told them she could do the pre-filming but not the studio recording, and it seems as if no contingency plan was put in place to deal with her absence. At the last minute, all of her lines in the final scene were cut, and she is doubled by diminutive assistant floor manager Dona DiStefano, who is hiding her face under a broad-brimmed hat. I don't know whether it was by luck or forethought that Kochanski is seen wearing an unusual black-hat-and-white-bathrobe combo in the pre-filming on location – but it could well be luck as it's not the same hat in the studio.

Danny John-Jules had brought Charles Augins to the **Red Dwarf** Series I wrap party. A fine choreographer, he had been a mentor to the young Danny and was also very recognisable to UK audiences as the guy who says 'I'll have a Babycham' in the twee adverts for the sparkling pear drink popular in the early eighties. With Norman Lovett lobbying for a Holly-centred story and having met this extraordinary performer, Rob and Doug soon cooked up the fan-favourite episode *Queeg* featuring Augins as Holly's replacement, Queeg 500.

In keeping with the drive to make the visuals more exciting, this episode featured a fairly major stunt for Craig Charles, who needed to hit a trampoline to match his standing posture in the previous shot, and then go hurtling over some computer consoles while sparks flew all around him. Captured from multiple angles and slowed down in postproduction, this footage was reused in several versions of the **Red Dwarf** opening titles and on Ed Bye's showreel for many years.

Also showing his particular talents was Chris Barrie in a sequence that saw him trot out his impersonations of his castmates and, supposedly, a rendition of BBC Manchester's own Peter Ridsdale-Scott, although I can't hear the resemblance. A more protracted scene of him acquiring the vocal characteristics of other members of the crew was trimmed for time. Barrie doesn't seem especially proud of these moments of mimicry, perhaps feeling that he was undermining his status as an actor and falling back on the impressions which had defined his early career, but I think they're great fun and he does a marvellous job.

There was no location filming for this episode, but that didn't mean that Ed Bye and his team got any additional recording time – or any more equipment. With Norman Lovett in one small cupboard at the back of the studio, staring into a camera, and Charles Augins in another small cupboard, staring into another camera, he only had three left to cover the rest of the action. Paul Jackson told him he was lucky to have five cameras at all – most BBC sitcoms only got four.

This episode is also famous for its fabulous ending, which manages to turn the events of the preceding twenty minutes entirely on their head without in any way feeling like a cop out. Remarkably, Rob and Doug claim that they had written fifty-eight out of sixty pages and didn't have that ending, or indeed any ending, until the day before the script was due, when inspiration fell upon them during a late-night drinking session at their local pub (Rob describes this as a 'three-pint problem', which I assume is a nod to Sherlock Holmes).

The series ended with the high concept *Parallel Universe* (recorded fifth but transmitted last) in which the boys from the *Dwarf* meet the girls from the *Dwarf*, and so Ed Bye had to find four actors who could summon up something of the spirit of the regular cast. He instantly knew who should play the female Rimmer, a stage actor he knew called Suzanne Bertish. He then spent the whole rehearsal week fretting that he'd made a terrible mistake, because Bertish would barely show them anything resembling a performance in Acton. It was only when she was in front of the Manchester audience that her version of Rimmer came to life, and everybody breathed a sigh of relief.

Playing the female Lister was Angela Bruce, who was already a familiar face on British TV from shows like *Rock Follies* and *Angels*. She matched Craig Charles's energy even more closely than Bertish had matched Barrie's, despite being in her late thirties when she played the part opposite a 24-year-old Charles. Even easier to cast was Hattie Hayridge as Hilly, given that a review of her stand-up had already described her as 'the female Norman Lovett'. Norman Lovett lent her his off-air tapes of the first series so she could get a feel for the part – but he drew the line at having her kiss him. For the shot in which Holly is shown covered in lipstick splodges, Hayridge happily volunteered to apply these herself, and was slightly taken aback when Lovett insisted that this was a job for make-up artists and that her smooching services would not be required. The Cat too had his amorous ambitions frustrated, since rather than the writers giving him a slinky feminine feline to molest, Matthew Devitt was cast as the Dog. All four made a great impression, maybe none more so than Hayridge, but we'll come back to her in Series III.

The episode – and thus the series – ends with the cliffhanger of Lister being pregnant. A couple of alternatives of this scene were considered, including a version where Rimmer admits that he was only pulling Lister's leg when looking at the results of the test, but two 'only joking' episode endings in a row probably would not have worked. As usual, Rob and Doug were having fun throwing ideas out and worrying about how to resolve them when and if they got another series – and what's wrong with that?

Still keen to mess around with the opening and closing titles, Rob remembered a song they'd written for *Son of Cliché* called 'Tongue Tied' and he and Doug wrote a new version based on the same gag (the singer becomes so love-struck that his song about being tongue-tied turns to gibberish) and gave the lyric to the redoubtable Howard Goodall, who composed a suitably jaunty tune. Everyone agreed that his demo, the melody inspired by Diana Ross's hit

'Chain Reaction', was very funny and so plans were made to incorporate the song into the opening of *Parallel Universe* as part of a dream sequence.

But experienced musical theatre performer Danny John-Jules had turned up to the recording of Goodall's music and wasn't best pleased with what he'd witnessed. 'Those weren't real musicians,' he said ruefully. 'There wasn't a single can of lager between them.' Before Ed Bye knew what was happening, John-Jules had got Charles Augins in to help with the choreography and had recorded his own version of the track in order to get a 'funkier' sound to the music. Doug Naylor's dismay at these changes is very evident in the documentary on the DVD. The new sound adds a bit of production value, but doesn't make the piece any funnier – if anything, it rather swamps the comedy.

The *Top of the Pops* style set for this three-and-a-half-minute song (cut down to just over two minutes in the edit) took up half the studio, and working on the steps with inexperienced dancers Barrie and Charles took up half the rehearsal time, to Ed Bye's mounting frustration. However, the song was popular. When it was released as a single in 1993, it reached number 17 in the UK charts, and was accompanied by a bizarre thirty-minute dream sequence-cum-pop video-cum-sitcom episode-cum-documentary featuring an array of **Red Dwarf** actors and friends of Danny John-Jules. This was released on VHS and almost qualifies for entry in the Apocrypha section (but not quite).

Paul Jackson organised a press launch for Series II, which took place at the 'Space Adventure' attraction on Tooley Street in central London. Ratings for Series II weren't a noticeable improvement on Series I; in fact they were generally lower, with no episode beating the high-water mark set by *The End* – but people were starting to watch and take notice. A few more favourable reviews crept out in the press, and Peter Ridsdale-Scott recalls his deep pleasure in seeing a young lad on the train wearing what must have been a home-made **Red Dwarf** t-shirt (home-made because no official merchandise was yet available). Maybe, just maybe, BBC Manchester had managed to craft a cult hit. Now, if they could just keep everyone on board for Series III, they might really have something.

Impressions of Series II

Written by Rob Grant and Doug Naylor. Designed by Paul Montague. Costumes by Jackie Pinks. Executive producer: Paul Jackson. Produced and directed by Ed Bye. Starring: Craig Charles, Chris Barrie, Danny John-Jules, Norman Lovett.

S02E01 Kryten ★★★★☆

TX: 6 September 1988 on BBC2. Ratings: 2.5m (12th for the week). Featuring: David Ross.

What a way to start. Instantly, everything is smoother, crisper, sharper, funnier. We're still starting with five minutes of idle *Dwarf*-time, but now when Holly and Lister shoot the breeze it's the classic 'dog's milk' routine instead of arbitrary gags about PE teachers or airline food. And the whole place looks livelier, more colourful and more textured. Even the mild obsession with Esperanto starts to pay off. Hoping to make the Jupiter Mining Corporation feel like an inclusive vision of the future, both here and in Series I, all of the signage on the ship is given first in English and then in Esperanto, the hoped-for universal language created out of whole cloth at the end of the nineteenth century. Here, Rimmer is shown trying to learn it, in scenes that do echo the doofus Rimmer from *Waiting for God*, but work rather better here (like so much in Series II, compared to Series I). When the ship sets were redesigned in Series III, the Esperanto was dropped.

We also get a slightly more vulnerable Rimmer here. Sure, he still tries to sabotage Lister's outfit when they all get dolled up to meet what they still think will be three young women, eternally grateful to have been rescued. But he also asks for help, confesses he was bullied at school, and appeals to Lister's better nature. The Cat meanwhile, although still not having a huge stake in the narrative, gets some excellent material, including having to be forcibly dragged away from a mirror, which is a fantastic moment in writing, acting and conception. Craig Charles, who had snagged a part in a BBC mini-series called *The Marksman* between stints on **Red Dwarf**, also looks completely relaxed and at home in front of the cameras now – not that he ever looked particularly tense or anxious.

But the episode belongs to David Ross. It's impossible to imagine what would have happened if he'd joined the cast – either here or at the beginning of Series III – and his early success in the part takes nothing away from Robert Llewellyn, who brilliantly reinvents the character. But Ross is perfect, whether it's trying to get Rimmer to confirm his hasty diagnosis of his three humans, wretchedly doing chores back on *Red Dwarf*, or in his final triumphant moments where he doesn't give even a hint that he's about to rebel, until finally, gloriously, he does.

Other episodes will probe the mind of a mechanoid with greater depth, plenty will have a bit more plot to sustain the full run time and the characters will continue to grow and deepen, but for the seventh-ever episode, this is an absolute triumph, and one of my top episodes to show somebody who's never seen **Red Dwarf** before.

The one with: Kryten.

That Rimmer's a solid guy: Even though he is a hologram sustained by the shipboard computer, there is no issue with Rimmer leaving *Red Dwarf*. It's not at all clear what he thinks he will be able to do with the *Nova 5* survivors, even had they not been centuries-dead. He can smell Lister's foul boots.

There's a time and a place: Art colleges are still a thing, and you get in via the usual boring way: fail your exams and apply. Rimmer refers to Norman Bates from Alfred Hitchcock's 1960 classic *Psycho,* and to Champion the Wonder Horse, equine companion to Gene Autry on American television in the early 1950s. Lister's choice of reading material is one of Eric Hill's *Spot the Dog* books, first published in 1980. He thinks Rimmer looks like Clive of India in his dress uniform – Robert Clive was a lieutenant colonel in the British Army who helped secure India for the British and who served as Governor of Bengal.

Influences, references and rip-offs: 'Androids' is an obvious riff on the Australian television series *Neighbours,* which ran from 1985 to 2022 and made stars of Kylie Minogue, Jason Donovan and many others. As the credits roll, the director of 'Androids' is shown to be one 'Kylie Gwenlyn', a nod to both Ms Minogue and the BBC's Head of Light Entertainment, Gareth Gwenlan. Holly's decimalisation of the musical octave is a routine recycled from the Grant/Naylor radio sketch comedy show *Cliché.* Kryten himself is inspired by J.M. Barrie's 1902 stage play *The Admirable Crichton,* in which a British Lord and his family are shipwrecked on a desert island and only their butler Crichton can keep them alive. Of the various filmed versions of this piece, the 1957 movie with Kenneth More as Crichton is the one best remembered.

Referred to but not seen in the closing minutes are the films *Rebel Without a Cause*, *The Wild One* and *Easy Rider*, with Kryten's leather gear duplicating Marlon Brando's look in *The Wild One*.

Best gag: 'I was only away two minutes.' Expertly set up in the script and perfectly delivered by David Ross.

Worst visual effect: This first iteration of Kryten's mask is pretty ropey, with no proper join around the eyes, lots of rough edges and those oddly coloured lips. Apparently, the special effects team had major problems with the foam latex and had to make it in two pieces, which wasn't the plan. Cat's approach to *Blue Midget* is some of the worst CSO ever seen on the show (and is cut from the Remastered version). On the other hand, the *Nova 5* model shot is very nice.

Continuity is for smegheads: Lister insists that he's read books, and indeed was keen to read the Cat's holy book in *Waiting for God*, but in *Future Echoes* he wistfully muses that he's never read… a book. Rimmer's obsession with aliens continues. First appearance of *Blue Midget*. Rimmer's preferred nickname here is 'Ace'. At school, he was known as 'Bonehead'. Rimmer refers to the encounter as 'our first contact with intelligent life in 3 million and two years', meaning that two years have passed since Lister emerged from stasis.

Remastered: There's no need to reshoot any of Holly's material here since in Series II he's presented with no video effect on him at all. An extra cartoon whiff has been added to Lister's smelly boots. The 'Mc' at the beginning of 'McNugget' – which was removed from the soundtrack on the transmitted version to avoid lawsuits – has been reinstated following the discovery that the product is actually called a 'Chicken Nugget' and not a 'McNugget' (although this 'discovery' was itself incorrect, and McDonald's does indeed own the 'McNugget' trademark). An extra shot has been added showing Kryten definitively leaving *Red Dwarf* on Lister's space bike. Tony Slattery is credited as playing the 'Andriod' actor in the closing credits. The reframing cuts off part of the text when the medical records for the *Nova 5* crew are displayed.

S02E02 Better Than Life ★★★☆☆

TX: 13 September 1988 on BBC2. Ratings: 2.45m (9th for the week).
Featuring: John Abineri, Tony Hawks, Judy Hawkins, Ron Pember.

There are at least two brilliant ideas here, and in true **Red Dwarf** style, we have to wait for them. And neither is quite executed as well as it might have been, making this a slightly frustrating, if nevertheless entertaining, watch. The late delivery of the post is at first just a pretext for some very twentieth-century Royal Mail and Inland Revenue gags, but the revelation of Rimmer's dad's death, complete with the ghoulish black humour of Lister being unable to read his mother's handwriting, takes us somewhere a little bleaker, a little realer.

What's bizarre is that they seize on the Total Immersion Video games at first sight, are filled with excitement at the prospect of playing them – and then just do nothing with them until almost halfway through the episode. When they do plug themselves in, we get hints of a bigger, bolder, crazier show than we've ever had before, but sadly the ideas are hobbled by the execution. Not that all the ideas are that wonderful. Fast cars, loose women, lavish meals and rapid promotions are all pretty much clichés of the wish-fulfilment genre, and while they all fit perfectly well with the characters that we know, it would have been nice to have gone a bit more niche – Cat's meal of live fish is more fun, for example.

The nearly insurmountable problem is that none of this looks remotely convincing because every detail of every shot tells us that we're about as far away from paradise as it's possible to get. Ed Bye does what he can with the interiors, but the exteriors look absolutely ghastly and even when the sun shines in a couple of shots, its conspicuous absence in the reverse angles only makes the problem worse.

The other brilliant idea is that Rimmer's mind can't accept nice things happening to him. Far more interesting than making him a doofus who can't learn a single word of Esperanto after literally years of study, this makes him into a fascinatingly wretched figure of self-loathing. The novel that covers the same ground, free of the problems of trying to summon up visions of literal paradise in two days' OB filming, goes even deeper into his self-lacerating psyche, but the glimpses we get here are still potent. I just wish that Rob and Doug had resisted the temptation to butter their bacon by having the Cat's fantasy of his father rejecting Rimmer first, as this fogs the issue. Always nice to see John Abineri though (and Tony Hawks, for that matter).

The one with: Paradise unconvincingly recreated on a freezing cold beach.

That Rimmer's a solid guy: Being 'keyed in' to the video game means that the fantasy world is as accessible for him as it is for everyone else. He gets turned back into a hologram at the end, but is still vulnerable to the claws of deadly crabs (and Ron Pember's mallet).

There's a time and a place: Hugely advanced video games look like film cans or biscuit tins painted green. Messages come on CDs (and paper letters). Holly references Berni Inn. *Casablanca* has been remade again, even though the version with Myra Binglebat and Peter Beardsley is definitive. There's a new *Friday the 13th* movie (the 1649th). The middle classes can't survive without Perrier. Three million years is about average for second-class post. Rimmer's sexual exploits remind him of *Playboy* publisher Hugh Hefner. He compares the skutters to Pinky and Perky, puppet stars of British children's television from 1957, whose sped-up voices were also heard on numerous records. Brooke Shields's buttocks are hard to get hold of. Gordon's ship is the *Scott Fitzgerald*, presumably named after the author of *The Great Gatsby*.

Influences, references and rip-offs: Dream worlds, easily confused with reality, have a long pedigree from simple fantasies like *The Wizard of Oz* to more sciencey versions like Isaac Asimov's 1955 short story *Dreaming is a Private Thing* or much of the work of William Gibson. Made ten years after this was broadcast, hugely influential film *The Matrix* opened the floodgates to a whole slew of such stories, but it's also worth noting the 1976 *Doctor Who* serial 'The Deadly Assassin', about a quarter of which takes place inside a surreal dreamscape, which the Doctor accesses by plugging into the Time Lords' supercomputer – known as The Matrix.

Best gag: Lister tries to hush a hungry Cat, telling him, 'Rimmer's dad's just died.' The Cat responds, 'I'd prefer chicken.'

Worst visual effect: All of the location stuff looks dreadful, as noted. Stars show through parts of Lister's body while they're in the observation dome.

Continuity is for smegheads: No mention of what currency Rimmer's tax demand is in (in the novels and later episodes, it's 'dollarpounds'). The J in Arnold J. Rimmer stands for Judas. In *Future Echoes* it sounded like Rimmer's dad had taken his own life, so it's surprising to hear him floored by news of his death. And speaking of *Future Echoes*, Channel 27 does indeed have a hologram reading the news, and it is a groovy channel, just as Rimmer said. The transmission dates to Friday the 27th of Geldof (presumably referring to Bob Geldof, lead singer of the Boomtown Rats, and organiser of the 1985 Live Aid benefit concert at Wembley). Rimmer's VR roll in the hay with Yvonne McGruder is only his second time having sex. First appearance of Marilyn Monroe (here played by Debbie Ash, sister of Leslie) and Napoleon, both of whom will rebook this gig. Rimmer has three brothers, one named Frank.

Remastered: A few shots in the observation dome have added nebulae and shooting stars. The newsreader has been inserted into a TV frame. There are some new music cues. A heroic effort has been made to coax Rhyl beach into paradise via the picture grade, but it still looks cold, rainy and grim.

S02E03 Thanks for the Memory ★★☆☆☆

TX: 20 September 1988 on BBC2. Ratings: 3.10m (6th for the week). Featuring Sabra Williams.

This starts quite promisingly, with some nice location work, and some great character stuff between Rimmer and Lister. They aren't just work colleagues who get on each other's nerves any more. They're friends from very different backgrounds and with very different outlooks on life, who still rub each other up the wrong way, but who have begun to grudgingly respect and appreciate – even care for – each other. Rimmer eating the holographic fried egg sandwich is some of Chris Barrie's finest non-vocal acting.

The rest of the story is structured like an Agatha Christie whodunnit, but there are only so many possible culprits, which makes unravelling the mystery rather less interesting than is really ideal. And the locker-room stench of much of the material around Lister's girlfriend doesn't help. Added to which, the whole notion of rummaging around in someone's memories and rewriting their personal history is kind of disturbing. When Rimmer describes the events of this episode as 'the most heart-breakingly tragic thing it's ever been my misfortune to witness', that's hyperbole, but only just. It's hard to keep laughing through the pain, but if you don't buy into the pain then the whole thing has no substance.

This isn't a failure on the level of *Waiting for God*, and it isn't dull the way that *Balance of Power* is. Indeed, in the moment where Lister realises, through his conversation with Rimmer, that he was the arsehole and that Lise deserved better than him, the story approaches something deeper – but it doesn't feel like this show. And then silly questions start intruding. Why does Rimmer plead with Lister not to tell anyone about his sexual history? They're the only two humans left. Who's he going to tell? And where exactly did Rimmer find these letters between Lister and Lise? What made him go looking for them? Has Lister never heard of sexting?

The punchline for this one is particularly limp: we end on the revelation that Lister has been putting together a jigsaw puzzle of the closing titles? Really? Thankfully, this is a blip in an otherwise strong series. What's baffling is that Ed Bye seems to have thought it was going to be the stand-out success of Series II. Maybe it's just not to my taste.

The one with: Rimmer's fake girlfriend.

That Rimmer's a solid guy: Rimmer, who had no problem wandering around the *Nova 5*, is only sustained on the planet's surface via a holo-cage. He plops heavily into a chair next to Lister. He's terrified of alien monsters, who cannot possibly harm him. Holographic drinks leave him with a holographic hangover.

There's a time and a place: Holly refers to Shake and Vac and Jimmy Osmond. Rimmer mentions Odor Eaters. Lister imitates Bogart when he says 'Play it Sam', and he refers to the Academy Award Best Picture-winning *From Here to Eternity*, famous for its scene of Burt Lancaster and Deborah Kerr smooching in the surf. Rimmer sings the Gershwin/Howard Dietz song 'Someone to Watch Over Me', which dates from 1926 but is now associated most with Ella Fitzgerald, who recorded it in 1950. The most romantic thing Rimmer has ever had down his ear is a Johnson's Baby Bud.

Influences, references and rip-offs: Oddly similar to an episode of *Star Trek: The Next Generation*, even down to the detail of including a broken bone. But 'Clues' aired over two years after this, in the show's fourth season, and it seems very unlikely that any of the writing staff in California was watching **Red Dwarf** (even if an overly excitable PBS executive did tell Doug Naylor around this time that his series was 'bigger than Monty Python' in the USA). The title comes from a song written for Bob Hope and Shirley Ross to sing in the film *The Big Broadcast of 1938*.

Best gag: Hungover Rimmer, peering at a clock when Lister asks him the time: 'Saturday. There are some numbers next to it, but they could be anything.'

Worst visual effect: All the *Blue Midget* stuff looks great compared to the horrid video game graphics in the remastered version.

Continuity is for smegheads: It's the anniversary of Rimmer's death (3,000,002nd anniversary, one assumes). In a rare moment of consistency, it is reiterated that prior to *Better than Life*, Rimmer has only had sex once. That also suggests that the running order was juggled late in the day – however, *Better than Life* was filmed before *Thanks for the Memory*, so maybe the change took place between writing and recording (*Kryten* was filmed fourth and *Queeg* was filmed last). Rimmer is still seeing aliens as the solution to every mystery. His preferred nickname now is 'Tiger'. During the conversation about Rimmer's sexual history, Lister is not wearing his hat, but it looks like he is on the memory recorder version. Lise Yates never comes up again, but we see another version of the hologram simulation suite in *Stasis Leak*. Hollister is Mr Fat Bastard 2044, which suggests that the Jupiter Mining Corporation will be beginning operations around twenty years from now. Rimmer's prized possessions include his telescope and his shoetrees. As noted, there is very poor plaster cast continuity from shot to shot.

Remastered: A video game-looking CGI *Blue Midget* AT-ATs its way across a poorly rendered planetary surface. New music cue in the observation dome. A gag about Spanish television has been deleted.

S02E04 Stasis Leak ★★★★☆

TX: 27 September 1988 on BBC2. Ratings: 3.15m (4th for the week). Featuring: Mac McDonald, C.P. Grogan, Tony Hawks, Mark Williams, Morwenna Banks.

Stasis Leak is good fun, but it's a bit too ambitious structurally. That ends up getting in the way of some of the character development, and you can occasionally hear the plot mechanism jangling as the story rattles over the points. Once again, we get the opportunity to see the pre-*The End* version of the ship, with welcome return appearances from Hollister and Petersen. And there are some more nifty split-screen effects, and some decent doubles for Lister and Rimmer – it's only on second viewing that you're likely to catch future Rimmer walking past during the early flashback. Classy.

The pretzel logic of the plotting sees Lister deducing that shortly before the accident, Rimmer saw future versions of themselves, mistaking them for hallucinations. Using this information, they find the stasis leak on floor 16 (which is a *very* inconveniently long way away, especially when you consider that the boys take multiple trips) and return to their past lives to try to save one of them. There's some neat writing here: Cat repeatedly asking 'What is it?' is very funny, but also a clever way of packaging up some much-needed exposition.

Of course, not all of this slots neatly into place with episodes past and to come (see various **Continuity is for smegheads** entries) but it breezes past in a jolly enough fashion. It's a bit confounding to have Rimmer given weeks, months or even years of punishment detail when there's no sign of that during the events of *The End* and it's even more confusing to see him given green paint to use on the outside of the very red ship. What really doesn't work is Captain Hollister's poultry-apology. Having him turn up in a chicken costume isn't funny enough to be worth the brief justification and the brief justification doesn't do enough heavy lifting on its own. But more seriously – why is Hollister apologising at all? I honestly expected that to be some kind of Rimmer-disguised-as-Kochanski fake-out. It's totally unnecessary and out of character for the hard-ass captain who put Lister in stasis for having a cat to be begging forgiveness from Rimmer. Why does he want to be friends with Rimmer? Rimmer's a smeghead.

The one with: Lister's fake girlfriend.

That Rimmer's a solid guy: He's constantly moving through things, hiding inside things and so on. It makes quite a change. He can travel into the past just as easily as everyone else. Does that mean that control of him is handed over to Past Holly? If that's the case, then it's lucky that George McIntyre is still alive in the past, as Holly can only sustain one hologram at a time.

There's a time and a place: Rimmer compares Hollister's wife to the simian characters in the 1968 film *Planet of the Apes*. Holly rips off **Red Dwarf**'s gag about what it means to have an IQ of 6,000. Desiccated humans look like Daz washing powder. Anything is better than an album by Olivia Newton-John. Living with Lister is like being in a Barbara Cartland novel. Rimmer is (probably) the only person ever to have bought a Topic bar with no hazelnuts. Holly was in love with a Sinclair ZX81, a tiny personal computer. Don't go and see *Run for Your Wife* in the West End (plenty of people did, though, it ran for nine years). As well as a showing of *Gone with the Wind*, the lift includes a 'cassette' for recording a last will and testament. Rimmer calls Hollister Captain 'Paxo' after the popular instant stuffing brand.

Influences, references and rip-offs: Rimmer's 'voyage to trip out city' recalls Paul Merton's classic 'Policeman on Acid' routine, which he had performed – of course – on *Saturday Live*. Although this episode resembles *Back to the Future Part II*, that film was not released for another year. This kind of 'Red Queen's Race' story (where the future creates the past) has been seen before in lots of places, though, including *The Terminator* from 1984, various *Doctor Who* episodes, and in the Isaac Asimov short story of that name.

Best gag: 'Now from this point on, things get a little bit confusing.'

Worst visual effect: All the split-screen stuff is very well done, but the entrance to the stasis leak is a bit *Doctor Who*-ish, and not in a good way.

Continuity is for smegheads: A clock on the wall identifies the year as 2077. Lister has five years to wait before he can marry Kochanski (he does acquire a time drive in Series VI and is reunited with Kochanski in Series VII, sort of). Rimmer implies that it's been three years since *The End*, when it had only been two earlier this series. Speaking of the accident, wouldn't preventing that from happening be a better plan than trying to save one extra person? Lister's reading habits now include Rimmer's diary. A wise old cat saying refers to dogs, but the Cat had never heard of a dog before Lister showed him a photo of one in *Future Echoes*. The very long lift journey is a one-off gag (but *Red Dwarf* lifts do feature prominently in Series XI). Rimmer has no qualms about there being two of him on board, despite his experience with just that in Series I. Holly appears as a watch for the first time. It can be assumed that Lister's punishment detail is what is depicted in the opening titles. Last appearance of Mac McDonald until Series VIII. Last appearance of C.P. Grogan until Series VI. Last appearance to date of Mark Williams, here credited as playing 'Petersen', as opposed to 'Peterson' as he was in *The End* and *Balance of Power*. (It's 'Petersen' in the books, so I've assumed the other spelling is the error.)

Remastered: A Holly joke about Felicity Kendall's bottom has become a joke about Marilyn Monroe's bottom. Everybody talking at once at the end, a moment cut from the transmitted version, has been reinstated.

S02E05 Queeg ★★★★☆

TX: 4 October 1988 on BBC2. Ratings: 2.3m (17th for the week).
Featuring: Charles Augins.

This is the Holly-centred story and it's a credit to all concerned that Norman Lovett doesn't get edged out of his own episode by the sheer presence of Charles Augins. But everyone's on their game here, from the sheer pettiness of Rimmer outwaiting the skutter in order to win at draughts, to Lister's shaggy dog story about Petersen's shoes, to the Cat despairing at the prospect of wearing Marigolds that don't go with his suit.

One example of how clearly Rob and Doug are seeing the world they've created is Rimmer's tale about being in the Space Scouts and nearly being eaten by the other boys. Without the prospect of cannibalism, this is just another bullied-at-school story and could easily have been dull. With the cannibalism, it could just as easily sound either completely ridiculous or profoundly disturbing. But the script is pitched perfectly, and Chris Barrie manages to recount the events with a tiny amount of self-mocking humour – a rarity for the blissfully un-self-aware Rimmer, but precisely judged here.

Everything is well set up, but nothing feels like chess pieces being moved into place (not even the chess game), and the pay-off when it comes is fantastic. I would have liked a bit more character development for the humans, and arguably the need for long conversations about things that happened off-screen (or never happened at all) suggests that – once again – there isn't quite enough plot for twenty-nine minutes, but I'm not going to knock off more than half a star for quibbles like those. This is my favourite episode of the first two years, and it's an absolute delight.

The one with: Queeg.

That Rimmer's a solid guy: Rimmer's legs separate from his body at one point, as Holly malfunctions. He briefly sounds like other members of the crew, including Cat, which is odd (maybe Holly made a personality disc for Cat at some point). He plops heavily into a chair. Why does a hologram need to exercise? And why does it make him feel tired?

There's a time and a place: Lister is filling in the quiz in a women's magazine. Cat's 'music' (purported to be Robert Hardy reading his namesake Thomas Hardy's novel *Tess of the D'Urbervilles*) is on a CD, although Lister claims 'the tape must have got twisted'. A survival course reminds Lister of Butlin's.

Influences, references and rip-offs: The name Queeg and the whole premise is a lift from Herman Wouk's 1951 novel *The Caine Mutiny*, filmed in 1954 with Humphrey Bogart as Captain Queeg, as well as the 1932 novel *Mutiny on the Bounty*, based on real events that took place in 1789, and filmed multiple times, most notably in 1935 with Charles Laughton. It's from here that Holly's line about swinging from the yardarm is drawn. Holly also whistles 'Colonel Bogey', which is a defiant anthem familiar to moviegoers from *The Bridge on the River Kwai*. His big hero moment is accompanied by 'The Ballad of High Noon' (vocal by Howard Goodall). His exit song is 'Goodbye to Love' by The Carpenters, which slows down in the manner of HAL 9000 in Stanley Kubrick's *2001: A Space Odyssey*.

Best gag: 'We are talking jape of the decade.'

Worst visual effect: When the ship is hit, everybody throws themselves across the set, in the best *Star Trek* manner, but the draughts pieces remain stubbornly in place.

Continuity is for smegheads: The shoes in Lister's shaggy dog story echo the boots in *Justice*. Exercise-mad, career-oriented Rimmer has now become a work-shy slob, who always wants a nice lie-in. Rimmer's blow-up girlfriend is called Ingrid. Holly's second game of chess, following his barely begun game with Gordon. This isn't Holly's first practical joke – remember Norweb?

Remastered: Added video effects when Rimmer glitches.

S02E06 Parallel Universe ★★★★☆

TX: 11 October 1988 on BBC2. Ratings: 2.9m (11th for the week).
Featuring Suzanne Bertish, Angela Bruce, Matthew Devitt, Hattie Hayridge.

As we come to the end of Series II, there's clearly much greater confidence in the whole team. Series I has some great moments, but it falters and stumbles at least as often as it soars and succeeds, and there's a definite uncertainty to much of it. In the second batch of episodes, there are still misfires and moments that don't come off – the precision has improved, but only somewhat – but now, the misses are delivered with a huge amount of confidence, and that confidence is often enough to carry the day. It's noteworthy that in an early draft script, we cut to the female Rimmer and Lister and see their point of view of the arrival of a version of *Red Dwarf* from a male-centred society. The transmitted version works much better – it's much more impactful to have Deb and Arlene revealed to us only when Dave and Arnold see them for the first time.

Despite that, *Parallel Universe* is one that Doug doesn't look back on very fondly, describing the battle-of-the-sexes material as sounding like it was written by a couple of schoolboys. Pretty soon, the series is going to discover some brilliantly funny and inventive ways of using science fiction concepts to dig into these characters and look at them from different angles. This feels like we're moving towards that, but we aren't there yet and while I'm not quite so down on it as the writers themselves, I can see what they're getting at. Maybe the most cringe-inducing moment for me is the 'Smurfette' skutters, which is where a lot of the unconscious bias seeps through: male is normal, neutral, typical, relatable; female is other, extraordinary, bizarre and pink with frilly bits on it.

On board the other ship ('It's identical in every detail to our *Red Dwarf*,' muses Rimmer in a budget-saving line) the two Listers mainly work well (Angela Bruce is inspired casting) and Cat's adventures with Matthew Devitt's Dog are pretty funny. It's a good start for Hattie Hayridge too, but the two Rimmers are far more problematic, both in terms of taste and in terms of plotting. Whereas the two Listers are instantly on the same page, it makes sense that Rimmer will screw this up, as he screws up everything else – and we know how little he can tolerate his own company.

But far from being a perfect duplicate of Arnold, Arlene is an overconfident sex pest who seems entirely different from Chris Barrie's portrayal of a stiffly English schoolboy, terrified of intimacy, maybe even asexual. (Likewise, it's hard to imagine Craig Charles treating a possibly pregnant girlfriend as callously as Angela Bruce treats him.) Both Chris Barrie and Suzanne Bertish make the most of what's on the page, but what's on the page doesn't really hit home, and the implied criticism of ladette culture (Or is it sexist male attitudes? It's hard to know.) sticks in the throat especially since this has always been a bit of a boys' club.

What's much more fun is the final scene, with Rimmer torturing Lister over the results of his pregnancy test. Any scientific implausibility is waved away. Who cares? 'I'm going to be an uncle!' There's that confidence I was talking about. Great stuff.

The one with: 'Tongue-tied' for some reason.

That Rimmer's a solid guy: One assumes that the exercise bike Rimmer is sitting on and adjusting is also a hologram. Holograms can touch each other – even when operated by different computers.

There's a time and a place: Shakespeare is now well known again, only here it's Wilma. She wrote *Rachel III* (instead of *Richard III*) and *The Taming of the Shrimp* (instead of *Shrew*). Jeremy Greer (instead of Germaine) wrote *The Male Eunuch* (instead of *The Female Eunuch*). The first woman on the moon was Nellie Armstrong. Ringo was a crap drummer (no he wasn't). Cat has heard of Carmen Miranda and her predilection for decorative headgear. Rimmer pretends to be a munchkin from *The Wizard of Oz*.

Influences, references and rip-offs: Both alternate universes and female-centric societies have long pedigrees, from the *Star Trek* Mirror Universe to 'The Worm That Turned' in the 1980 series of *The Two Ronnies*. Charlotte Perkins Gilman's 1915 novel *Herland* is often cited as the first story to depict an all-female society. The gender-flip device is also used in various episodes of *Star Trek* and the Polish satirical film *Seksmisja* ('Sexmission') from 1984 among many others.

Best gag: Danny John-Jules's face when he sees the Dog is priceless.

Worst visual effect: The Holly Hop drive is a pretty dreadful prop, which they've hung a lantern on by pointing out how crap it looks, but it still resembles something out of a school play, with no weight to it and no detail. Cat's sped-up dancing looks very silly and you can clearly see the fishing wire pulling the baby skutters.

Continuity is for smegheads: Rimmer, whose antipathy towards physical activity was clearly established in *Queeg*, is voluntarily on the exercise bike here. Cat refers to Lister's smelly moon boots from *Kryten*. For the first and only time, they bring a skutter with them when visiting another ship. Holly explicitly refers to *Future Echoes* in which a version of Lister is shown with twin sons – and maybe having their mother be another version of Lister is intended to be an explanation as to why Lister's son looks identical to him, so much so that Rimmer thinks he has seen Lister's death. If that was the idea, it isn't referred to again, and in any case, eventually gets swept aside in Series VII's *Ouroboros*.

Remastered: We get the regular titles before 'Tongue Tied'. There are new video effects for the Holly Hop drive (but not very good ones) and there's new music in the disco.

Series III

The Making of Series III

Getting the second series had been suspiciously easy. Getting a third series was more of a struggle. In making the decision to recommission it, the BBC had grudgingly admitted that, yes, some people did seem to have been watching the show, and that it was possible that some of them had even liked it. But if there were going to be any more episodes – and mind you, we did say if – then there needed to be more female characters, less of this two-men-arguing the whole time, and can you please get them off that spaceship once in a while? Peter Ridsdale-Scott was forced to bite his tongue and refrain from reminding his bosses that the series had only been allowed to proceed on the basis that it was *Steptoe* in space and not a crazy science fiction show. Regardless of these inconsistencies, when the word came that a third series was wanted, Rob and Doug knew they wanted to make some changes. Chief among these was making the mechanoid Kryten into a regular character.

But David Ross was doing a play. To be exact, he was doing *A Flea in her Ear* at the Old Vic, and so there was no way he could make the recording dates on Friday evenings in Manchester. If Series III had been recorded on Sunday nights like Series II, possibly he could have made it work, but as it was he had to bow out. This was deeply disappointing for Rob and Doug, who had fallen in love with Kryten the robot, and were banging their heads on the limitations of their format. With one insubstantial hologram, one insubstantial computer, and one cat who doesn't really care about anything, they only had one character they could put in danger or who would have relatable fears or desires. The search was on for another mechanoid.

Someone who had previous relevant experience was Robert Llewellyn. He'd been on the fringes of the eighties alternative comedy boom with his sketch group The Joeys and had taken a play to the Edinburgh Fringe called *Mammon: Robot Born of Woman*, which had been nominated for the prestigious 'Perrier' comedy award. This brought him to the attention of Paul Jackson, and he quickly set up a meeting with Rob and Doug and Ed Bye.

Llewellyn recalls that the meeting involved quite a lot of experimentation with different styles, voices, walks and so on. In particular, he remembers demonstrating what he called his 'Douglas Bader special' – a stiff-kneed, hip-swivelling gait named after the British Second World War fighter pilot who lost both legs, which he enthusiastically essayed, complete with little squeaking noises for the wooden joints. Having not met either of the writers before, he was then appalled when they got up to leave and for a second it seemed as if Doug was amusingly doing his own version of the Douglas Bader special, but the laugh caught in Llewellyn's throat as he realised that the writer was genuinely walking on a prosthetic leg.

Despite the possible *faux pas*, Llewellyn was offered the part and gladly accepted, although he was a little anxious about being typecast as a robot. 'Don't worry,' Ed Bye told him cheerfully. 'Nobody will recognise you.' At this stage, Llewellyn – who hadn't watched the episode in which the Kryten character had already appeared – imagined that the costume would be something like *RoboCop*, which had been such an influential hit only a few years before. Yes, he thought, my face probably will be quite well hidden. Even while being covered with alginate (as David Ross had been before him) he appears not to have quite grasped what was going to happen to him. 'This must be a very snugly fitting helmet,' he mused as the stuff set hard. When he saw himself in the full make-up for the first time, he got quite a start. The change in actor has caused some fans to speculate that 'Kryten' is a code name, passed from mechanoid to mechanoid, but this is not considered canon.

As the writing continued, pre-filming began for various scattered episodes as scripts were ready and locations became available. Robert Llewellyn's first day on set involved being blown around by industrial fans on a set covered in soap flakes for the episode *Marooned*, but his first dialogue scene was some pre-filming for *Bodyswap*, where Rimmer, in the body of Lister, is relaxing in a Jacuzzi. With his head encased in rubber and with his limbs restricted by a fibreglass suit, the sauna-like environment didn't help him to relax, and nor did Peter Wragg rigging a cigarette lighter to his finger, which kept giving him mild electric shocks. Eventually, he passed out due to heatstroke and exhaustion. Welcome aboard, mate.

That scene was eventually cut from the finished episode, but it would have been redubbed if it had been included. Experimentation with voices and accents was continuing, and at this point Llewellyn was basically doing his version of David Ross's Kryten, a sort of nervy upper-class English. When rehearsals started properly for *Marooned* – the first episode of Series III to be recorded – this had been abandoned and for a while, the new Kryten was going to have a sing-song Swedish accent which at first everybody thought was very funny but after only a few hours of saying the lines it was driving everybody crazy.

Chris Barrie recalls Llewellyn's Job-like patience as his entire performance was scrapped and had to be reconfigured time after time after time. Finally, Llewellyn recalled a woman he'd known in Vancouver and attempted a version of her British Columbia accent. Plenty of Canadian fans have told him since then just how far from the mark his vocal performance was, but something about those mid-Atlantic strangulated vowels seemed to fit the put-upon robot perfectly. Kelsey Grammer's slightly prissy performance as Frasier Crane in *Cheers* also informed both the voice and the attitude. As for the walk, in the end that was dictated entirely by the restrictive costume he was given.

Llewellyn wasn't the only performer stepping into someone else's shoes, or rather black polo neck. Norman Lovett's Holly had been a key element of the original line-up, but Lovett had recently moved to Edinburgh with his new wife and was shooting his own TV show, *I, Lovett*, in Glasgow. Travelling to Manchester once a week to record the show was no problem, but spending five days in Acton to sit in the corner of an empty rehearsal room didn't seem like an enticing prospect, especially for a man still recovering from the heart attack he'd suffered a few years earlier, and so Lovett rang up the production office to discuss how he saw the next series working. He'd still be Holly, he explained, but he was going to be much more 'professional', by which he meant he wouldn't be attending rehearsals in London; instead, he'd just turn up on the recording dates in Manchester.

Nobody thought this would work. Sure, Holly is just the computer, but getting everyone together, going through the lines, working out the timing with the other actors, is a big part of creating a comedy television half-hour. 'I'll come to one rehearsal,' offered Lovett. 'You have to come to *all* the rehearsals,' said Paul Jackson. 'In that case, I'm not doing the show,' responded Lovett. 'Fine,' replied Jackson – and there the matter rested.

Looking back, Rob and Doug feel that this was a situation that could have been resolved, but with neither producer nor actor willing to back down, Holly too had to be recast. Plenty of people were seen (including Janine Duvitski and, according to rumour, Kathy Burke) but Hattie Hayridge was an obvious person to ask, given her success as Hilly at the end of the previous series. Hayridge recalls that when she first met Ed Bye and Paul Jackson, they gave her some script pages to read, which she duly did, and pronounced them very amusing. 'No,' said a puzzled Ed Bye. 'Could you read them out loud?' She still got the job, and both she and Robert Llewellyn had to fit into a tight-knit team, as by now the other three actors had got to know each other very well. (Craig Charles was still calling Robert Llewellyn 'new boy' on the set of *The Promised Land* in 2020, three decades after he joined the cast.)

Hate-watching from his Edinburgh home when the episodes started going out, Norman Lovett was mysteriously enraged to see that 'the female Norman Lovett' – of all people – was 'stealing his act'. He seemed to have formed the idea that he had been assured that when the part was recast, they would move as far away from his version of Holly as possible. It isn't clear how or from where this notion arose, but Doug Naylor was very clear that they had no reason for giving such an undertaking. They didn't want Lovett to leave the show, they felt let down by his decision to quit (two weeks before the start of production), so why on earth would they be offering him special favours as he walked out the door, leaving them in the lurch?

Over the next several series, it became apparent that the dynamic Kryten had with Rimmer, Lister and the Cat was loads of fun, and that Kryten could serve a similar purpose to Holly in terms of being an exposition-delivery-machine, all of which made Holly less necessary and less appealing to write for. Holly was written out after Series V, and although Norman Lovett made various return appearances, Hattie Hayridge wasn't seen again on the show.

She did, however, make quite an impression at the first rehearsal for Series III, which was shooting in September–October 1989, starting immediately after the Edinburgh Fringe in August. Having had a successful Edinburgh run, and unwilling to miss the final night celebrations, Hayridge stayed in Edinburgh on the last Sunday and arranged a car to take her to London the following morning. The car duly arrived to find a sleep-deprived Hattie Hayridge, sitting miserably on the front step of her Edinburgh apartment, having found herself locked out, and unable to track down her housemate after the party. She dozed in the back of the taxi and then walked into the Acton rehearsal room, hungover in a blue cocktail dress.

Now, this might make it sound as if hangovers and late nights were a rarity for the **Red Dwarf** crew but while Robert Llewellyn might have learned the wisdom of an early night preceding a 5:00 a.m. wake-up call, to give time for the Kryten make-up and costume to be applied, and while the slightly older Chris Barrie might have spent more time with his collection of Victorian enamelled advertising signs, the two younger cast members were going out clubbing most nights. Craig Charles ruefully recalls, 'I did most of the third series with a hangover.'

Both Charles and Danny John-Jules had missed the plane from London to Manchester more than once, and so for the third series, Paul Jackson hired a coach to take everybody up and down the motorway, making sure that he knew where his unruly cast was at all times. This was another opportunity for the team to bond, watch science fiction movies (or sleep off the effects of the night before) and it did make sure that nobody was left behind – although Danny John-Jules looks back and wonders why as the success of their show grew, the quality of their transportation declined.

Craig Charles and production manager Mike Agnew almost came to blows during the Liverpool-based pre-filming for *Backwards*. After setting up a complex shot for several hours, suddenly the actors were nowhere to be found, Charles and Danny John-Jules having borrowed a crew vehicle to do some sight-seeing. 'What's your problem?' asked a chipper Craig Charles, wandering back onto set, half an hour after he was needed. 'You're my smegging problem,' responded a furious Agnew – although I don't think he said 'smegging'. Ed Bye quickly emerged and stopped the situation from escalating further. (Mike Agnew is at pains to point out that he and Craig Charles now get along very well indeed.)

Robert Llewellyn, meanwhile, wasn't there at all. He was juggling commitments to his own Edinburgh Fringe play, this time dealing with pornography and masturbation, which meant he wasn't available for some of the August pre-filming – that's not him on the speed boat in *Backwards*, but a stand-in named David Billington.

Both Rob and Doug felt that the slightly longer gap between Series II and Series III had given them time to recharge their creative batteries and they were full of ideas for new stories with their new characters. But first, they had to deal with the cliffhanger ending which they'd left themselves with at the end of *Parallel Universe*. Doug, who had recently become a father, began noticing amusing changes in his own behaviour, including preparing a bottle for his son as if he was working in a secret government lab, handling a virus that could wipe out humanity.

He suggested to Rob that they go ahead and have Lister give birth, and they duly began writing an episode called 'Dad', which included Kryten delivering Lister's son by caesarean, but Rob didn't feel as if he had much to add to this script, because he had not yet had any children, and – with Kryten and the recast Holly to introduce as well – they finally scrapped the whole idea and wrote out Lister's pregnancy in a deliberately too-fast-to-read opening crawl at the top of the first episode.

They had also spent some of the time between series writing the novel *Infinity Welcomes Careful Drivers*, which was published in November 1989, just before the third series began transmitting. This book, credited to 'Grant Naylor', drew on material from the televised episodes *The End*, *Future Echoes*, *Kryten*, *Me²* and *Better than Life*. As with the various versions of *The Hitchhiker's Guide to the Galaxy*, assembling the different tellings of the story in various media into a single coherent canon is completely impossible and no sane person should attempt this. While the TV series was still only getting modest ratings, the book became a best-seller, further contributing to the impact that **Red Dwarf** was having on British popular culture.

As the time came once more to turn words into actions, Rob and Doug approached Paul Jackson about their position on the show. 'We want to be producers, because…' they began. 'I couldn't agree more,' interrupted Jackson. 'This is your show.' Series III still carries the credit 'A Paul Jackson Production for BBC North West', but from this point on, Jackson would take a step back and let Rob and Doug (and Ed Bye) make most of the major decisions.

Among the changes that they made was getting designer Mel Bibby to work on **Red Dwarf**. In the late 1980s, the BBC still operated a system in which camera crews, costume designers, make-up artists, lighting designers and so on were on full-time contracts. Producers could request individuals to come and work on their shows, but the allocation of people to programmes was ultimately decided by BBC bureaucracy. Ed Bye had wanted Mel Bibby to design the sets for Series I, but Bibby had been assigned to *The Satellite Show* instead. Now, he was free, and with the BBC purse strings loosening slightly, he was able to design a whole new set of ship interiors, with clever use of light shining through wooden flats to create much more visual interest, while barely spending more money. Bibby remained on the show for the rest of the BBC episodes, before dying unexpectedly at the age of just 54.

Another key collaborator was costume designer Howard Burden who also joined the team at this stage. He'd worked in a more junior capacity with Ed Bye on *Filthy Rich and Catflap*, but **Red Dwarf** was his first time taking sole responsibility for a show's costumes, and he seemed to immediately understand what was needed, helped perhaps by reading that first **Red Dwarf** novel, which was already in bookshops by the time he started work on Series III. The new sets and new clothes brought everything up a notch in terms of production value, and Burden was still working on **Red Dwarf** at the time of the 2020 special, *The Promised Land*. In fact, I've no reason to think that he won't be called on next time the boys from the *Dwarf* have an adventure to go on.

Next to go was *Blue Midget*, which the writers felt looked like a bread bin from the outside, and the interior of which was a cramped set to shoot in. The original plan was to replace it with a new vehicle called 'White Midget', and Peter Wragg and his team got to work creating a model. The new craft was made up of several linked spheres, giving it an almost insectoid appearance, and the designers in the workshop nicknamed it 'Starbug', which Rob and Doug both thought was perfect. *Blue Midget* was retained in the end, and seen in the episodes *Marooned* and *Bodyswap* (where Lister calls it 'White Midget').

As with Series II, they'd also been talking to their collaborators about what could and could not be done on a BBC budget. 'We can do good snow,' Peter Wragg had mused. 'We can get some big fans and some soap flakes. Looks great for miniatures or with actors.' With that in mind, the *Starbug* model ended up being painted bright green, rather than white, and it makes its debut in the first transmitted episode, *Backwards*. Mel Bibby designed an interior that plausibly could have fit inside the structure shown in the model – but under protest, and he let it be known that in future he would prefer to design the interior set first and then have the model makers construct what they thought the outside should look like.

Because much of this episode had to be a) shot on location and b) reversed in post-production, it was quite a headache for all concerned. Ed Bye had to adjust to thinking about how what seemed like the *beginning* of one shot was going to edit on to *either* the beginning *or* the end of the next shot, depending on whether it was two reversed shots in a row, or a reversed shot followed by a forwards shot. He ended up drafting in Paul Jackson to help with some of the more intricate editing. Poor Craig Charles had to wade into a lake with weights in his pockets, get thrown through a plate-glass window and he'd already been knocked off his feet into a blizzard of soap flakes during the pre-filming for *Marooned*. Although stunt co-ordinator Gareth Milne supplied a few experienced daredevils for the big 'unrumble' at the episode's climax, Charles gamely did all his own stunts for this sequence, including several retakes.

Chris Barrie and Robert Llewellyn, meanwhile, had to walk backwards through a busy shopping centre while Ed Bye filmed them from a distance. Once reversed, it appeared that they were walking forwards and everyone else was walking backwards. In his new green costume, and accompanying a man with a rubber head, Chris Barrie assumed that he was going to be walking backwards into some kind of trouble, but actually, Liverpool shoppers just walked straight past them and minded their own business, and the shot was quickly in the can.

Tony Hawks's services as warm-up man were still required and he was opting to do these in character as 'The Fabulous Tony', wearing a spangly suit and taking off television entertainers of an earlier (but still quite recent) age. Like the magpies that all good writers are, Rob and Doug wrote The Fabulous Tony into the script of *Backwards* and Tony Hawks made his second on-camera appearance (after *Better than Life*) but not quite his last. He also saved Howard Burden a job by wearing his own clothes, but this time none of his dialogue was intelligible because all of his scenes were reversed in post-production.

These technical considerations meant that comparatively little of *Backwards* was acted in front of the audience in the traditional manner, and great chunks were just played to them on television screens to capture their reactions, meaning that the actors had to do their best to judge the timing without the benefit of a live audience to bounce off. This will come up again, both later this series and in series to come. One scene that was played in front of the audience, even though it would later be reversed, was the one featuring comedian Arthur Smith who ad-libbed a hilarious tirade aimed at anyone 'sad' enough to take the audio, reverse it, and find out what he was actually saying. The studio audience, of course, could hear him clearly but it was only during the edit that

Ed Bye realised that reversing the dialogue meant reversing their laughter too. A painstaking dubbing session followed in which he and sound supervisor Jem Whippey had to do their best to lift off the laughter and lay it back on the right way round, all the while preserving the dialogue.

Marooned, the first show shot but the second transmitted, is virtually a Rimmer/Lister two-hander – Craig Charles has even talked about wanting to perform it as a play. Stranded on a freezing planet, the two men share some intimate details as well as fighting for survival. Ed Bye elected to shoot the whole 'marooned' section – the great majority of the episode – with handheld cameras, which he believes may have been a first for a UK television sitcom. The dynamic camerawork adds a lot to the tense, claustrophobic atmosphere, but by now the laughs are much easier for the writers and actors to find. A famous moment revolves around Lister having to eat dog food to survive, and for some time, Craig Charles cheerfully told fans that it was real dog food. In fact, it was canned tuna, plus some pork pie jelly. It still looks pretty nasty, if you ask me, and he spat it out off-camera.

By now, of course, **Red Dwarf** had built its fan base so there was no question of dragging bewildered Mancunians in from the pub over the road to fill out a half-empty studio audience. Instead, people clamoured for tickets and delighted in being able to watch their favourite characters act out these stories live. During the filming of the third episode, *Polymorph*, the crew got more than they bargained for out of the studio audience. When Lister puts on his boxer shorts, unaware that a psychotic shape-changing killing machine is on board, he barely takes two steps before contorting in pain as his underwear starts contracting around his nether regions. When he collapses on the floor, Kryten has to straddle him and try to wrench off the homicidal clothing, resulting in the two being seen by Rimmer in a compromising position.

Both Charles and Llewellyn recall that the gales of laughter from the studio audience weren't just loud, they were almost literally deafening, to the point where neither could really hear the other's dialogue, meaning they just had to start speaking when the other person's lips stopped moving. Comedy shows are often criticised for 'sweetening' laugh tracks, some of which definitely does go on – for example when the reaction from a bad first take is dubbed over the visual from a technically better, but less laughter-inducing, second take. But here, the laughter had to be partially removed in the dub, and the sequence cut by about half in the edit, otherwise the episode would have been in danger of overrunning.

Also very amusing to the studio audience, but hugely nerve-wracking for Robert Llewellyn, was a long speech he was supposed to give in which he apologises repeatedly for a thoughtless remark about Rimmer's mother – his every contrition only making matters worse. The repetitive but unpredictable dialogue had proven impossible for Llewellyn to recall during rehearsals and so Ed Bye had arranged for cue cards to be prepared so Llewellyn could read the words during the take. Not wanting the audience to be able to see these in advance, the boards had been placed leaning against the set, but nobody got to them in time to hold them up. Mike Agnew recalls crawling across the floor to try to reach them as Llewellyn started on the speech – and he didn't make it. Miraculously, for the first time, Llewellyn managed to get almost all the words out in basically the right order – if you know what to look for, you can see a few hesitations, but if you don't, it's easily put down to Kryten's heightened emotional state, rather than the actor's uncertainty about the lines. Triumphantly exiting the scene, Llewellyn was careful to step over the prone body of the desperate floor manager to avoid ruining the take.

In the second half of this episode, all four main characters have their personalities altered as a major emotion is removed from them. While Cat, Kryten and Lister's new incarnations worked very well at the first read-through, nobody was quite happy with the version of Rimmer without his anger, which was more like Neil from *The Young Ones*. Chris Barrie suggested that the new Rimmer be a sort of peacenik, trying to see the situation from the homicidal monster's point of view, and organising a fundraiser for it. He happily improvised paragraphs of material on this theme, which an amazed Rob and Doug hurriedly jotted down, returning the next day with a new script, largely inspired by Barrie's on-the-spot invention, but given a bit more shape and structure. While too much of this kind of thing leads to madness (as the behind-the-scenes documentary for *Blackadder Goes Forth* ably demonstrates), this anecdote shows just how much the whole team is pulling together here to make the shows as strong as possible. And it works – this is possibly the most consistent series in **Red Dwarf**'s entire history (even if there are all-time best episodes still to come).

The fourth episode to go out was *Bodyswap*, which had been inspired by a conversation Rob and Doug had about what it's like borrowing someone's car. Rob recalled that there was often a laundry list of things to watch out for: 'When you steer to the right, you need to oversteer, because the back wheel comes out a bit, because the handbrake's never truly off.' What, they wondered, would it be like if you borrowed someone else's body? Regardless of the realities of such things, the way Rob and Doug had written the script was that when the mind of Rimmer was in the body of Lister, we would see Craig Charles, but hear Chris Barrie. Who cares whether or not David Lister's vocal cords would sound like Arnold Rimmer with a different intelligence controlling them – this was a brilliant way of dramatising the situation, and reminding the viewer that while this might look like Lister, it's actually Rimmer.

After some experimentation, Ed Bye realised that if he filmed the two actors impersonating each other, he could dub their voices back on afterwards and get pretty good lip synchronisation. But to avoid a muted soundscape, he also got them to perform every scene twice, once where they just mouthed the dialogue, in order to create a clean audio track with no talking, but with all the footsteps, chair-scrapes, door closes and so on.

This would have been incredibly confusing and boring for a live studio audience, and so the decision was taken to shoot the entire episode without an audience present and then play it for them to capture their reactions – just as had been done with large chunks of *Backwards*. Rather than take up an extra studio day just for this, the production team booked the (now defunct) BBC Paris Studio in Regent Street, where radio comedy shows were frequently recorded. Peter Ridsdale-Scott recalls that the over-enthusiastic crowd laughed so long and so hard at many of the jokes that the track was unusable, because the setup lines that followed were being drowned out by laughter from the previous punchline. Eventually, the finished episode was shown to a less excitable studio audience attending the recording of another story, in order to get something they could work with. The lack of a studio audience did mean much more freedom for lighting designer John Pomphrey, who created a much more detailed and filmic look for this episode.

The other challenge this story presented was getting Chris Barrie and Craig Charles to impersonate each other. For Chris Barrie, an experienced impressionist, this wasn't difficult, and Craig Charles also found that nailing the timing of his lines when redubbing his dialogue came very naturally. But, as Charles himself points out, he naturally speaks much more rapidly than Chris Barrie, and he isn't the talented mimic that his co-star is, so the scenes involving Rimmer's voice coming out of Lister's face were much harder for everyone involved. The end result, though, is eerily convincing, regardless of who is speaking.

To create Lister's dreadlocks, Craig Charles had to have appendages sewn into his head, generally at the beginning of each series, not to be taken out until filming was done for the year (he sometimes hacked them off at the end-of-series party and threw them into the crowd like a bridal bouquet). This meant a one-time only shot of Craig Charles sawing them off with an electric carving knife, and a revisit to the hair and make-up department before shooting the next episode. As for the pile of mashed potato which Charles buries his face in – that was real mashed potato half-inched from the Oxford Road canteen (and it went up the actor's nose).

Timeslides was the 'pretzel logic' episode for this series, in which the crew discover they can mess with the past by jumping into photographs. This presented further technical challenges for Ed Bye, and it's a testament to his hard work and the skill of the crews he was working with, that shots like a pan across a series of animated prints, or moments like Lister jumping out of a photograph – not simply in mid-sentence but actually in mid-word – are pulled off without any seeming difficulty. As the ambition of the writing climbs, the ability of the production to match it is (almost) never left behind.

The series was also getting more ambitious when it came to guest stars, and Ed Bye had lined up comedy royalty to play the self-contained part of the host of *Lifestyles of the Disgustingly Rich and Famous* – none other than Graham Chapman. Sadly, the Monty Python star died only days before the recording date, and the director quietly booked his wife, Ruby Wax, to take over the part instead.

To play Lister's 17-year-old self, the production recruited Craig Charles's 17-year-old brother Emile, and to play his band, Smeg and the Heads, Jeffrey Walker and Bill Steer, the only constant members in the ever-changing line-up of Liverpool extreme metal band Carcass. Their music, including the 'Om' song (and other music heard in this and the previous episode) was provided by Craig Charles's band, The Sons of Gordon Gekko. Charles maintains that these were used without permission and that Howard Goodall owes him royalties – but he sounds like he's joking.

A brief scene of Lister interacting with a pair of holidaymakers up a mountain was the subject of a last-minute edit. The joke is that Lister got his pictures mixed up with someone else's (because in the future, we'll still be taking holiday snaps to the chemist to be developed) so he's never met these people and doesn't know who they are. In dialogue, they were to recall the horrifying images of Dave Lister's party, which they received, but Craig Charles pointed out that at the time the photo was taken, they would not yet have seen these. Thus, all their dialogue had to be removed, but having been booked as speaking artists not as extras, they still got on-screen credit. The male skier is firebrand comedian Mark Steel, whose career hadn't quite taken off yet.

The final story of the series, *The Last Day*, saw Gordon Kennedy's Hudzen try to terminate Kryten. This script was delivered quite some time after the other five – due to the decision to scrap the 'Dad' episode which was taken very late in the day. So, with time and money running out to dress this new character, Howard Burden grabbed whatever he could find from the BBC costume store – there's that *RoboCop*-esque helmet, which Robert Llewellyn had fondly imagined he would be wearing (although actually I think I recognise it from the *Doctor Who* story 'Earthshock') – and was able to cobble something together that would be suitably menacing.

Dropping by the edit, Rob suggested that it would be nice if the Hudzen mechanoid were to make little motorised sounds every time he moved. And with that, he left Ed Bye and Jem Whippey to it. This was a long dub anyway, and they finished well after midnight with only the Rob Grant-mandated Hudzen noises to go. To dub a servo noise over every movement took them another two hours, meaning that they finished at almost 4:00 a.m.

Hattie Hayridge was dismayed to note that all of the rest of the cast got a nice moment when they gave Kryten a present, but no such gift was forthcoming from Holly. She spoke up about this during rehearsals and a little extra exchange was added, including some tongue-twisting technical gibberish for Robert Llewellyn, in which Holly gives Kryten a computer chip he's always wanted. Over the next couple of series, Hayridge would continue to suggest extra things for Holly to do, sometimes successfully, such as her delightful faint at the sight of Ace Rimmer, sometimes without success, as when she didn't get her own GELF partner in *Camille*.

One final thing needed changing. Those opening titles that had so impressed John Lloyd definitely helped to establish the show as having a bit more ballast than a typical BBC sitcom, but it was a low-key, almost depressing, way to kick off a show that was getting livelier and more energetic all the time. Ed Bye had been playing around at home with his VCR and showed Rob and Doug a series of quick cuts of some **Red Dwarf** footage with the jaunty closing theme music over the top. 'Let's do that,' chorused the writers, and so Howard Goodall was asked to provide a shorter instrumental version of the closing titles to go at the top of each show.

Perhaps influenced by Lister's fantasies of guitar supremacy, Goodall employed a session guitarist to help create this new arrangement of the music, and encouraged him to mess around with the melody, rather than playing it exactly as written. This is not something that session musicians are used to doing and it took a lot of takes before he got a loose enough rendering. Maybe Danny John-Jules had a point, and he should have provided some cans of lager. The new opening theme also includes Goodall's own voice, processed through a machine called a Vocoder, singing the words 'Red Dwarf' four times. There was no particular plan to conceal these, but nobody noticed them there until 2016, when their presence suddenly set the internet on fire.

Announced in the *Radio Times* as 'Red Dwarf III', but only identified on-screen as such during the opening crawl of episode one, the new series was the first to be consistently in the BBC2 top ten ratings for the week, and in all departments shows a huge increase in confidence over Series I and II. Adding to the glossy look, Rob and Doug paid London-based graphic design agency Dewynters £1,000 to come up with an image for their show, which Doug thought should be influenced by the swooping shape of the NASA logo. This made its debut on the cover of the first **Red Dwarf** novel, and a variation was used for their company, Grant Naylor Productions. When the familiar image of the red ellipse, intersecting the Ds of 'Red' and 'Dwarf', makes its first appearance in the newly upbeat opening titles of Series III, it feels like the last piece of the puzzle is finally now in place.

Impressions of Series III

Written by Rob Grant and Doug Naylor. Designed by Mel Bibby. Costumes by Howard Burden. Executive producer: Paul Jackson. Produced by Ed Bye, Rob Grant, Doug Naylor. Starring: Craig Charles, Chris Barrie, Danny John-Jules, Robert Llewellyn, Hattie Hayridge.

S03E01 Backwards ★★☆☆

TX: 14 November 1989 on BBC2. Ratings: 4.29m (3rd for the week). Featuring: Arthur Smith, Tony Hawks, Maria Friedman.

In Series I, everyone figured out whether or not this was even possible. In Series II, they discovered that it was. Series III is where **Red Dwarf** as we know it finally emerges. You can think of Series III as the end of the beginning, as I have, or as the beginning of a new phase. Regardless, it's certainly an enormous evolution from the previous episodes. The changes begin with the titles, which sucker you in with a brief shot of *Red Dwarf* and a few ominous musical tones, before smashing into an upbeat instrumental version of the theme song with American sitcom-style clips of the main cast. The series is still relatively constrained in terms of what it can achieve physically and visually and so these are mainly close-ups of the actors turning to look at something, but it does kick the episodes off with a bit more energy than we're used to (unless you've been watching the remastered versions).

This is the debut, of course, of Robert Llewellyn, and it's a very impressive start for him. *Kryten* was one of my favourite episodes from the first two years, and it isn't immediately apparent from watching that story what else can be done with a fussy robot who's learning to rebel. But Llewellyn slips seamlessly into the setup and immediately develops a wonderful rapport with the others, creating a brand-new version of the character that nevertheless has a clear lineage back to Series II. As later episodes will show, it's inspired casting and Llewellyn's charm and versatility rapidly becomes a huge asset among an already enormously talented ensemble.

Weirdly, adding an extra cast member has made it easier for the Cat to have a stake in the action, not harder, as one might have assumed. With three regular main characters, the stories all tended to be about Lister vs Rimmer, with the Cat routinely sidelined. With four regular characters (four who can get up and walk around at least), there's the opportunity to split them into two teams of two, as here. That having been said, this is a pretty weird introduction to Kryten, who rarely gets much to do that is specific to him or to his personality. In fact, it's not until the third episode that he gets much to do at all, and it's only in the last episode of the series that a whole story is centred on him. It's possibly due to the, now-usual, juggling of the running order, which means that here we're just expected to take him for granted. But given that he's already had his origin story, perhaps that makes sense.

As discussed in the previous section, visually the show has had a huge upgrade, with only Rimmer's bottle-green *Captain Scarlet* outfit letting the side down – and even that is much slicker than his previous beige-tie-over-beige-shirt combo. It does look a bit silly, though, especially the peaked cap with its own H on it and the ridiculous aerial coming out of the side. There's a new confidence to the writing too, shown most clearly in the opening exchange between Lister and Cat, which has gone down as a classic. Hattie Hayridge also makes a tremendous first impression as Holly. Her 'showing her working' as she grapples with the question of what time period they're in, followed by her guess that it's 'around lunchtime, maybe half-one!', complete with her wide-eyed, hopeful 'did I get it?' micro-expression, is an absolute delight. She has a subtle (and fairly consistent) video effect applied, which works well.

The rest of this episode, sadly, isn't for me. Firstly, it really helps to find the mere sight of footage being played in reverse terribly funny. If you do, my friend, this is the show for you. Fill yer boots. I don't remember finding that particularly novel or amusing when I first saw this in 1989 and I feel the same way now. But also, Rob and Doug can't pick a rule and stick to it. Sometimes the orders of letters are reversed, so the signpost to London reads 'NODNOL' – but that wouldn't be the result of time running backwards. Sometimes everything is reversed, like the number plate of the taxi in the final scene (because they've inverted the whole shot in the edit). Sometimes causes precede effects (Lister and Cat ask for a lift and then they get one, Tony Hawks introduces the Reverse Brothers and then they begin their act). At other times, causes happen after the effects they caused, like the Reverse Brothers being fired before the brawl (although after their final performance). Just what causes that fight? And what ends it?

All of this would be easier to tolerate if there were wonderful character beats for our regulars, but after those earlier establishing scenes, very quickly we get to the point where these could be any four guys and it's only the world they're in that is supposed to be interesting or funny. In particular, why does Rimmer find that success comes so easily to him here? Why isn't he screwing up being one of the Sensational Reverse Brothers, the way he screws up everything else? Why isn't he suffering from crippling stage fright, or becoming a dreadful diva, or doing anything at all Rimmer-ish?

There's always bound to be a certain tension between character, gags and plotting – the best scripts braid these three together until they become one, and that isn't easy. It's nevertheless going to happen to great effect in some of the episodes that are coming up next, but here plot wins, gags are beaten into a poor second place and the characters are lost in the shuffle. It's the characters that win audiences and keep them, though, and you overlook them at your peril.

The one with: sdrawkcab gniog gnihtyrevE.

That Rimmer's a solid guy: Any hint of Rimmer being a hologram projection sustained by Holly on board the ship goes completely out the window here. Sitting next to Kryten in *Starbug* is no issue – he even manages to be shot out of the top of the craft when Kryten fires the ejector seat. He falls through a time hole and continues to exist. On the backwards Earth, which can't be mapped anywhere in Holly's databanks, he walks up stairs, sits on chairs, hides under tables, stands on stages, rides in a taxi, acquires a change of clothes and so on. It's also profoundly odd that – looking for a way to make money by doing impossible feats on stage – they focus entirely on being the Sensational Reverse Brothers and not at all on Rimmer being The Amazing Insubstantial Man, which would, if anything, be even more impressive. Maybe Alfred Molina was right!

There's a time and a place: Driving tests haven't changed much in hundreds of years. Rimmer, trying to work out what time period they're in, wonders if they'll see Doug McClure, rugged star of such seventies movie classics as *The Land that Time Forgot*. Lister asks Cat if he's seen *The Flintstones* and the Cat responds, 'Sure.' When? How? The newspaper on Backwards Earth is 'Yesterday', a gag at the expense of Eddie Shah's publication *Today*. This was Britain's first colour newspaper, launched amid great hullabaloo in March 1986, sold to Tiny Rowland four months later, then to Rupert Murdoch in 1987, before it ceased publication altogether in 1995.

Influences, references and rip-offs: The opening crawl is inspired by *Star Wars* and the closing line 'Red Dwarf III, The Same Generation, nearly' is a nod to *Star Trek: The Next Generation*, which had yet to come to British television, although early episodes were available to rent on VHS. An invisible spaceship landing in a field had recently been seen in *Star Trek IV: The One With The Whales*. Philip K. Dick explored time running backwards in his

1967 novel *Counter-Clock World*, as did J.G. Ballard in his 1964 story *Time of Passage*, which is thought to have been inspired by F. Scott Fitzgerald's 1922 short story *The Curious Case of Benjamin Button*. Running film backwards to create novel effects goes all the way back to silent cinema. The 1984 film *Top Secret* from the *Airplane!* team includes a scene in which a visit to a Swedish professor played by Peter Cushing turns out to be a single hugely elaborate backwards shot. The 'Red Dwarf Shuffle' is a riff on the 'Super Bowl Shuffle', a 1985 single from the American football team the Chicago Bears. The crew read about a criminal named 'Michael Ellis', which might be a reference to the episode of *Monty Python* in which a man by that name is at the centre of several Harrods-related shenanigans – or it could just be a coincidence.

Best gag: LISTER: This is crazy. Why are we talking about going to bed with Wilma Flintstone? CAT: You're right. We're nuts. This is an insane conversation. LISTER: She'll never leave Fred, and we know it.

Worst visual effect: Rimmer being ejected from *Starbug* is laughable, both the on-set stunt with clearly visible bungee cord and the awful video effect from the outside. On the other hand, the new *Starbug* model is gorgeous.

Continuity is for smegheads: Much of the established continuity from Series I and II is tossed overboard in the opening crawl. Kryten has never been to Earth before. *Starbug*'s cloaking device is never used again. Lister and Cat find the inhabitants of Backwards Earth utterly unintelligible, but the audience at Rimmer and Kryten's cabaret performance seem to understand them perfectly. Lister is 25 years old, same as he was in *Future Echoes*. Rimmer's H has gained a little bit of extra detailing.

Remastered: The titles are basically the same as for the other remastered episodes (all of which featured a shot of Robert Llewellyn as Kryten) but the shot of Norman Lovett consulting *The Junior Encyclopaedia of Space* has been replaced with one of Hattie Hayridge going cross-eyed. The wide shot of Rimmer being ejected from *Starbug* has been redone (it's only a marginal improvement). The time hole effects have been gussied up and there's a longer, more elaborate crash sequence, and some extra invisible-spaceship effects.

S03E02 Marooned ★★★★☆

TX: 21 November 1989 on BBC2. Ratings: 3.9m (8th for the week).

This one starts at a hell of a clip. Barely have the titles left the screen than Holly is heard announcing 'Abandon ship! Abandon ship!' and suddenly, with no explanation, Lister and Rimmer are in one craft and Kryten and the Cat are in another. Before long, an asteroid hits *Starbug* and Lister and Rimmer are stuck together in a knackered spaceship on a remote planet with almost nothing to eat. So, what do they do? They wait. And they talk.

Back in Series I, when this was tried with even a bit more plot, it fizzled out very quickly. But we know who these guys are now, and that makes a galaxy of difference. And far from being generic **Red Dwarf** banter, what they talk about matters. It might be the last conversation they ever have, and even if story logic tries to ruin the whole thing for you by whispering in your ear, 'I don't think Dave Lister will starve to death. It's only episode two of a six-episode series,' that still doesn't spoil it, because the question is not: will Lister survive? It's how will this experience change these two men?

We go through hell with them. Not just in the Jean-Paul Sartre hell-is-other-people sense – we've been doing that since Series I – but the feeling of cold and deprivation is expertly summoned up. And Ed Bye's brilliant decision to shoot the whole thing handheld gives it a liveliness and an authenticity that is very unexpected, culminating in that brilliant shot through the guitar-shaped hole in the trunk – a wonderful piece of direction that allows us to see the hole and Rimmer's reaction at the same instant and in the same shot (it's the same reason why Billy Wilder chose a compact mirror as the object that tells Jack Lemmon that his boss's girl is also his girl in *The Apartment*).

But what's really fascinating about this episode is that this is the one in which Lister is faced with the moral choice and *he* does the cowardly, selfish, deceitful thing. We don't really lose sympathy for him. Rimmer is well established as the punching bag of the show, and it's easy for many people to place some old trunk on a lower rung than a precious guitar – especially an authentic Les Paul copy. But Lister does get it wrong. And then Rimmer pours on the praise. He's unstinting. It's excruciating and brilliant, and it gives both of them such depth and dimension. Rimmer's petty grievances seem much more understandable and while we hope that we wouldn't do what Lister did, if we're honest, we all probably would.

Are there niggles? Of course. There's a *long* list of things that Rimmer does which don't make any sense of his holographic nature (see below), Lister cuts that guitar shape out of the back of Rimmer's trunk very quickly (and very quietly) and there's just the tiniest hint of doofus Rimmer creeping back in, when he surmises that Lister's guitar must have been made of camphor wood. But, on the whole, this is top-drawer stuff, not just terrific compared to the slightly lacklustre opening instalment, but maybe even better than previous front-runner *Queeg* – alas, my star ratings don't quite have the necessary fidelity to distinguish between them.

The one with: Lister eating dog food.

That Rimmer's a solid guy: Rimmer is seen early on leaning his elbow on one of *Starbug*'s consoles. Once more, there's no issue with him being entirely off *Red Dwarf*, completely out of Holly's control. (Holly has no idea where he even is.) He sits on a folding chair. He can clearly be seen operating the radio on board *Starbug* after the crash. He somehow avails himself of a quilted green jacket with the Dewynters logo on it at some point during the journey. He found various things in the first aid box and tool cupboard, but how could he have opened them to see inside? He doesn't want Lister to burn books that he can no longer pick up or open. He can smell the odour of burning camphor wood, even though his nasal receptors are only made of light.

There's a time and a place: Snobbish Rimmer can't believe Lister doesn't know how to pronounce 'Pinter' but himself has no idea that 'May day' is a corruption of '*m'aidez*'. 'Topic' reminds Lister of food. He hates Pot Noodles. Lister's rear end is like two badly parked Volkswagens. Rimmer has seen *West Side Story* but can only quote a single word of *Richard III* (which he does while impersonating Laurence Olivier). Lister compares him to Roadrunner. Page 61 of *Lolita* is worth saving. You can't change the clothes on Rimmer's tin soldiers like you can with Sindy. Generals don't smash Newcastle Brown Ale bottles into your face. Lister plays 'She's Out of My Life', which was a hit for Michael Jackson in 1980. Everyone can remember where they were when Cliff Richard was shot.

Influences, references and rip-offs: Some of the books Lister burns echo previous episodes, notably Herman Wouk, who wrote *The Caine Mutiny*, which inspired *Queeg*. Any number of stories have trapped two warring characters together in dire circumstances – the most obvious venue being a stuck elevator. The icy surroundings also recall Scott's expedition to the Antarctic as well as films like *The Thing from Another World*.

Best gag: 'You can't have been a full member of the golf club then! You didn't pay any green fees or anything?'

Worst visual effect: As they prepare for take-off, nothing is visible through *Starbug*'s windows except for some CSO fringing.

Continuity is for smegheads: Sums of money discussed include 'twenty-four grand' and 'fifteen quid'. Lister has already heard a vivid account of Rimmer's first (and only) sexual encounter – twelve minutes with Yvonne McGruder including pizza – but he subsequently erased his memory. However, Rimmer's story here contradicts his story in *Thanks for the Memory* and it's hard to understand why he would be lying on either occasion. Lister's guitar only has five strings and three of them are G, and his step-dad taught him to play it. The trunk is the only thing Rimmer's dad ever gave him (apart from his disappointment).

Remastered: A siren has been added to the beginning of Holly's announcement (which does make sense of her line a moment later 'Oh god, now the siren's bust'). There's also a brief shot of the CG *Red Dwarf* before *Starbug* launches, and more CG shots of all three vehicles during the evacuation. There's still some dreadful CSO fringing around the actors but now there are some images seen through *Starbug*'s windows (the handheld camerawork creates problems here). Jokes about future history (the Earth having a toupée, Cliff Richard being shot) have been removed. Most (but not quite all) of the excellent snowy model work has been retained. A bad CSO shot of Kryten in the snow has been snipped out.

S03E03 Polymorph ★★★★☆

TX: 28 November 1989 on BBC2. Ratings: 4.35m (6th for the week). Featuring: Simon Gaffney, Kalli Greenwood, Frances Barber.

These first three episodes of Series III represent three different approaches that **Red Dwarf** can take. And even though I think *Marooned* is a slightly better example of its type than *Polymorph* is of its, this is a crucial episode in the development of the show. *Backwards* is an example of 'the boys go to the planet of the [BLANK]s' (mechanoids, waxworks, GELFs etc.). How much fun that is depends on how interesting the blank is, and how well the characters are used in the adventure. *Marooned* takes us back to *Steptoe* in space. It's all about two men who hate each other, forced to share the same environment. But this is something new. *Polymorph* uses a science fiction concept to interrogate our main characters. When each of the main four has a key emotion removed, we get to see a new version of them, which is simultaneously very insightful and laugh-out-loud funny. We got a hint of this in *Confidence and Paranoia* but here's where the idea really takes flight. This, more than anything else, is the **Red Dwarf** secret sauce, and it will lead us to all-time favourite episodes like *Dimension Jump* and *Back to Reality*.

Of course, part of the fun stems from how well we know the characters and therefore how funny it is when a major component of their personality is taken away. And you can't do that in series one, episode one. So it's by no means a criticism to point out that it takes around half a dozen episodes to get here. But now we are here, the possibilities are enormous.

And, although third transmitted, this is our first 'proper' Kryten episode. He's barely in *Marooned* (Robert Llewellyn's first studio day), and in *Backwards*, he isn't very 'Kryten-y'. But his impossible-to-learn 'blubbery fish' speech really establishes who he is and how he fits in to the existing dynamic. He'll get his big episode at the end of this series, but he's already becoming a core part of the ensemble. The only thing I don't like is the mask. It fits much better than David Ross's but the cheekbones make him look like he's got Spock ears. We also get our first really fancy guest star of the series in the seductive form of Frances Barber, already Olivier-nominated for the RSC production of *Camille* (not that one), and here she's the perfect embodiment of the Cat's libidinous desires.

So, if the main comedy idea is brilliant and the guest cast is so shiny, why isn't this a five-star masterpiece? Not for the first time, there's nothing for Holly to do – Hattie Hayridge only gets to deliver exposition. The polymorph prop is pretty lousy and didn't work properly during the pre-filming. In fact, it broke in two, and when the special effects team frantically tried spot-welding it back together, they were told that no such procedure could be performed on BBC Manchester premises without a hot work permit and Rocky Marshall and his team ended up doing the hasty repair work outside in the car park, in the dark.

The heat-seeking bazookoids, seen here for the first and last time, are a bit silly, in conception and execution (they're awfully slow-moving), and there are a couple of very weird video effects, especially on Chris Barrie when he turns from Rimmer into the creature. And the ending seems a bit pointless, setting up a rematch that never comes (although it's better than the caption gag in the *Remastered* version). Ultimately, though, when Lister is waggling that baseball bat around, Rimmer is gesturing with his pipe, Cat is slumped in the corner and Kryten is plotting to sacrifice them all so he can live – all's right with the world. The final piece of the **Red Dwarf** engine has been slotted into place. Now let's see what this baby can do.

The one with: The major, and I mean major, leaflet campaign.

That Rimmer's a solid guy: It's not clear how Rimmer is operating the device which is showing him his old home movies. He's deathly afraid of the polymorph, which has no trouble attaching its sucker to his formless forehead.

There's a time and a place: The episode opens with a warning courtesy of the rumbling tones of Canadian voice artist Bill Mitchell, who was a favourite of British advertising agencies in the 1980s. This is pure storytelling, as nothing in the episode would have warranted a real warning, given the 9:00 p.m. transmission time (the VHS release was given a 15 certificate but that was due to the sex-talk in *Marooned*, on the same tape). The polymorph has more teeth than the entire Osmond family. Nothing enrages Rimmer more than the thought of his mother getting frisky with Alphabetti Spaghetti.

Influences, references and rip-offs: The creature that can be disguised as anything recalls *The Thing from Another World* – not the last time that will be evoked. The appearance of the polymorph is inspired by the Xenomorph in the *Alien* franchise, and the hunt for it recalls James Cameron's sequel, *Aliens*, specifically.

Best gag: 'So, now Lister's got no fear? What are we going to do?' 'Well, I say let's get out there and twat it. I could have had it in the sleeping quarters, but you saw it – it took me by surprise.'

Worst visual effect: The rubber snake is only briefly glimpsed but it looks very silly.

Continuity is for smegheads: First appearance of Kryten's groinal socket. Cat, who was previously seen preferring to eat with his hands, and picking chicken off the floor, is revolted at the thought of eating out of human operating instruments, which he presumably would never have seen before. He seems to have attended at least one bris, however. Rimmer's other brothers are named: Frank is joined by John and Howard. First mention of a Space Corps directive from Kryten.

Remastered: The opening warning has been removed. A series of CGI ducts introduces the polymorph. An extra ball-bouncing shot has been added. The rubber snake has been trimmed a little. Some of the polymorph transformations have been redone. Rimmer's mother has been given a more middle-class accent. An additional shot of the closed airlock door has been added and the creature's demise has been souped up. A text caption has been added at the end explaining that the second polymorph died of old age in Lister's underwear drawer, replacing the shot of the duplicate Lister.

S03E04 Bodyswap ★★★★☆

TX: 5 December 1989 on BBC2. Ratings: 4.06m (7th for the week).
Featuring Lia Williams, Mike Agnew.

This is the second total triumph of the series (after *Marooned* and closely followed by *Queeg*), and it's also the introduction of the much-heralded (in this book, that is) Grant/Naylor sitcom structure device. Plenty of television episodes set up a situation in the opening minutes, develop and complicate that situation through the middle, and then resolve it at the end. In sitcoms in particular, it's also common to have an A-plot and a B-plot, which helps to make use of the larger cast. The two plots run parallel, and we cut between them. Sometimes they collide at the end, sometimes they don't. Some shows regularly cut between three different plots. A typical episode of *Scrubs* manages four.

That hasn't really happened on **Red Dwarf** so far – maybe on *Waiting for God*, but that's nobody's idea of a template worth copying. *Me^2* is about what happens if there are two Rimmers. *Queeg* is about what happens if Holly is replaced by Queeg 500. *Marooned* is about what happens if Rimmer and Lister are marooned. This episode appears to be about what happens when a skutter goes mad and rewires the ship – but that's the B-plot. The solution the gang tries involves downloading a senior officer's mind into Lister's body. And if that works once… Thus the A-plot is created by the B-plot, but they run consecutively, not in parallel.

This is unusual and can feel awkward. It also robs the episode of some of its thematic unity – however, it does wonders for the pacing, since now both sections can expand or contract depending on how much story material is available, and when each portion is as entertaining and as well worked out as these two are, it seems a price eminently worth paying. So, with hindsight, we can see that this isn't really about the rewiring/self-destruct storyline at all, but let's take a minute to admire how funny, well-constructed and even exciting this is. As a little self-contained adventure, it works very well indeed.

Rimmer getting Lister to swap bodies makes perfect sense of their situation and Rimmer taking horrific advantage of the agreement makes perfect sense of his character. This then escalates brilliantly, culminating in Rimmer taking Lister's body hostage and making himself scarce in *Starbug*. As well as being a very funny piece of television, it's also a remarkable technical and acting challenge, with Craig Charles and Chris Barrie having to adopt the other's mannerisms and speech patterns. Chris Barrie obviously finds this easier, but it's no trouble to accept Arnold Rimmer in Charles's body after a while, especially when he puts the uniform on. There's also real attention to detail throughout. The mind-swap process has been given a distinctive sound effect, which means that – on only the second time it's deployed – we can hear that sound while looking at a model shot of the ship and know exactly what is happening. It's very efficient, fast-moving storytelling.

What stops this from being a full five-star masterpiece (other than the fact that I'm keeping my powder dry) is a few niggles. There's precious little for the Cat to do here, and not much more for Kryten. As someone who does not appreciate doofus Rimmer, I really enjoy seeing him take charge of the self-destruct situation calmly and with crisp authority, but the childish practical joke and double V-signs at the end seem to be from another character entirely. Plus, the fact that – of necessity – this wasn't filmed in front of the audience means that the laugh track sounds off sometimes and treads on a few important lines of dialogue. These are minor problems, though, in what's a great episode, overall.

Continuing the newly minted tradition of hiring top stage actors to play one-scene roles, that's Lia Williams as the voice of Carol Brown, popping in to do half an hour's audio work a year or two before her Olivier-nominated breakthrough role in Alan Ayckbourn's *The Revenger's Comedies*. Floor manager Mike Agnew, who had started his career as an actor, voiced the homicidal Crispy Bar machine.

The one with: Rimmer and Lister swapping bodies.

That Rimmer's a solid guy: He can sit at the console and swing the chair around but has to give verbal instructions to Kryten. It is confirmed that holograms can't smell (except camphor wood). Presumably, there is a qualitative difference between the holographic taste sensation of the fried egg sandwich provided by Holly in *Thanks for the Memory* and the real food Rimmer gorges on here. Lister in charge of Rimmer's holographic body sounds like Lister, whereas in *Balance of Power*, Rimmer in charge of Kochanski's holographic body sounded like Kochanski.

There's a time and a place: Lister's mind is recorded on a quarter-sized microcassette, of the kind often seen in Dictaphones and telephone answering machines in the eighties and nineties. (In *Confidence and Paranoia*, holograms were stored on CD-sized shiny discs.) Rimmer references Mr Spock from *Star Trek*, compares Lister to Alfred Hitchcock, and quotes Dirty Harry in *Sudden Impact*. Even Lister thinks that Chris Barrie's costume looks like something out of Gerry Anderson. Ajax and Domestos are still going strong. If you paint 'Goodyear' down Lister's sides, you could float him over the Superbowl. Cat is familiar with Rolls-Royce cars.

Influences, references and rip-offs: This is a holographic spin on *Freaky Friday*, first filmed in 1976 with Jodie Foster and Barbara Harris swapping bodies, although earlier versions of the same concept exist, including 1948's *Vice Versa* with Peter Ustinov, in turn based on an 1882 novel by Thomas Anstey Guthrie.

Best gag: 'Keep that safe, it's Lister's mind.' Splosh.

Worst visual effect: The model work is excellent, but the oncoming mountains seen behind Lister/Rimmer as he pilots *Starbug* to its doom look a bit… small.

Continuity is for smegheads: Why would Holly, who knows she's got rid of the bomb, suggest that the best option for the crew is to get blown up? She is senile, so I suppose we can't expect her to be completely consistent. It's been 3,000,002 years since the drive plate accident. Lister calls *Blue Midget* 'White Midget'. Lister's severed locks grow back in time for the next episode. It isn't clear why Brown's authorisation is rejected. And what happened to Brown after the crisis was over? Did they just switch her off? Did she protest? Yikes.

Remastered: Souped-up sound effects when the Crispy Bar is delivered. The precisely deployed mind-swap noise has been replaced with music when Lister and Rimmer first switch. 'White Midget' has been overdubbed and now becomes 'the Midget'. Excellent model work has been replaced with sometimes dodgy CGI. The final shot of Cat playing with his food has been slightly extended.

S03E05 Timeslides ★★★★☆

TX: 12 December 1989 on BBC2. Ratings: 4.35m (6th for the week). Featuring: Robert Addie, Emile Charles, Simon Gaffney, Koo Stark, Mark Steel, Ruby Wax, and tonight's special guest star: Adolf Hitler as himself.

There's lots to like about *Timeslides*, which doubles down on the pretzel plotting of *Stasis Leak* (with which, as noted, it forms a loose trilogy along with *Future Echoes*), and it's got lots of good character stuff, especially for Rimmer and Lister (Cat and Kryten are once again along for the ride, and Holly gets no laugh lines at all). But the implications of the technology that the crew stumbles upon aren't fully, er, developed, which makes this whole episode somewhat of a fridge logic nightmare.

Let's start with the basic gag: photos that come to life and provide a window into the past. This has an almost fairy tale quality to it, and typically for **Red Dwarf** our heroes take a discovery of almost unimaginable power and use it to mess around, have fun, and get into fights (mainly get into fights). But then they realise that what they do in the scenes depicted in the photographs of the past can affect the present, and so Lister hatches a plan to better his life.

When Lister has all the money he could wish for, the vision of paradise which we get a glimpse of is still fairly clichéd – a stately home, self-aggrandising statues, hot and cold running butlers. But, it is a bit more specific than the version presented in *Better than Life*, a sign once again that the writers are really getting to know the world they're creating. And Chris Barrie steals a scene that isn't really about Rimmer at all, when he lavishly praises the young

Lister's songwriting abilities, proof that the regular cast are really starting to inhabit the characters, not just play the lines on the page.

Of course, I'm not going to worry about the fact that 'the developing fluid has mutated' is a pretty feeble justification for all of this scurrying back and forth through time. Just as with 'solid hallucinations' in *Confidence and Paranoia*, that's a feature, not a bug. But if 'photos are portals to the past' is a gimme, then I do have some questions about how some of the guys react. Given how sex-starved everyone seems to be, it's strange that messing around with bubble wrap is the first thing they think of. It's also surprising that they don't pick a photo of a really wonderful place and just live there – the idea is discussed, but then abandoned. (See also *Tikka to Ride* from Series VII.)

And, I guess we also have to give a pass to when-you-change-the-past-it-takes-a-while-for-the-future-to-notice. That's just one of those things that happens in time travel stories, regardless of how little sense it makes. But while I can accept Lister (who never joined the Space Corps) disappearing, and Cat not being there any more (because Frankenstein was never smuggled on board), I cannot understand why hologram Rimmer is still on the ship. For what possible reason would Holly bring him back after 3 million years, even given that he made the same mistake and irradiated the whole ship, with or without Lister by his side? A later Rob and Doug (or just Doug) would probably conjure up a completely different vision of the future; a sort of *It's a Wonderful Dwarf*, full of fun new details about this Rimmer's new life. But this episode streamlines its way past obvious consequences to get us to the next beat of the story, and it feels hasty and incomplete.

And then, yes, Rimmer absolutely would go back into the past and try to smeg up Lister's hopes and dreams. And if he does that, and we accept that the present only changes when it's narratively convenient, then, yes, I suppose Lister, Kryten and Cat would all reappear. But why is the amazing power they have to travel into the past forgotten about? You can absolutely understand that Lister would destroy the mind-swap machine after what Rimmer put him through, but you'd definitely keep the magic developing fluid around, wouldn't you? Yet, it's never heard of again.

Finally, when Rimmer is crowing 'I'm alive! I'm alive!' von Stauffenberg's exploding briefcase is very prominent in the frame, but Rimmer leaves it behind and then appears to detonate some packing crates with 'Explosives' written on them, having hardly touched them – the cargo bay must be a health and safety nightmare. And, actually not quite finally, because – a bit like the end of *Back to the Future* – we're left with a situation where one member of the 'family' recalls events completely differently than everyone else. Presumably as far as Cat, Kryten and Lister are concerned, Rimmer has been alive for the last two or three years (and nobody thought to bring back a hologram of anyone else – Kochanski, say, or Petersen or Hollister). Now, he's been killed (and we skip over the mourning, gruesome dealing with dismembered body parts and so on) and then – oh yes! – senile old Holly remembers that crewmembers can be brought back as holograms.

But in that case – as far as Lister is concerned, did last week's episode ever even happen? And why does Rimmer remember being a hologram if he never died? A lot of this, to be sure, is the kind of logic that you only stop to think about two hours after watching the episode as you open the fridge, but not all of it. And it does give what should a be a really high-stakes and exciting episode a slightly synthetic air. Deep down, when watching this, I know it doesn't really make sense, and therefore it doesn't really mean anything. The gag of Rimmer being alive for less than thirty seconds before being blown up is really, really funny, though, so maybe the trade-off is worth it.

Tedious fan theory: One explanation for Rimmer being alive in the final moments of the episode is that because he travelled back in time and talked to his younger self, even though he let Thicky Holden beat him to the Tension Sheet patent, the possibility of time travel stayed with him, and so this time, the events of *Stasis Leak* unfolded differently. Now when pre-accident Rimmer sees his future self's head emerging from a coffee table, he's less likely to dismiss this as a hallucination, and more likely to make sure he's safe in a stasis chamber when the accident occurs – this time, presumably, because no one was available to mend the drive plate. Now you just have to figure out how future hologram Rimmer was able to travel back into the past if he never died in the accident in the first place.

The one with: The Tension Sheet.

That Rimmer's a solid guy: Travel into the past is no problem. He sits down at a table in the pub with everyone else. Holly provides him with a torch. He doesn't immediately feel the difference between being a hologram and being alive.

There's a time and a place: *Lifestyles of the Rich and Famous* was an American TV show presented by Briton Robin Leach, which was on the air when this was made. Camera technology on board ship is still stuck in a photochemical world of darkrooms, developing fluid, Polaroids and 35mm slides. Kryten's music is on a cassette tape. Lister would like to tell Dustin Hoffman not to make *Ishtar*, the notorious 1987 flop that cost Elaine May her career as a film director. Cat is reading a Marilyn Monroe magazine. According to Blaize Falconberger, Lister's mansion is named 'Xanadu' not in homage to the 1941 movie *Citizen Kane* (nor the poem by Coleridge) but the 1968 UK number one 'The Legend of Xanadu' recorded by English rock band Dave Dee, Dozy,

Red Dwarf publicity still. (*MovieStillsDB*)

Chris Barrie as Ace Rimmer. (*MovieStillsDB*)

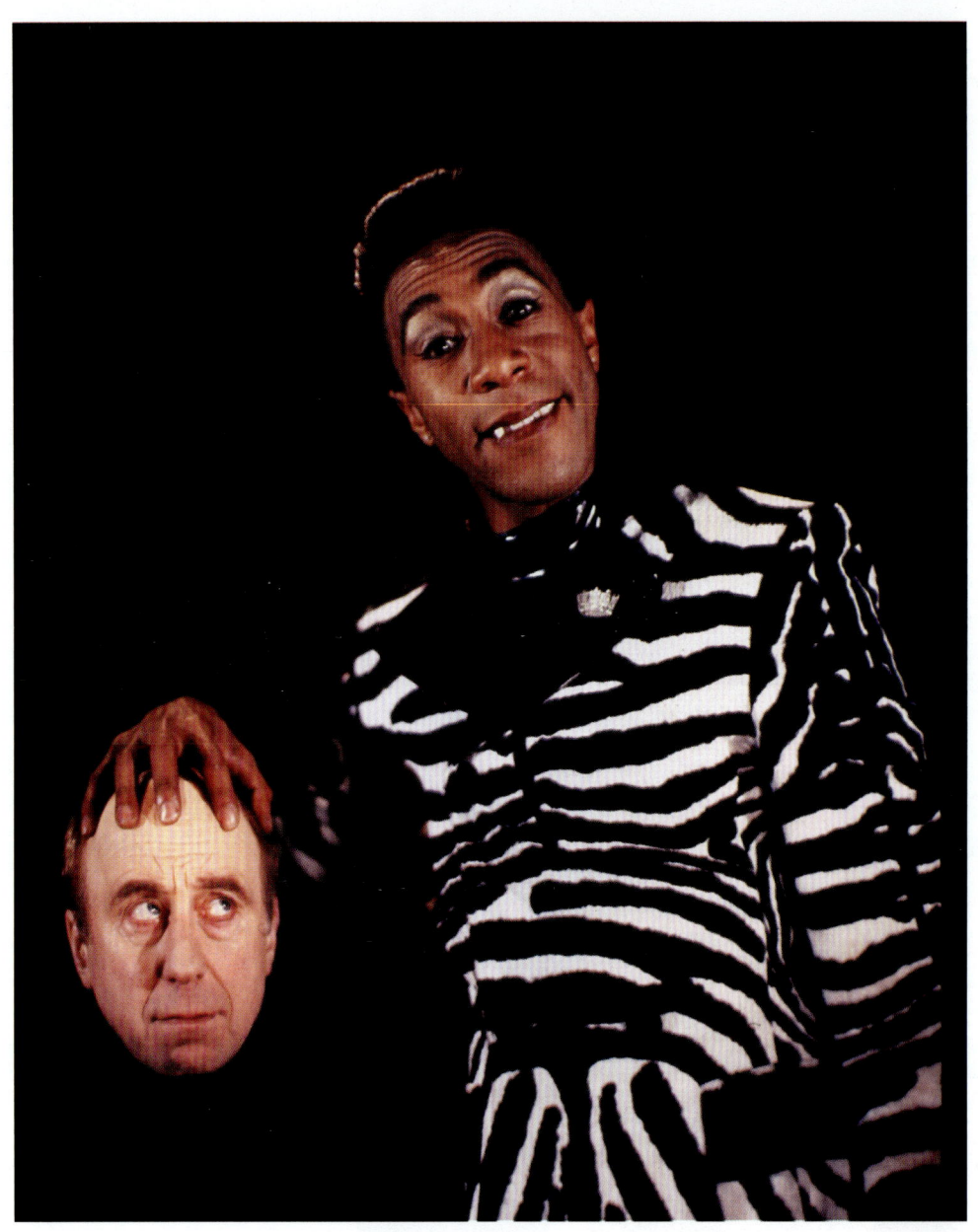

Norman Lovett and Danny John-Jules. (*MovieStillsDB*)

Chris Barrie in *Quarantine*. (*MovieStillsDB*)

Publicity still of Norman Lovett. (*MovieStillsDB*)

Danny John-Jules. (*MovieStillsDB*)

Chris Barrie on stage at Dimension Jump XIX (2017). (*Andy Walker*)

Danny John-Jules on stage at Dimension Jump XIX (2017). (*Andy Walker*)

Doug Naylor on stage at Dimension Jump XX (2018). (*Andy Walker*)

Hattie Hayridge on stage at Dimension Jump XIX (2017). (*Andy Walker*)

Lee Cornes on stage at Dimension Jump XXI (2021). (*Andy Walker*)

Rob Grant and Paul Jackson on stage at Dimension Jump XXI (2021). (*Andy Walker*)

Robert Llewellyn on stage at Dimension Jump XIX (2017). (*Andy Walker*)

Two Hollies on stage at Dimension Jump XXI (2021). (*Andy Walker*)

Starbug model on display at UKTV Play Exhibition (October 2022). (*Andy Walker*)

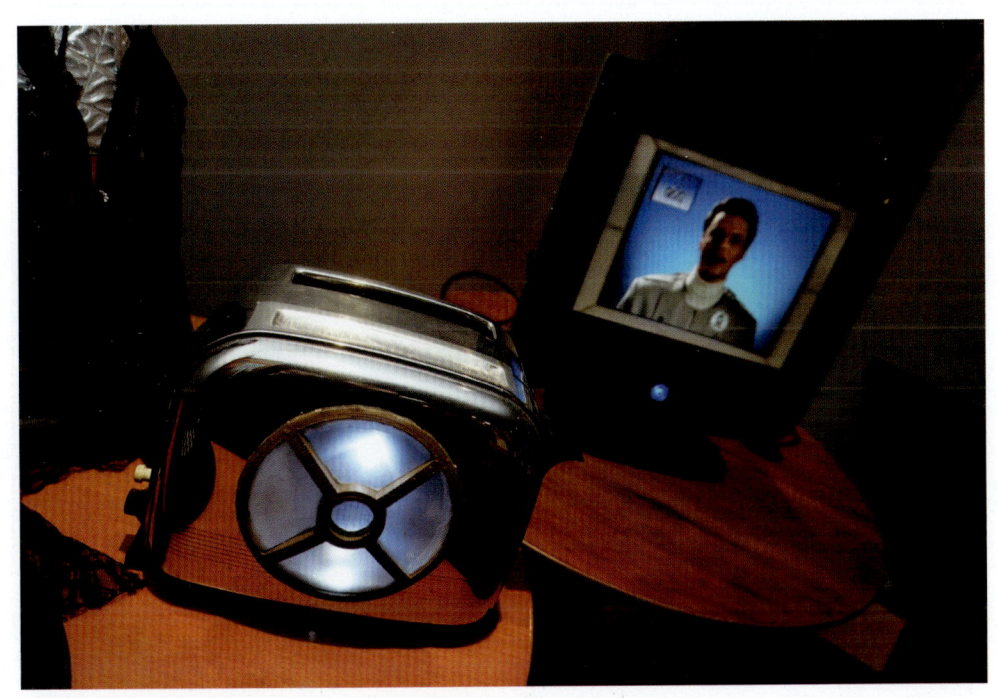

Talkie Toaster and Jim Reaper props. (*Andy Walker*)

Mark Williams (Olaf Petersen) in *Doctor Who*. (*MovieStillsDB*)

The Brittas Empire publicity still. (*MovieStillsDB*)

Publicity still of Timothy Spall, guest star in *Back to Reality*. (*MovieStillsDB*)

Publicity still of Jane Horrocks – guest star in *Holoship*. (*MovieStillsDB*)

Alfred Molina – first choice for Rimmer. (*MovieStillsDB*)

Publicity still of Patrick Stewart, who thought that *Gunmen of the Apocalypse* was ripping off one of the *Star Trek: The Next Generation* episodes he directed. (*MovieStillsDB*)

Alien publicity still. (*MovieStillsDB*)

Arnold Schwarzenegger as The Terminator – frequently referenced in **Red Dwarf** episodes. (*MovieStillsDB*)

Dark Star publicity still. (*MovieStillsDB*)

It's a Wonderful Life – frequently homaged in various episodes. (*MovieStillsDB*)

Marilyn Monroe – appears in episodes *Better than Life*, *The Last Day* and *Meltdown*. (*MovieStillsDB*)

Peter Weller as RoboCop – frequently referenced or homaged in **Red Dwarf** episodes. (*MovieStillsDB*)

Beaky, Mick & Tich. Rimmer sings 'If I Were a Rich Man' from the 1964 musical *Fiddler on the Roof*.

Influences, references and rip-offs: Rich people sitting at opposite ends of very long dining tables was a familiar image in single-panel cartoons like those in *The New Yorker* and had recently been seen in the Tim Burton/Michael Keaton *Batman* movie. Stories about people travelling into the worlds of pictures include C.S. Lewis's *The Voyage of the Dawn Treader*, where a painting of a sailing ship provides the gateway into Narnia; the *Sapphire & Steel* story 'The Man without a Face', where people become trapped in photographs; and, weirdly, the bonkers 1980 Olivia Newton-John movie musical *Xanadu*, in which a mural is a portal to the realm of the gods. Counterfactual versions of the reality we know recalls the 1946 classic movie *It's a Wonderful Life*, which is extensively homaged at the end of the first and the beginning of the second **Red Dwarf** book. Stories about time travel profiteering include a brief mention in *The Hitchhiker's Guide to the Galaxy* – you pay for your lavish meal at The Restaurant at the End of the Universe by depositing a small amount in the past and waiting for compound interest to do the rest. Combining both these elements, a 1960 edition of Rod Serling's *The Twilight Zone* featured a camera that could take pictures of the future, which our unscrupulous heroes use to try to win big at the races. That also recalls a key plot element of *Back to the Future Part II*, in which Biff from 2015 goes back to 1955 with a sports almanac so that his past self can make a killing at the bookies. Despite the obvious similarities, it's hard to see how Rob and Doug's episode of **Red Dwarf** recorded in September 1989 could have been influenced by a movie released in November 1989. Unless…? No…

Best gag: 'It's my duty – my duty as a complete and utter bastard.'

Worst visual effect: As noted in the making of section, Ed Bye makes some very, very difficult video effects look very, very easy. I'll give this to Cat's golfing knitwear (complete with Dewynters **Red Dwarf** logo).

Continuity is for smegheads: The footage of Hitler is from the 1935 propaganda film *Triumph of the Will* and depicts the 1934 Nuremberg rally. Lister's newspaper proclaiming that Hitler survived a bomb plot is dated 4 May 1938. While it isn't impossible that further attempts on the Führer's life were made, Operation Valkyrie, von Stauffenberg's assassination plot involving a bomb in a briefcase, took place on 20 July 1944 at Hitler's military headquarters in East Prussia. Mechanoids like Kryten were unknown when Lister was a teenager. Kryten suggests visiting Dallas in 1963, which the team will do in *Tikka to Ride*. Lister, who has no conception of his inability to play the guitar, tells his 17-year-old self that they don't make it as a rock star, because they're crap. Rimmer's preferred nickname is 'Old Iron Balls'. At school he was known as 'Bonehead' (as first noted in *Kryten*) and there's some kind of chapel on board ship, where he attends some kind of services. His enthusiasm for fascist dictators extends to a magazine collection devoted to them. We briefly meet Rimmer's brother Frank (played by Chris Barrie). Rimmer appears to have no recollection of the events of last week's episode where he tasted, smelled and ate a great deal while body-swapped with Lister. Ingrid has become Rachel, but she has a puncture. Cat's golfing prowess has improved since *Better than Life*. Simon Gaffney makes his first appearance as young Rimmer.

Remastered: The explosion out of the slide now has an extra tongue of flame. The *Ishtar* conversation has been deleted (as has the Xanadu gag in the middle of Ruby Wax's monologue, by way of a quick cutaway to a revolted-looking Rimmer). The opening caption about Adolf Hitler being the special guest star is missing. Rimmer appears in Lister's mansion in a flash of light. The statue, which according to the dialogue can't be made to urinate champagne, does now appear to be urinating something via an unconvincing video effect.

S03E06 The Last Day ★★★☆☆

TX: 19 December 1989 on BBC2. Ratings: 4.06m (7th for the week). Featuring: Gordon Kennedy, Julie Higginson.

Once again, despite being 3 million years into deep space, *Red Dwarf* is located by not one, but two different pods, one containing news of Kryten's demise and one containing his replacement. Speaking of which, this script was written to replace the planned first episode, 'Dad', and a few bits and pieces make it through from that draft to this, but this does bear signs of being written in a hurry, starting with those two pods. Wouldn't it have been more elegant to have one pod, bearing Hudzen, who gives the news but doesn't give any hint of malice until Kryten refuses to self-terminate? Or a dormant replacement who wakes up when he's needed?

Anyway, there is some good stuff here, mainly in the middle. The party that the gang throws for Kryten is full of great jokes, strong character moments and a lovely sense of camaraderie. Even Hattie Hayridge gets a couple of solid laugh lines. And we also get the sight of Robert Llewellyn *sans* rubber and talking in his own voice as the aptly named 'Jim Reaper'. But when Hudzen-10 turns up, it becomes difficult for the production to rise to the level of jeopardy that the script is going for. And, I hate to say it, but I think Gordon Kennedy is miscast (apparently, Rutger Hauer was the first person they thought of).

The impish Scotsman is so unlike the Terminator, that he's forced to do a silly growly voice, and it makes the whole thing feel a bit panto. It's not integrated enough to feel either funny or scary. And then I start wondering how this hulking, weapons-bedecked killing machine is in any way the obvious next purchase for someone happy with Kryten?

His defeat at the hands of Kryten's revelation about silicon heaven feels perfunctory and poorly explained too. If only the suggestion that silicon heaven isn't real is enough to shut down any mechanoid, then Kryten should have been shut down when Lister made the same observation. Silicon heaven is a neat idea, though, and it satirises religion more effectively than *Waiting for God*, while still being unlikely to deeply offend even the very devout.

We also discover that for one morning, Rimmer worked for the Samaritans, the helpline for people in emotional distress. During that morning, five people he spoke to took their own lives (and one was a wrong number, asking for the cricket scores). Very oddly, according to his wife, Gordon Brittas of *The Brittas Empire* had a similar experience. In the fifth episode of the first season, 'Stop Thief', broadcast just over a year after this, we learnt that Brittas worked for the Samaritans for a single evening, dubbed Black Friday. They lost four in an hour and a half, and one of them was just a wrong number. Gordon Brittas is, of course, played by Chris Barrie.

I don't think there's much to be concluded from this, except to note that the Samaritans were quite often evoked as punchlines by British comedy writers around this time. Richie calls them in the first *Bottom* stage show (and they hang up on him). In *Drop the Dead Donkey*, sad sack George knows the number by heart, and rattles it off, barely prompted. Rigsby in *Rising Damp* rings them to ask about a troubled tenant (but they're out). Basil Fawlty claims that the line was engaged and thus he has to resort to singing and rubbing his hands to get through the day – and no doubt other examples exist.

Anyway, it's certainly nice to get a Kryten-centric episode, and it's great to see the boys from the *Dwarf* enjoying each other's company, without becoming an anonymous gang of four, and still able to needle each other – but the pieces don't quite slot together here. So, this is not my favourite episode of the series, but it's very heartening to see that even if the story gods aren't smiling, the character jokes can still put air in the script's sails and the regular cast can still sell it with vigour and charm.

Some people, notably Robert Llewellyn, assumed this would be the last ever **Red Dwarf**. Three series is quite often the max for a British sitcom, especially one with only middling ratings – but Series III was never out of the BBC2 weekly top ten, which was a first for the show, so a further commission wasn't far away. If these eighteen episodes had been all we got, then I think they would still be fondly remembered. In fact, the best is yet to come.

The one with: Silicon heaven.

That Rimmer's a solid guy: He does turn up with the others to face Hudzen, but then he literally wets himself and panics when he's standing between the guns and the target, despite being made only of light. It's not at all clear how Hudzen intends to kill him.

There's a time and a place: Without any mental or physical activity, Kryten could still get a job as a disc jockey. Kryten has absent genitals like Action Man – the UK version of the American GI Joe posable figure for children. Lister doesn't want to hear any of this *Star Trek* crap. Kryten's Owners Manual comes in a blue A4 lever arch file. Eighties Danish movie star and model Brigitte Nielsen is Lister's idea of silicon(e) heaven – a concept which he thinks is 'wacko Jacko', a nickname for Michael Jackson often found in tabloid newspapers. Holly's concoction for Kryten tastes like a cross between fruity soft drink Vimto and liquid nitrogen. Lister's vomit resembles the works of American abstract artist Jackson Pollock.

Influences, references and rip-offs: What was at the time called 'built-in obsolescence' was memorably applied to synthetic humans in the 1982 film *Blade Runner* where replicants have pre-set lifespans. Hudzen has a heads-up display similar to that seen in the 1984 film *The Terminator*. Kryten's method for dealing with Hudzen is essentially to fry its brain with a contradiction, as Captain Kirk did with various computerised adversaries, notably Nomad in *The Changeling*.

Best gag: The traffic cone.

Worst visual effect: Hudzen microwaving that chicken looks like it was a bit of an afterthought.

Continuity is for smegheads: Kryten's full name is Kryten 2X4B 523P. He's a Series III mechanoid made by Diva-Droid International. A second incarnation of Marilyn Monroe appears, this one in robotic form. Rimmer's uncle Frank shares his name with one of Rimmer's brothers, and he was having an affair with Rimmer's mother, inadvertently giving 14-year-old Rimmer his first French kiss. Some details of Lister's family history emerge too – he was found in a box under a pool table in a pub at six weeks old. This will be re-examined in Series VII's *Ouroboros*. The ship's armoury can supply one quick-disassembly bazookoid and a sawn-off shotgun. Kryten's ability to lie freely is not something he retains for very long.

Remastered: The two pod-approaching shots have been redone as weirdly static CGI. There's new pulse-pounding music as Hudzen comes on board.

Part Two

Boys from the Dwarf

Series IV

The Making of Series IV

Paul Jackson had been instrumental in getting **Red Dwarf** on the air, and episodes in the first three series had all ended with the caption: 'A Paul Jackson Production'. Jackson also had a stake in Noel Gay Television, the company founded by Richard Armitage, and named after his songwriting father. Armitage had made a fortune from his 1980s reworking of the stage musical *Me and My Girl* (a project he had devised as a vehicle for his father's songs). When he died, his sons Alex and Charles took over the business, and it was effectively run by Charles Armitage and Paul Jackson for many years. Noel Gay Television was one of the very first major independent television production companies in the UK.

When Noel Gay purchased Paul Jackson Productions, it seemed inevitable that **Red Dwarf** would be swallowed up along with everything else, but Rob and Doug were still on very good terms with Paul Jackson, and they were able to come up with a deal whereby Jackson would keep a small stake, but Rob and Doug would form their own company, Grant Naylor Productions (GNP), which would control all the rights to **Red Dwarf**. They still used Noel Gay as agents, and in fact, Noel Gay also represented composer Howard Goodall and actor Chris Barrie. Rule one of show business: where possible, keep it in the family.

By now **Red Dwarf** was becoming something of a cottage industry. Rob and Doug had written a second novel, *Better than Life*, which continued the story begun in *Infinity Welcomes Careful Drivers*. Ratings for Series III had been strong, and a fourth series was only a matter of time. Releasing the first three series on VHS was now being actively discussed, but Rob and Doug still weren't sure if they wanted Series I to be seen again. They discussed a re-edit, but the budget wasn't there for it (yet).

The freedom of the novel-writing process impacted the writing of Series IV, and for the first time, story material from one of the novels turned up in the television series instead of the other way round – although the planned 'Garbage World' sequence was another idea which temporarily caused Ed Bye to lose the power of speech, and so the white hole storyline was used instead. Several other decisions that they had taken in writing the novel were deemed superior to those they'd taken while writing early episodes of the television series, and so – secure in the knowledge that Series I wouldn't be repeated any time soon – they quietly ret-conned details such as the number of people on board the ship, the extent of Lister and Kochanski's relationship and so on. See **Continuity is for smegheads** for further details.

Doug was very blasé at the thought of all of these contradictions, finding a certain humour in the thought of angry science fiction fans being driven crazy as the puzzle pieces failed to click into place. Rob was a bit more anxious but conceded that the changes were all for the better. Having Kochanski barely know who Lister is lowers the stakes on everything, and given the character they were now writing, it seemed incongruously teenage for him to have only mooned over her from a distance.

Meanwhile, the Manchester Oxford Road studio was closed for refurbishments and so the days of flying and/or bussing up north were over. Eschewing the usual option of Television Centre, the team eventually ended up at Shepperton Studios in Surrey. This expansive facility had decades of film history. Productions shot there include *The Third Man*, *2001: A Space Odyssey*, *Alien* and *Blade Runner* and it became **Red Dwarf**'s main home for the remainder of the BBC years, and beyond. Now owned by Pinewood, it is still a major centre for film and TV production in the UK, with Netflix controlling seventeen sound stages there on a pretty permanent basis.

Freed from both the grim rehearsal rooms at Acton and the tiresome journeys up and down the M6 motorway, for the cast this definitely felt like an upgrade. Of particular benefit was the fact that – unlike filming in a BBC studio – the sets that were erected would stay on the sound stage until they were no longer needed, which meant that instead of having to work out moves, performances and physical 'business' in a featureless room with walls marked on the floor in electrical tape, rehearsals could instead take place on the set where the action would later be recorded. Everybody thought this was a huge improvement, except, slightly oddly, Chris Barrie, who was distracted by the fact that people were sometimes working on refining the scenery while they were trying to rehearse, and was bothered by the draughty nature of what is essentially a large aircraft hangar in the middle of the English countryside in November.

Someone else who was streamlining working practices was new make-up designer Andrea Pennell (sometimes credited as Andria, sometimes credited as Pennel, and now known as Andrea Finch). Previously, Kryten's prosthetic make-up had been applied in individual pieces, each of which had to be carefully glued to the actor's face, then painted and blended in – a process that, as noted, could take upwards of four hours. By devising a new version of the mask, which could be slipped over Robert Llewellyn's head like a balaclava, and doing most of the painting beforehand, the make-up team managed to get the process down to under an hour. This proved to be a boon for the first transmitted episode, *Camille*, in which Robert Llewellyn's real-life partner, Judy Pascoe, played the mechanoid version of the pleasure GELF which comes on board the ship.

Having heard Llewellyn complain throughout the making of the previous series about the agonies he'd suffered, Pascoe was delighted to find herself avoiding the 5:00 a.m. calls which she'd heard tell of. This was very frustrating for Llewellyn, who had expected to find himself vindicated for his months of moaning. 'Wait till she has to spend all day with her head in rubber,' he thought, but actually, again, Pascoe found the ordeal no worse than mildly uncomfortable. Kissing each other with rubber lips proved to be a very unsatisfactory experience, however, which Llewellyn likened to snogging after having had an anaesthetic at the dentist's.

Since the GELF takes on a different appearance for each member of the crew, other guest actors were needed. Getting C.P. Grogan back as Kochanski was discussed, but it was realised that suddenly having Lister's 3-million-years-dead girlfriend appear would give the game away even more quickly, and so Tracy Brabin was cast in the hope of getting a hint of Grogan's energy. It was apparent in front of the audience, though, that it wasn't working out. Possibly observing the chemistry between Robert Llewellyn and Judy Pascoe, Craig Charles suggested that if they were going to reshoot Brabin's stuff, why not ask his girlfriend Suzanne Rhatigan? Lister's scenes with his ideal woman were re-recorded during a later episode. Even though she's never referred to as such on-screen, Rhatigan was nevertheless credited as 'Kochanski Camille'.

Neither Danny John-Jules nor Chris Barrie were able to obey rule one of show business. Barrie was paired with Francesca Folen as a hologram in shimmery red, to contrast with Rimmer's shimmery green. And the Cat's idea of the most beautiful person imaginable was, of course, himself. By now, a simple split screen was child's play to Ed Bye and even having John-Jules high-five himself didn't create any serious problems. Hattie Hayridge was a bit put out not to have the GELF create an ideal computer for her to be seduced by, but the episode didn't have room for an extra scene.

Once the creature's true nature is revealed, things take a turn for the romantic, and Kryten and the GELF develop something of a relationship, even though it is doomed from the start. Despite the many references to the classic Warner Bros. film *Casablanca*, no actual clips were included. According to Ed Bye, licensing that material would have left them with only enough money for two bits of scenery, half a bazookoid and a shoe. Resident composer Howard Goodall came up with a piece of music similar enough to 'When Time Goes By' to set the mood, but not so similar as to incur lawsuits. And Peter Wragg's team created another disgusting animatronic monster, but endless retakes were needed of the creature and Kryten having drinks together, because it couldn't hold a glass in its appendage without dropping it.

The next episode transmitted, *DNA*, saw Kryten transformed from mechanoid to human. (According to the script, 'DNA' stands for 'Do Not Alter'.) For Robert Llewellyn, it should have been a relief to be able to act without having his head encased in rubber – all of the mechanoid Kryten scenes were taped during the pre-filming session. Ed Bye, however, recalls having occasional moments of panic watching the monitors, during the main recording. Even though he was used to seeing and hearing an un-made-up Llewellyn acting as Kryten during rehearsals, the sight of him without all the latex seemed so jarring that he kept catching himself thinking, 'They've forgotten to put Bobby's make-up on! How has that happened? Wait…'

In fact, Llewellyn found that playing Kryten without make-up was rather more nerve-wracking than he expected. Without the mask to hide behind, he suddenly felt vulnerable and uncertain in front of the audience – naked without all the latex (and indeed very nearly naked regardless, since in the first scenes to be recorded, he's only wearing a hospital gown). Also unimpressed were his two young nephews who had been invited to watch the taping, but they had been hoping to see mechanoid Kryten, not 'boring Uncle Rob'.

In one of the series' most famous moments, as the once-mechanoid is grappling with his newfound humanity, he takes a personal photograph of himself – or rather two of them – and hands them to Lister, who has to arrange them correctly to see what is depicted. Quite what the art department prepared for him to look at has never been definitively revealed but Craig Charles has suggested that very little acting was required from him as he stared at the 'double Polaroid'.

As part of their preparation for writing the fourth series, Rob and Doug had asked the cast if there was anything they wanted to do. Chris Barrie, who had by now completed filming the first series of his new sitcom *The Brittas Empire*, said he felt he was suffering from 'git overload'. Couldn't he play somebody normal and nice for a change? Rob and Doug didn't see what would be funny about that but promised to keep Barrie's thoughts in mind. Robert Llewellyn had an idea about Kryten having a spare head with a gruff northern accent, and this was a request the writers found much easier to implement. Thus were born Kryten's spare heads numbers one, two and three, with number three suffering from an advanced case of 'droid rot'. Again, Ed Bye's abilities to marshal the still fairly primitive video effects of the day came to the fore, as three different takes of Llewellyn sticking his head through a hole were combined, with a fourth element removing everything below the neck to create the illusion of three disembodied talking heads.

Further video effects were needed to reduce Lister to only a foot tall, and this was a rather longer, more involved process, which required Craig Charles to play his scenes in a separate part of the studio, festooned with blue drapes. All of this was prerecorded and played to the live audience at the appropriate juncture.

Justice, recorded first but transmitted third, featured prosthetics for Craig Charles, who usually had the easiest time of anyone in the regular cast. Danny John-Jules needed to have the Cat's teeth fitted and even Chris Barrie had to have his H stuck to his forehead. This time, however, the script called for him to – once again – be suffering from an exotic space virus and to have developed an enormous, swollen, pus-filled forehead. Although the appliance only began at his eyebrows, the extent of the seam between the latex and his skin meant that several hours had to be spent carefully blending, painting and matching colours to hide the join. As a result, for the first time in **Red Dwarf** history, Robert Llewellyn was out of make-up faster than Craig Charles, who – at last – managed to develop a little sympathy for what his castmate had been going through all these weeks.

Some pre-filming for this episode took place at a new location for the team – Sunbury Pump House, used by countless television shows from ITV's *Kenny Everett Video Show* in the 1970s to Channel 4's *Gamesmaster* in the 1990s, as well as many future episodes of **Red Dwarf**. Despite this, Ed Bye and Mel Bibby were still struggling to make real everything that Rob and Doug were describing. Bye had worked on another show recently where the designer had created a false perspective corridor which appeared to stretch to infinity and he and Bibby attempted to use the same technique here, but for whatever reason it didn't quite work, and they were forced to hide the end of the too-short set with a bright light shining at the cameras. As written, the Justice Complex was supposed to be on a planet and location filming had been planned with the Dwarfers walking around a park while Rimmer was incarcerated. This was dropped, the Justice Complex was moved to a space station, and the closing speech from Lister about free will was added in order to keep the episode from underrunning.

White Hole, as noted, was less ambitious, but for this one Ed Bye had problems of his own. Not only had he just become a father, but during the rehearsal week he contracted some kind of gastric flu, and on the day of the live taping, he threw up twice in his own lap while driving to the studio, before eventually deciding to turn around and go home. Luckily, Paul Jackson was still in the habit of attending recordings, and although he hadn't directed television for seven years, he was able to take over Bye's camera script and keep the show on the road. Everybody was pleased to see the man who had had such faith in the project back to supervise things once more – maybe apart from Danny

John-Jules, who arrived late, not for the first time, to find in the place of the expected affably eye-rolling Ed Bye, a quietly furious Paul Jackson, who gave him a dressing down for several excruciating minutes.

The plot of this episode required Holly to be transformed into an actual genius supercomputer and various ideas were discussed regarding how to suggest this visually. A make-up test was done using a bald cap and some round glasses, but nobody seems to have liked the results, so in the end, Hattie Hayridge's own hair was slicked back, and she was given a kiss curl on her forehead. She also got a change of outfit, swapping her black polo neck for a blue one so that her head could be superimposed over the rest of the set.

White Hole also saw the return of the redoubtable Talkie Toaster, but with John Lenahan now otherwise engaged, the OG Kryten, David Ross, was called in. The change in actor has caused some fans to speculate that 'Talkie' is a code name, passed from toaster to toaster, but this is not considered canon. Robert Llewellyn was understandably anxious about meeting the man whose part he'd stolen, but the fact that Ross was himself coming in as a replacement for another actor must have calmed him a bit. And in the end, Ross was delighted to meet Llewellyn and congratulated him on making the part his own so successfully – although some of the cast didn't take kindly to Ross asking each performer in turn if they were 'legitimate' (in other words, a trained stage actor). The poet, dancer, impressionist, stand-up comedian and cabaret performer all had to find ways to change the subject.

Fifth in the running order was perennial fan-favourite *Dimension Jump*. This introduced us to 'Ace' Rimmer, Rob and Doug's solution to Chris Barrie's 'git overload' problem, and you can tell watching the finished episode that he loves every moment of playing this swaggeringly heroic figure – still in his own way kind of an arsehole, but miles away from the characterisation he'd been used to. Key to the performance was the excellent wig that Andrea Pennell came up with. Styled and fitted to Chris Barrie's head, it genuinely is seamless, and Barrie recalls striding down the corridors at Shepperton and having close colleagues, including Paul Jackson, fail to recognise him, at least for a moment. The character returned in later episodes, but the wig went mysteriously missing. Pennell wonders if Chris Barrie himself half-inched it, but in that case, why would he complain so bitterly about how poor the replacement was?

In the climactic scenes, Craig Charles, Chris Barrie, and the Ace wig are seen clambering around on the outside of *Starbug* as they work together to repair it and escape the ocean planet they've crash-landed on. Being sprayed with water from huge industrial fans wasn't Barrie's idea of a good time, but when he complained, Craig Charles responded – loud enough for the rest of the crew to hear – 'Shut up, man, we're supposed to be space heroes.' This did little to build the rapport between the two men, whose relationship at this stage often resembled the one between their characters more than the trust and affection they have for each other today.

Hattie Hayridge again felt she got short-changed, having no interaction at all with Ace once he got on board *Starbug*, but time was found to shoot a quick scene of her fainting at the sight of his charms – possibly the comedy highlight of a very, very successful episode. The rest of the cast got to play new versions of their characters too: Lister becomes Ace's trusty mechanic 'Spanners', Hattie Hayridge is the Moneypenny-like 'Mellie', Ace's mission is given to him by Robert Llewellyn's 'Bongo' and Danny John-Jules appears as the kindly chaplain. This last part was changed during rehearsals. Initially, Rob and Doug had simply inverted the character that John-Jules was playing in the rest of the series and so had reinvented the cool and immaculately presented Cat as a scruffy janitor who was seen sweeping the floors. But it suddenly seemed wrong for the show to be presenting a Black actor working as a janitor, and so Rob and Doug – who had heard John-Jules doing a benevolent West Indian voice over lunch – reimagined the character as a padre instead.

In the DVD documentary, both Craig Charles and Danny John-Jules talk about their role on the show and the positive impact of having a mainstream BBC sitcom in which two out of four (or five) of the main cast are non-white, but where race is never an issue or a plot point. Even in the episode *Queeg*, where the Cat and Lister are seen scrubbing floors, it's hard to ascribe a racial motive to this, since another Black actor is playing the character who has ordered them to do this. Both actors are at pains to point out that they don't believe Rob or Doug to be the slightest bit racist, but sometimes an unfortunate image can be created with the best of intentions, and it's good that there was the flexibility in the writing and production teams to make the change from janitor to padre in time – although the debate seems to have irritated Rob Grant, who felt the show had earned the right to show any of its regular actors in any role, having had two non-white leads for so long.

Another unfortunate collision of fantasy and reality nearly occurred with this episode and the next one. As originally planned, *Dimension Jump* would have opened the series, but in January 1991, Operation Desert Storm had just begun in Iraq and for as long as television news reports were full of very real images of warfare, the BBC was not keen to put out either the scenes of heroic fighter pilot Ace Rimmer, or the depictions of armed combat in the sixth episode, *Meltdown*. In fact, it looked for a while as if *Meltdown* might not be transmitted at all.

Some hasty rearrangement of the running order resulted in the series opening with the romantic episode *Camille*, which now, as luck would have it, transmitted on Valentine's Day 1991. A couple of weeks later, on 3 March, Iraq accepted the terms of a ceasefire from the United Nations and now the

BBC relented, and both *Dimension Jump* and *Meltdown* were released from television jail, making up the fifth and sixth episodes of Series IV, respectively. Repeat screenings in May 1992 and July 1994 returned the episodes to their planned order, although *Meltdown* still went out last, but the original transmission sequence is now regarded as the 'correct' one and has been used for all subsequent airings and the DVD releases. VHS releases, which split six episodes over two tapes, regularly moved episodes around in order to get one popular episode at the start of each tape.

Meltdown has proven to be a less popular episode than its predecessor and it required a lot of location filming and a lot of guest actors playing an array of well-known figures from pop culture, including Elvis, Hitler, Einstein, Lincoln, Napoleon, Noël Coward and Stan Laurel. Additionally, Pauline Bailey made a more convincing Marilyn Monroe than we saw in *Better than Life*. Howard Burden was able to find many of the costumes he needed from BBC stock, but professional Elvis impersonator Clayton Mark turned up in his own gear. I recommend not Googling that name if you enjoy this episode and would rather not have your memories tarnished. The elderly actor booked to play Gandhi, Alex Tetteh-Lartey, was suffering in the cold and clearly wasn't going to be able to manage the push-ups which the script called for, and so he was replaced by the younger, fitter, Charles Reynolds.

Seen on screen for the last time in **Red Dwarf**, Tony Hawks got his best role to date as the face-slapping Roman emperor Caligula. His replacement for the warm-up was an up-and-coming comedian called Eddie Izzard, but Craig Charles remembers that Izzard didn't connect with the audience in the same way that Hawks had, and he wondered if this new comic would ever amount to anything.

Finally, the BBC had given the team a bit more money to spend. A total of £1.5 million was allocated to Series IV, but everyone was so concerned to keep costs down that as production came to an end, it became clear that they were going to come in around £150,000 under budget. As this realisation dawned, panic began to spread, with people being sent home in taxis who would normally have been expected to take public transport, post-recording takeaways suddenly being offered – anything to get rid of the excess cash. If you have money left over at the end of producing a series for the BBC, you don't get any thanks, you just get less money next year. Doug Naylor despaired at the corners that had been cut early in the series – why couldn't more have been spent on Mel Bibby's infinity set? – and vowed to prevent the same thing from happening in the future.

Red Dwarf was going from a scrappy show shot up north so that the BBC could deny all knowledge of it, to being one of the jewels in their comedy crown, and Series IV includes some all-time classic episodes – including my personal favourite, *Dimension Jump*. Meanwhile, **Red Dwarf** was finally coming to home video. In October 1991, Series III was released on VHS in two volumes: 'Backwards' and 'Timeslides' – and the official Red Dwarf fan club was launched while Series IV was in production.

Impressions of Series IV

Written by Rob Grant and Doug Naylor. Designed by Mel Bibby. Costumes by Howard Burden. Produced by Rob Grant and Doug Naylor. Produced and directed by Ed Bye (and Paul Jackson). Starring: Craig Charles, Chris Barrie, Danny John-Jules, Robert Llewellyn, Hattie Hayridge.

S04E01 Camille ★★★☆☆

TX: 14 February 1991 on BBC2. Ratings: 4.32m (4th for the week). Featuring: Judy Pascoe, Francesca Folan, Suzanne Rhatigan.

A new series means new opening credits, and these are on the same pattern as last year, just with new clips. A minor change is that the episode titles now scroll across the screen sideways in giant red type. A new bunk room set gives a cleaner, whiter, more modern feel to the place – a little less truckers-in-space, but also looking a little bit less grey cardboard, which is all to the good. The viewscreen showing an aquarium screensaver when not in use gives it a vaguely corporate lobby feel. Elsewhere, Holly has longer hair, Lister has a furry hat on, and the new Kryten mask is a tremendous improvement. It's the first episode I was able to watch without thinking, 'That doesn't look like Kryten.'

As noted, the episode order was changed at the last minute. It's obvious that *Dimension Jump* would have got the series off to a better start, but would any of the remaining stories have lived up to the promise of that cast-iron classic? The upshot of the revamped running order is that the most disappointing offerings are the first and last, which is not the usual way of designing these things (usually you want to bury your weakest material towards the end, but start and finish strong). It does help to ease us in, though.

That's especially true of Kryten, who didn't really get an episode to (re)introduce him last time. Even the episode centring him, *The Last Day*, is more about mechanoids in general (and having a big shooty bang bang guy to kill) than this mechanoid in particular. The opening scene, with Lister trying to teach Kryten how to lie, tells us more about him than almost any scene in the whole of Series III – even if it does flatly contradict Kryten's big moment at the end of the last episode.

Like *Bodyswap* in Series III, this is a show of two halves. In the first half, the gang are hornswoggled by a Genetically Engineered Life Form, which makes itself into the perfect object of desire of whomever is looking at it. In the second half, Kryten romances the GELF, even when he knows its true nature. Unlike *Bodyswap*, where the first half is both funny and exciting, and the story segues naturally into other uses for the same technology, here the first plot is not so much resolved as just abandoned. When Camille simply 'fesses up to her true nature, it squanders any story or comedy potential in everyone being in love with her and trying to keep her to themselves. If Rob and Doug wanted to tell a story about Kryten in love, it might have been better to just have another mechanoid come on board and to find some other reason why the relationship couldn't last – or stick to the Pleasure GELF idea and have the gang turn on each other, instead of being very nice and understanding, which tends to make for less than compelling viewing. Very odd for a series devised on the 'two men who hate each other' model.

That wouldn't be so bad if the second half of the episode took us to somewhere much more interesting and novel, but alas, it simply follows the outline of the movie classic *Casablanca* – seemingly without understanding what makes it work. There's a noble purpose to Rick giving up Ilsa for Victor – he's finally going to stick his neck out for something. Kryten just lets Camille go back to Hector because that's what happens in *Casablanca*. It's clear that the intention was to set up the fact that he learns to lie to spare her feelings, but that gets lost in the shuffle somewhat. And why does a Pleasure GELF have a spouse anyway? 'We'll always have Parrot's' is a noble pun but I can't help thinking that we should have had more laughs and/or character work along the way. Or stuck with the first idea.

The one with: *Casablanca*.

That Rimmer's a solid guy: Lister urges Rimmer to go and help Kryten, and Kryten calls out for him when he falls off that gantry, but it isn't clear what kind of help a hologram would be able to provide. Since holograms can touch each other, Rimmer does have a chance with Camille (or he would have, if she was actually a hologram who fancied him).

There's a time and a place: Kryten's first successful attempt at lying has him identifying a banana as 'a small, off-duty Czechoslovakian traffic warden', despite the fact that Czechoslovakia ceased to exist at the end of 1992. Lister has seen every episode of *St Elsewhere*, but he only knows the folk version of Napoleon's refusal to acknowledge the order to retreat given at the Battle of Copenhagen. Steve McQueen also met a blob, but he tried to kill it. Lister is watching *Tales of the Riverbank: The Next Generation* (and compares Hammy

Hamster to Marlon Brando). *Tales of the Riverbank* was a real show, but the 'Next Generation' part of the name is a *Star Trek* joke. Kryten thinks Camille must find him as stupid as a photocopier. She wears WD-40 as a fragrance. Robert Llewellyn pronounces the acronym ASCII as 'A-S-C-two' (it's normally said 'askey' and it doesn't include a Roman numeral) and 'E5 A9 08 B7' in ASCII is 'å©[BACKSPACE]·' not 'LOVE' or 'love'. Prime numbers don't have 'prime roots', but they do have primitive roots, which may be what was intended. Karl Malden is less attractive than a GELF.

Influences, references and rip-offs: The last third of the episode is a grinding rehash of *Casablanca*. The different appearances of the GELF recall the salt monster in the original *Star Trek* episode 'Where No Man Has Gone Before', and her name is a hint at her chameleonic nature. The snatch of Strauss's 'The Blue Danube' over a model shot of a wheeling *Starbug* is a nod to *2001: A Space Odyssey*.

Best gag: Cat's vision of physical perfection is himself. Gold.

Worst visual effect: The GELF creature is a fairly poor animatronic, and weirdly phallic.

Continuity is for smegheads: In *Better than Life* it was established that the remake of *Casablanca* with Myra Binglebat and Peter Beardsley was definitive, but here Lister refers only to the Humphrey Bogart original. Rimmer's preferred nickname is 'Duke'. Cat calls him Captain Sadness. Rimmer's ideal woman looks like his sister-in-law Janine. First appearance of the GELFs, who will stand in for the forbidden aliens in several future episodes. Kryten is now a 4000 Series mechanoid instead of a Series III, as he was in *The Last Day*.

S04E02 DNA ★★★☆☆

TX: 21 February 1991 on BBC2. Ratings: 3.78m (6th for the week).
Featuring: Richard Ridings.

Again, this one is a bit oddly structured. For the second week running, the plot is kicked off by the discovery of another craft in the vicinity of *Red Dwarf*. This time instead of a crashed GELF ship, it's a DNA machine floating in space. Holly is presumably having an early night, because the crew has to track it manually, something that doesn't make much sense, but which is the source of some good gags as the Cat keeps unplugging things to dry his hair.

As is often the case, the crew splits up, with Rimmer and Kryten on one team and Lister and Cat on the other. The Cat being a technological doofus is also very funny ('Touch nothing! Get Kryten!') and it's a great use of his character to get Lister into trouble. Once again, though, we go the long way round to get to what the episode is really about. Nothing whatever comes of Lister being turned into a chicken, but when Kryten becomes a human, there's suddenly loads to explore.

Granted, we have to assume that Kryten has forgotten a great deal about human anatomy since he was looking after the crew of the *Nova 5*, but given that he didn't exactly do a bang-up job there, I think we can let that one slide. There's masses of good stuff here, with Kryten's journey from bewilderment, to adjustment, to jerky arrogance, to finally accepting that he was better as he was originally – and Robert Llewellyn plays it all beautifully. Rimmer and the Cat, alas, are shunted off into a dandruff-related side plot that goes nowhere, so this feels a bit incomplete as it stands.

Eventually, and with very little justification, they are attacked by a curry monster, and we essentially reprise the ending of *Polymorph*, only without the great character work – although with a cleverer method of despatch for the enemy, to be fair. So, this feels like one-third of a really great episode, preceded by a rather clumsy setup and followed by a rather by-the-numbers climax, which is frustrating. Was there really nothing else to be done with human Kryten?

The one with: The double Polaroid.

That Rimmer's a solid guy: Arnie runs away in panic when the curry monster attacks. A three-headed mutant corpse is said to have fallen through him, but we don't witness this.

There's a time and a place: Kryten can't receive Jazz FM. Once again, photography is stuck in the photochemical world, specifically Polaroids. If God had intended us to fly, he wouldn't have invented Spanish air traffic control. Cat has heard of *The Elephant Man*. Rimmer is concerned that they'll get Glenn Miller back. Cat doesn't want to look like the Bride of Frankenstein. Kryten misses Quantel, the digital image processing system used on TV in the 1980s to make snazzy transitions. Rimmer wonders if Lister is a closet squirrel, and uses the name 'Nutkin', after the Beatrix Potter character in her stories for children. Spare Head Two's eyes might spin like fruit machines. Perry Como sang 'Memories are Made of This' with one of those stashed in his slacks. It wasn't Descartes who said 'I am what I am', it was Popeye. Lister once went into a wine bar (which is a slippery slope leading to pine kitchens, futons and tapas). Cat calls the curry monster 'chomp thing', which is presumably a pun on DC Comics's 'Swamp Thing'.

Influences, references and rip-offs: Superhuman mini-Lister is costumed like RoboCop from the 1987 movie directed by Paul Verhoeven. The curry monster is essentially a reprise of last year's *Polymorph*, which the Dwarfers acknowledge, misquoting *Die Hard II* in the process. The final despatch of the creature is a nod to *Jaws*, with a lager can instead of a pressurised oxygen tank.

Worst visual effect: The curry monster is shot more craftily than the polymorph was, and also might be a better prop. The mini-Lister stuff is pretty good, all things considered (although he doesn't cast any shadows).

Continuity is for smegheads: It's established that Lister and Kochanski did date, contrary to what we were told in Series I. That being the case, what does that say about Holly's decision to resurrect Rimmer and not her? We never see Kryten and Lister returned to normal. Rimmer's enthusiasm for finding aliens appears to have evaporated. Lister hails from the twenty-third century, not the mid-twenty-first, as established in *Stasis Leak*. Kryten's brain is part organic (although why that means his entire body is susceptible to the DNA machine is not clear). *Polymorph* was twelve months ago to the day.

S04E03 Justice ★★★★☆

TX: 28 February 1991 on BBC2. Ratings: 3.97m (4th for the week).
Featuring: Nicholas Ball, James Smillie.

Again, we kick off the episode with the discovery of another craft, this time a pod that might or might not contain the no doubt very foxy Barbara Bellini. It makes space seem very small when we can barely leave one pod behind before stumbling across the next one. It then seems to take an awful lot of reverse engineering – involving a pod, a prison planet, a penal colony and a black box flight recorder – just to get the gang into Justice World, and although there are some decent one-liners along the way, this all feels very laborious. Contributing to that feeling is the lengthy digression involving Lister's space mumps, which never feeds into the rest of the plot, and is never particularly interesting or funny.

When we arrive on Justice World, things improve significantly. We get a genuinely insightful take on the meaning and purpose of justice, in a novel science fiction setting; and we get a situation where – rather like Jeeves and Bertie Wooster in the stories by P.G. Wodehouse – the only way in which Kryten can save Rimmer is by humiliating him utterly. But the episode ends the same way the last one did – a horrible creature is stomping through corridors trying to kill the crew of *Red Dwarf*. This time, the nature of Justice World means that it doesn't present an actual threat, so the stakes are very low, but the slapstick is excellent. Nicholas Ball seems to have been shown a tape of Gordon Kennedy in *The Last Day* and been told, 'Do it like that, but about 15 per cent better.'

At halfway through the series, we seem to have settled into a not altogether satisfactory groove. Three stories in a row have given us ten minutes of largely irrelevant messing about, followed by ten minutes of properly exploring the theme, followed by ten minutes in a different genre altogether, usually involving everybody running around and shouting. It's not bad TV exactly, but I know this show can do better – far better. Hattie Hayridge is now getting so redundant that she has her voice dubbed by a rich-toned male actor twice in two episodes. It's quite close between *Justice*, *DNA* and *Camille* for me. I think *Justice* is cleverer than *DNA*, and *DNA* is funnier than *Camille*, thus my star ratings, but they're all middle-of-the-pack episodes which feel like they could have been top-tier with just a bit more work.

The one with: Stop hitting yourself.

That Rimmer's a solid guy: The auto-shoes work as well on Rimmer as on everyone else because: 'that has been accounted for'. Uh-huh. Lister brings Rimmer a book to read, which presumably he would be unable to pick up or open. Lister taps Rimmer's arm to get his attention as they stand on the gantry, looking for the Simulant.

There's a time and a place: Kryten has looked after Lister like 'Florence Nightingdroid'. Rimmer intends to show Lister a slide show of his tour of the diesel decks and has been loading the carousel. At least the projection appears to be holographic without a physical screen. Musical theatre producer Cameron Mackintosh gives his name to one of the engines. Kryten compares Rimmer to Long John Silver's parrot from Robert Louis Stevenson's classic novel *Treasure Island*, which did much to cement the iconography of pirates in pop culture (including their fondness for parrots). Cat is familiar with *Ripley's Believe It Or Not*, and compares the auto-shoes to Frankenstein's hand-me-downs. Kryten's mechanoid proverbs are expressed in the programming language BASIC, developed as an educational tool in the mid-1960s. Rimmer calls Cat 'Pussycat Willum', a reference to the glove puppet star of 1960s Rediffusion children's television show *The Five O'Clock Club*. He parties less than Rudolph Hess. The Simulant's gun quotes Dirty Harry.

Influences, references and rip-offs: The Justice Zone recalls Kafka's *The Trial*. The Simulant looks like a cross between The Terminator and the Borg from *Star Trek: The Next Generation* (which had now come to BBC2). Although the series was slightly inspired by *Porridge*, very little of this resembles HMP Slade.

Best gag: Cat clonking the Simulant on the head with a spade and promptly keeling over himself.

Worst visual effect: *Starbug*'s approach to the prison colony looks very nice, as does the overhead matte shot when they first arrive. The shoes-with-wings-on are pretty pony, however.

Continuity is for smegheads: Lister is sitting on the right side of *Starbug*, not the left as would become the standard configuration. There were 1,169 people on board *Red Dwarf*, compared to 169 as stated in *The End*. Rachel still has a puncture. Rimmer failed the astro-navigation exam thirteen times instead of ten times (*Future Echoes*) or the engineering exam eleven times (*Waiting for God*). First Simulant, and – along with the GELFs – they will return as not-alien baddies in several future episodes.

S04E04 White Hole ★★★★☆

TX: 7 March 1991 on BBC2. Ratings: 4.41m (2nd for the week).

Finally, we're back to: *the crew makes terrible decisions and faces the consequences* – as opposed to: *the mysterious pod of doom floating in space the contents of which stalks and tries to kill everyone* stories which made up the first part of the season. The novel Toaster's-eye-view shooting of the opening scenes reminds me of the opening of the later episode *Tikka to Ride*, which also features Lister talking into a camera.

The plan to 'fix' Holly makes perfect sense as a thing that the crew might attempt, and the result is very funny and well worked out. Hattie Hayridge is brilliant as genius Holly, although the continuity about how many minutes or seconds she has left is very poor. What's also striking is how helpless they all are without Holly, and yet how happily the ship seems to run without her in later episodes.

The titular white hole spewing anti-time seems like it turns up at the worst possible moment, unifying the two elements of the story in the way that other episodes in Series IV have struggled to do. Only the section in the middle, about the crew having to generate their own power, feels like a bit of a narrative cul-de-sac. Again, nothing wrong with a self-contained comedy set piece if it's funny enough. But if it's only there to be funny, then it needs to be consistently super-hilarious to get over the fact that it isn't pushing the story along, and it isn't revealing anything about the characters.

However, the solution to their problem – Lister playing pool with planets – is pure, delicious **Red Dwarf** fun and made me laugh like a drain when I first saw it. All the pool talk – 'it's a felt-ripper', 'in someone's beer', 'played for and got' – is perfect and the juxtaposition of the very high stakes of the situation and Lister's insouciant attitude to the means of their escape is brilliant. The time-is-behaving-oddly scene is great too.

The one with: Lister playing pool with planets.

That Rimmer's a solid guy: The hologram made of light is unable to walk through the doors, requiring the use of Kryten as a battering ram. There is much talk of the need to keep him powered up, what other ship's systems could use the power, the inability to restore him from a back-up if they ever turn him off – most of which is contradicted in earlier episodes, later episodes, or actually in this episode. For some reason, Rimmer accompanies Kryten on a quest to find supplies, none of which he will be able to touch, pick up or carry.

There's a time and a place: They used to call Lister 'Cinzano Bianco' because once he was on a table you couldn't get rid of him. There's no Eskimo word for 'Eastbourne'. Cat is familiar with the Grand Canyon. Kryten urges Rimmer to remember Captain Oates, who abandoned Scott's *Terra Nova* expedition of the Antarctic in the futile hope that the remaining men would be more likely to survive. Rimmer compares time-slowed Kryten to 'Paul Robeson on dope'. Cat refers to Rimmer and Kryten as 'Stan and Ollie' (i.e. Laurel and Hardy).

Influences, references and rip-offs: Holly's fate is a riff on *Flowers for Algernon*, Daniel Keyes' short story and later novel in which a janitor has his IQ tripled through experimental surgery. Cat reprises his 'What is it?' routine from *Stasis Leak*.

Best gag: 'I'm fine thank you, Susan.'

Worst visual effect: The white hole video effects are all pretty poor.

Continuity is for smegheads: Talkie Toaster is a product of Crapola Inc. and retails for $£19.99. Lister later claims that his arm is 'as sound as a dollarpound'. The events of this story are unwritten after Lister's successful planet-potting, which will create continuity issues later. First mention of The Aigburth Arms.

S04E05 Dimension Jump ★★★★★

TX: 14 March 1991 on BBC2. Ratings: 4.10m (2nd for the week).
Featuring: Simon Gaffney, Kalli Greenwood.

Okay, cards on the table, this is my favourite episode of **Red Dwarf**. I love *Back to Reality* as well, of course (and *Quarantine*, and *Polymorph* and *Queeg* and – look, that's not the point) but this one is my favourite. It's brilliantly clever, genuinely insightful, very funny all the way through and it's a story that only **Red Dwarf** could tell. We start not one, but two, steps away from our familiar situation. Beginning with a flashback to Rimmer's childhood shows a lot of confidence. To bounce from there to an alternative universe in which Rimmer is a swaggeringly cocksure ace fighter pilot, beloved by all, is supreme self-belief. It takes guts to show every member of the regular cast playing unfamiliar versions of their characters first, and only then show us business as usual – but it works perfectly.

If I was going to quibble, the gags about sex involving Greek deli foods are a bit seaside postcard (and it's amazing how – in every dimension – Robert Llewellyn always gets the long exposition speeches) but, honestly, it's packing so much into such a small space, we can forgive a few shortcuts. And it's immensely gratifying that there's barely a hint of the homo-giggly when both Mellie and Bongo throw themselves at Ace.

The 'hanging out with the Dwarfers' sequence is definitely one of the better ones, full of good lines as everybody – even Holly – attempts to sneak off the ship to go fishing without waking Rimmer. And it's on theme as well. Rimmer really is a weasel. He can make anything un-fun. Then, when Ace turns up, you can sense Rob and Doug's joy at being able to give him zinger after zinger, and every time he gets contrasted with 'our' Arnold, the delight becomes greater. There's seamless split-screen work here from Ed Bye too, and Chris Barrie is magnificent in his dual role.

True, there's a hint of transphobia, or homophobia, as Rimmer sneers at Lister and Ace, but this is meant to be a portrait of a nasty, twisted individual at his lowest ebb, and we're a long way away from the toxic 'I bet she's a man' bit in *Dear Dave*. The final revelation that it was Ace who was kept back a year is incredible. It makes perfect sense, but it's impossible to see coming.

This isn't the first time that we've seemingly discovered the key to Rimmer's awful personality, and it won't be the last. But it's probably the most insightful, the funniest, and the one which also gives the rest of the cast a chance to shine – we even get to see Hattie Hayridge below the neck. Coming near the end of a slightly wobbly series, this is absolutely first-class stuff. I'd show it to anyone who wanted to know what **Red Dwarf** was all about.

The one with: Ace Rimmer.

That Rimmer's a solid guy: Arnold finds it helpful to assume a crash position. He is assumed to be of use when it comes to helping Ace to fix things he can't touch. The planned final shot of the episode would have been the kippers intended for Ace falling on 'our' Rimmer instead – but presumably they would have passed straight through him. The scene was shot, with fish bouncing off

Chris Barrie, but not used and the text scroll added instead to maintain the necessary run time.

There's a time and a place: In-flight magazines are therapeutically boring. Rimmer's Hammond organ music is on CD. How he 'brought them with him' is not clear. Rimmer thinks 'Ace and Skipper' sounds like *Skippy the Bush Kangaroo*, the Australian kids' TV show from the late sixties. The elastic has snapped on *Starbug*'s furry dice. In his delirium, Cat imagines he will look cool wearing bicycle clips. Rimmer speculates that Ace 'Masonic-handshook' his way into flight school.

Influences, references and rip-offs: Ace Rimmer has more than a hint of Pete 'Maverick' Mitchell from the 1986 film *Top Gun*, along with a dash of James Bond. As noted under *Parallel Universe*, the idea of parallel universes is one with a long list of antecedents. As *Starbug* starts submerging, Holly suggests finding a dance band to play 'Abide with Me', although she may have been thinking of 'Nearer My God to Thee', said to have been the last song played as the RMS *Titanic* sank in 1912.

Best gag: Hattie Hayridge falling off her stool as Rimmer compliments Holly.

Worst visual effect: Bongo, Spanners and the rest look pretty poor chromakeyed into the model hangar.

Continuity is for smegheads: Simon Gaffney and Kalli Greenwood return as Young Rimmer and Mrs Rimmer (who has plummed up her accent since *Polymorph*). Rimmer's obsession with telegraph poles continues (and now he's into Morris dancing too). Mechanoids can be rendered unconscious by a right hook to the jaw. Lister briefly gains the nickname 'Skipper'. A Hammond Organ version of the theme music plays over the end titles, which very oddly credit Robert Llewellyn as 'Kryten/Bongo' but the rest of the regular cast just get referred to by their main character names. Was it thought that Llewellyn would be unrecognisable as Bongo?

S04E06 Meltdown ★★☆☆☆

TX: 21 March 1991 on BBC2. Ratings: 3.56m (4th for the week).
Featuring: Clayton Mark, Kenneth Hadley, Martin Friend, Stephen Tiller, Jack Klaff, Tony Hawks, Michael Burrell, Forbes Masson, Roger Blake, Pauline Bailey.

I've criticised some of the episodes in Series IV for taking too long to find the theme, or introducing extraneous material which takes us away from the main plot. You can't accuse *Meltdown* of not being focused. It takes one comedy idea and sticks to it like hot wax. As with *Backwards*, it really helps if you can think of nothing funnier than the sight of the entire complement of a lookalikes agency stepping on landmines and shooting machine guns at each other, because that's a great deal of this half-hour.

It's probably unreasonable to point out that the matter paddle that drives much of the plot early on is never used again in any subsequent story (at least not in this way). That's just the form of a comedy series in discrete half-hour episodes (although tell that to the comic shop owner in *Back to Earth*). But it is curious that the possibility of using the device to go, well, back to Earth isn't even discussed. Instead, the show immediately zeroes in on its *Westworld* / boot camp / *Guns of Navarone* parody and won't let it go.

To be fair, Lister and Cat's adventures with the Third Reich are pretty funny, and Lister describing the execution of Winnie-the-Pooh to the Cat isn't bad. (But why do they need both gallows and a firing squad?) It is ever so slightly incongruous, though, that Lister is full of fascinating facts about Nazis and Romans, the way Rimmer would be. But once Rimmer gets it into his head to turn the wax goodies into a fighting force, the whole episode becomes repetitive and dull.

The script can't make up its mind whether the waxdroids are mindless automatons or whether, like Kryten, they've broken their programming and have become people in their own right. If they're mindless automatons, then Rimmer can shoot them, blow them up, melt them (off camera, that's expensive) and so on, all he likes – but the stakes are very low, so why should we care? Of course, if they're people, as Lister claims, then this is horrifying.

The only real twist is that Rimmer's suicidal decoy charge 'works' insofar as Kryten is able to adjust the thermostat and melt all the baddies, but this is a weak justification for such a cavalier action, and there's a real dearth of good jokes here too. An odd series, this. At least one all-time classic, several episodes with genuinely brilliant concepts at their core, but at the same time, a slight feeling that the storytelling and the characters are taking a bit of a back seat to science fiction hijinks and – god help us, given these budgets – spectacle.

The one with: All the lookalikes.

That Rimmer's a solid guy: Insubstantial Rimmer refuses to face the dangers on the unknown planet below. He dons a Second World War style uniform. His breath is visible in some shots. I assume that's a holographic motorbike he's riding.

There's a time and a place: James Last is as bad as Hitler. Cat has heard of Winnie-the-Pooh and Tweety Pie and knows what a gallows looks like.

Rimmer plays the board game Risk (or maybe he doesn't, some of the details are wrong, I'm told). Lister compares Rimmer's antics to the 1967 film *The Dirty Dozen*. Naturally, all of the famous people from history who are recreated as waxdroids became famous before 1980.

Influences, references and rip-offs: Has obvious echoes in *Westworld*. Rimmer's boot camp alludes to *An Officer and a Gentleman* and *Full Metal Jacket* among other things. He later resembles General George S. Patton. The transitions feel like the 1960s *Batman* TV show with Adam West and Burt Ward, or possibly *The Man from UNCLE*.

Best gag: Caligula smacking Lister whenever he doesn't like Cat's answers gets funnier every time.

Worst visual effect: The Dino-birds taken from stock footage look unbelievably shoddy, and are – for some bizarre reason – included in the opening titles of all six episodes.

Continuity is for smegheads: Rimmer now has a floating 'light bee' projecting his image around it. This makes more sense of his cowardice but fails to explain how he was able to walk through walls in earlier series (or have people walk through him). 'Elvis' provides his own take on the closing theme. Third appearance of Marilyn Monroe, second appearance of Hitler. The matter paddle is the first teleporter to be seen on the show – something avoided almost as much as aliens and cute robots, because it kills the format. Rimmer's code name is 'Iron Duke'.

Series V

The Making of Series V

The story of **Red Dwarf** covers the period when most UK households only had access to four television channels, to today's media landscape dominated by streaming services. Sky TV launched in the UK in April 1982, six months before Channel 4 started transmitting, but you needed a very large dish to receive the signal (large as in over 3m in diameter) and it remained very niche – possibly less than fifty British households had the necessary equipment. It wasn't until 1985 that consumer satellite dishes were even on the market. In the second half of the 1980s, as demand increased and technology improved, the size of the dishes started to come down, and some telephone companies began offering cable television to homes. Multi-channel television was coming, and it was coming fast.

Eager to compete in this new market, a consortium was formed consisting of companies such as Virgin, Granada, Pearson and Amstrad (although Amstrad pulled out relatively early) and they successfully bid for the remaining space on the UK satellite that was already transmitting BBC and ITV shows. Rebranded as 'British Satellite Broadcasting', or 'BSB', this new venture launched in March 1990. This was a full eighteen months after Rupert Murdoch had successfully got his Sky Television Network onto the Astra satellite, and had begun broadcasting four channels in the UK television PAL standard. BSB had given an aggressive rival with very deep pockets a very long head start.

Their ace in the hole was their 'Squarial' technology, which didn't require a bulky dish in the back garden (even if Sky dishes were now only about 90cm in diameter instead of 3m). The Squarial was supposed to be only 25cm wide and when it was unveiled, there was some head scratching about just how it was going to work. As it turned out, at that stage, no working prototype existed, and what was unveiled to the press may have been nothing more than an inert lump of painted wood. The eventual model sold to consumers was 38cm wide.

At launch, BSB carried five channels covering movies, sport, news, music and entertainment. Having original programming was critical to BSB's success (Sky was mainly competing via glossy American imports) and the new channel began courting Britain's top programme makers. One beneficiary of this expansion of available networks was comedy writer Geoff Atkinson.

Atkinson had been a professional comedy writer for five years, following quite a similar career path to Rob Grant and Doug Naylor. He began in the early 1980s, writing material for *The Two Ronnies* and Bobby Davro, became part of the core writing team on *Spitting Image* and countless other TV sketch shows besides, and now he was looking for a series of his own. A fan of golden age American sitcoms like *The Dick Van Dyke Show*, *Bewitched* and *I Love Lucy*, he hatched an idea that was completely crazy, but was certainly eye-catching. What about a show that looked and sounded like a 1960s American sitcom, but was set in Berlin in 1938 and had Adolf Hitler and Eva Braun as the central characters?

Heil Honey I'm Home! was produced by Paul Jackson, and BSB ordered a full season for its 'Galaxy' channel, broadcasting episode one on 30 September 1990, one hour after the Jewish festival of Yom Kippur ended at dusk. By this stage, seven more episodes had been shot, but no more would ever be broadcast. Not because of a huge outcry from concerned citizens, Mary Whitehouse, or conservative newspapers (probably only a few thousand people even saw it) but because on 2 November 1990, BSB merged with Sky, creating a UK monopoly on satellite television. This would normally have been referred to the regulator, but Rupert Murdoch was sufficiently pally with the Conservative government to make sure that it would be waved through. The new outfit was known as 'British Sky Broadcasting', or 'Sky' for short, and almost immediately the new proprietor killed the BSB Galaxy channel and the outlandish sitcom it had ordered.

This was no doubt a bruising experience for all concerned. The show, only the first episode of which has ever been made public, isn't very good: it feels like an over-extended sketch at just under half an hour, so heaven knows what a whole series would have been like. But, as with most artistic endeavours, it had been made with passion and dedication, and nobody involved ever expected it to wither on the vine quite as suddenly as it had. The director was a young woman named Juliet May, who had got her start on entertainment shows like *Wogan* and *The Oxford Road Show* before she broke into comedy with a sitcom called *Morris Minor's Marvellous Motors*, produced by (who else?) Paul Jackson and starring (who else?) Tony Hawks. When *Heil Honey* was cancelled so suddenly, Jackson told her he'd keep her in mind next time something came up.

Around the same time, Ed Bye had a decision to make. He'd been working steadily on **Red Dwarf** since 1987 and while it was great fun, it was absolutely exhausting. His wife Ruby Wax, meanwhile, was looking for a producer/director she could trust for her new series *The Full Wax*. While parting on good terms, Bye elected to pass on **Red Dwarf** Series V. Hilary Bevan Jones (who had worked on *Not the Nine O'Clock News* and *Blackadder*) came in as producer and Paul Jackson told them he had just the person to take over from Ed Bye – Juliet May.

Now, listen, I don't mean to hang *Heil Honey I'm Home!* around Juliet May's neck, but her participation in **Red Dwarf** was troubled to say the least, and I felt a little context would be helpful. This was a turbulent time in UK television; lots of people were trying new things, and an established show like **Red Dwarf**, entering its fifth series, probably looked like all it needed was a safe pair of hands to write a camera script and jolly the cast along. But Rob and Doug meanwhile had been talking about where to go next and had made a conscious decision to push the science fiction further, push the action further, and trust that the comedy would always still be there. You can say this about **Red Dwarf** pretty much every year, but it's particularly relevant this time: Series V was going to be the most ambitious set of episodes yet. Rob and Doug essentially wanted Hollywood feature film production values out of a £1.5 million budget and a five-camera sitcom setup in an electronic TV studio.

As luck would have it, the Series IV underspend didn't come back to bite them. Series V got a £6,000 bump (a bit less than half a per cent, unlikely even to keep pace with inflation, but not a cut), so very quickly Juliet May had to get to grips with an awful lot: six high-concept science fiction scripts (a genre she knew nothing about), a budget stretched as tight as a drum, a cast who had been working together in some cases for five years and who didn't like change, and technical challenges that she'd never encountered before. There were very few split-screen effects on *Wogan* and hardly any model spaceships in *Heil Honey I'm Home!* Rob and Doug gave her science fiction movies to watch on VHS, but in her own words, they had a twenty-year head start on her, and she could never hope to catch up.

Doing his best to be fair to all parties, Doug Naylor on the DVD documentary says that her biggest problem was that she wouldn't ask for help. If she'd been paired with a technical expert who could take care of all the effects stuff, freeing her to work with the cast to help them nail the comedy, she would probably have been quite effective. But as it was, on her first day in the studio she found herself grappling with scenes for episode five, *Demons & Angels*, in which three different versions of the regular characters shared the screen and interacted – something none of her previous jobs had prepared her for. And when cast and crew asked her to explain the intricacies of the complex scripts, she was unable to provide any answers.

Incredibly, on one episode, Craig Charles recalls trying to get her to position the camera in order to capture the Kryten POV shot specified in the script and only realised after several minutes that the breakdown in communication was occurring because Juliet May had never seen the abbreviation POV before and didn't know that it meant 'point of view'. I wasn't there, of course, but I do use the word 'incredibly' with precision, because I find this account very hard to believe. Possibly, she was flustered and not thinking clearly, but anyone with her experience would have to have seen that term before. However, it speaks to how she was seen by the almost all-male cast that Craig Charles tells this story.

Despite all of this, it must be admitted that the finished episodes look great. The camera crew – led by expert operator 'Rocket', who had been with the team since Series II – were all very experienced, the effects team were clear about what they could and could not accomplish, and the regular cast by now knew their characters inside and out. But getting six episodes rehearsed, shot, edited and finished would be even harder and more stressful than usual.

As ever, the recording order was decided late in the day. First to go out was *Holoship* in which the crew meet an entire crew of holograms, including some of the series' fanciest guest stars to date: sitcom royalty Don Warrington, famous for his role in *Rising Damp*; and future sitcom royalty Jane Horrocks, who had not yet started work on *Absolutely Fabulous*, in which she would play Bubble. Not knowing that this would be pretty much her next television job, she based her performance on Joanna Lumley. Warrington's work really only amounted to one scene, in which he drily surveys the non-hologram crew of *Red Dwarf* and faces a tongue-lashing from Lister. Craig Charles was so in character, that at one point, he spontaneously ate the cigarette sticking out of the packet he was pretending was a radio. As soon as the floor manager called cut, he spat the mess out, wondering why he'd done that.

Adding to the problems faced by Juliet May, the script was way too long and the first edit came in at well over forty minutes, requiring an enormous amount of postproduction surgery to bring it down to something that could be transmitted in a half-hour slot. Some of the first material to go was Holly's, further disappointing Hattie Hayridge, who felt she'd been underused in the previous series and now was pretty much reduced to saying 'Hailing frequencies open, Captain,' every other episode.

The finished product isn't a particular favourite of anyone in the cast, especially not Craig Charles, who continued to be infuriated by the fact that as the show had progressed, the dead guy who everyone hated had been getting girlfriend after girlfriend, while he hadn't had so much as a kiss on the cheek. In a post-coital scene, Chris Barrie appears half-undressed, which caused several of the other boys to double-take at the sight of his physique and wonder just what it was that he'd been doing in his spare time. Barrie also takes credit for Rimmer's farewell line to his *Red Dwarf* family: 'I just want to say, over the years, I've come to regard you as… people I met.'

Episode two, *The Inquisitor*, added another member of Scottish comedy team *Absolutely* to the roster of **Red Dwarf** guest stars. Joining his stablemates Gordon Kennedy and Morwenna Banks was Jack Docherty, who genuinely was inside the colossal Inquisitor suit on set (John Sparkes also auditioned for Kryten in Series III). This was another script that confused everybody, with its complicated plotting, time travel intricacies and philosophical musings. Without Ed Bye to cheerfully keep everyone on track, or Paul Jackson to tell them to shut up and get on with it, confusion reigned on set, especially when multiple cast members had to wear the clunky Inquisitor costume and play scenes opposite themselves.

Docherty's initial instinct had been to play against the lines and make the Inquisitor rather camp and high-pitched. In rehearsals, that didn't seem to be working, and so for the pre-filming he was furiously roaring all the dialogue. Then he happened to see an interview with acting legend Robert de Niro, who commented, 'Evil doesn't shout, it whispers.' Inspired by this observation, Docherty played the rest of his scenes in a low growl, and redubbed his earlier, shouty performance where necessary – an easy task given that his mouth wasn't visible inside the costume. For a while, it was planned to end the episode revealing the actor's face, made-up to resemble a withered old man, but Rob and Doug changed their minds and had the final scene reshot with the mask in place.

Episode three, *Terrorform*, opened with a complex sequence in which a wrecked Kryten despatches a severed hand to alert his fellows – and Lister, mistaking it for a tarantula and frozen with fear, can only communicate with Cat via text messages. The usual pre-filming day was used partly to capture the material needed for this interaction, which would then be edited and shown to the studio audience at the right time during the main recording. Anxious about how this would turn out, and by now used to being in the edit, Doug Naylor wanted to work with Juliet May on this – but she insisted on doing it herself without supervision. Doug couldn't believe what she eventually showed him – it was completely unusable, and he worried that they hadn't got the shots they needed. He went into the edit bay himself and, thankfully, was able to construct the sequence that eventually made it to screen. Juliet May's stock with the writer-producers was dropping virtually by the day.

In a crucial scene, the crew come face to face with The Unspeakable One, the latest in a series of hideous monsters to threaten the Dwarfers. Just as the curry monster had improved upon the polymorph, The Unspeakable One was an even more sophisticated animatronic puppet, standing 6 feet tall and operated by a team of technicians. But Rob and Doug had also learned the wisdom of keeping monsters in the shadows, and the result is that the very expensive contraption is barely seen on screen. Hardworking effects creators Peter Wragg and Mike Tucker are philosophical about this treatment of their handiwork, commenting that the shadows on the wall only look as good as they do because of all the effort they put in. Whether this actually required the design and construction of a fully textured and painted 6-foot animatronic is open to debate.

Finally, as work finished on *Terrorform* and rehearsals started on *Quarantine*, Juliet May quit. *Quarantine* had been intended as the season's 'cheapie', requiring little more than the regular cast, the standing sets and a red gingham dress. But even a 'cheapie' won't direct itself. With neither Ed Bye nor Paul Jackson available, Rob and Doug had no option but to take over and direct the last two episodes themselves. Rob was very gung-ho about this, but Doug remembers being intensely worried about whether or not they were in over their heads. However, they'd been watching Ed Bye closely for four years and – as noted – were often heavily involved in the edit, so they came to believe they could do it. And, as there was no one else, they were going to have to.

The system they worked out was that they would construct the camera script together, and then Rob would talk to the actors and the crew from the gallery, leaving Doug free to do last-minute rewrites and other general producer-ish problem solving. *Quarantine* turned out to be an abnormally long recording. Even when everything is going according to plan, it can take a couple of hours to record a thirty-minute sitcom episode, with costume changes, technical requirements, set alterations and so on. As the publicly available 'smeg-ups' show, the regular cast enjoyed each other's company (mainly) and would make fun of each other to further entertain the studio audience if anything did go wrong. But Paul Jackson had taught them well, and they were usually very strong on the lines – especially Craig Charles, who generally not only knew all of his dialogue perfectly, but everyone else's too (in several episodes, including as late as Series VI, he can occasionally be seen mouthing other people's words as they say them).

On this night, for some reason, a perfectly ordinary interaction between Cat, Lister and Kryten proved impossible to get through, with all three getting the giggles, and nobody able to accurately recall what they were supposed to be saying. That single two-or-three-minute scene took almost an hour to record and the whole episode took around four hours. Quite the ordeal for the first-time directors. The story, however, is now seen as a classic, with the character of Mr Flibble (a stuffed penguin glove puppet that was grabbed at random out of stock) having had quite the life outside the show.

Episode five, *Demons & Angels*, as well as needing all of those split-screen effects, also featured a spectacular shot of *Red Dwarf* exploding. This presented a problem as the huge and detailed 8-foot model ship built back in 1987 had fallen off a shelf and been damaged beyond repair and the production had been making do with existing footage. A whole new (much less detailed) ship had to be built simply in order to be destroyed for this sequence. Luckily, the next series would not require any model shots of *Red Dwarf*, but before we get to that, we have to get to the last episode to be recorded for Series V – *Back to Reality*.

Rob and Doug had considered putting this one out first. The plot of the episode seemingly reveals that all of the previous adventures of the Dwarfers have been part of a Total Immersion Video Game, and our central foursome are actually four completely different guys. Not only that, they have screwed up the game, and failed to enjoy many of its most exciting possibilities. The writers had endless fun teasing the cast about whether or not this script was going to actually reinvent all of their characters – or write them out completely – and part of the debate regarding its position in the running order was about whether the deception would be more convincing if it went out first or last.

Again, this one was a difficult shoot. Another very impressive guest star, Timothy Spall, came in to play 'Andy' but it was only on the day of the recording that he revealed that he had never done a sitcom in front of a live studio audience before. Almost immediately, nerves started to get the better of him. He began racing through his dialogue, tripping over his words and then trying to get to the end of the line. By now experienced at this kind of acting, the regulars all knew that if they screwed up they should stop immediately, in the hope of preventing the audience from fully hearing the joke, and so increasing the chance that they'd get a genuine laugh on the retake. But Spall was blowing laugh line after laugh line and eventually, Rob got him to go right back to the beginning of the scene and start again. Remarkably, given this 're-set', he walked back out and instantly nailed the performance – to everyone's enormous relief.

The episode's other big guest star was another good 'get'. Lenny van Dohlen was already making a name for himself in David Lynch and Mark Frost's off-kilter soap opera *Twin Peaks*, and he wasn't sure what to make of the script when it came through. He was convinced to accept the offer after chatting to his friend Frances Barber, who had already appeared in the show back in Series III.

Chris Barrie has commented that while various aspects of his and Craig Charles's personalities have been incorporated into their characters, their dress sense is rather closer to how they appear in the 'real world' of this episode – if they go out in the evening, Charles is always very smartly turned out, but Barrie just pulls on jeans and an old jumper with holes in it. Howard Burden created a new look for everybody, helped by make-up designer Andrea Pennell, who also needed to find a new wig for Danny John-Jules. He recalls visiting a top London wigmaker and getting an outrageous quote for making a new hairpiece in the style that they had in mind. But they went through an old cardboard box of leftovers brought up from the basement, and in an amazing stroke of luck, they found exactly what they were looking for, and discovered that it was a perfect fit.

On screen, all four alter egos are very well thought through and Cat's reinvention as 'Duane Dibbley' proved to be particularly popular, with John-Jules inserting Dibbley's enormous teeth in at least as many subsequent episodes as Chris Barrie donned Ace Rimmer's wig and leather jacket. But on the night, the reaction from the studio audience was muted and Rob Grant went home in despair, not returning to the **Red Dwarf** offices for several days. Doug Naylor spent that time reconstructing the episode in the edit, incorporating Juliet May's pre-filming of the scenes on board the SSS *Esperanto*, and was eventually quite pleased with how it turned out. Since then, it has become a perennial fan favourite, regularly topping polls of the best ever episodes.

Normally, that would just leave the end-of-series 'wrap' party, which was – as usual – a fairly boisterous affair. But as the cast and crew drank, and partied, and drank, and ate, and drank, a problem was emerging. Viewing the footage shot for *Demons & Angels*, which had been the first episode recorded, but would go out fifth, it was clear that much of it was unusable. Now more comfortable in their role as joint directors, Rob and Doug reassembled the cast and crew the following day, and guided the very hungover team through a series of reshoots, which amounted to around half the finished episode. As with their novels, Rob and Doug used the name 'Grant Naylor' as their directing credit on *Quarantine* and *Back to Reality*. Juliet May retained her credit on *Demons & Angels*, sharing it with 'Grant Naylor', and she's credited as 'SSS Esperanto Director' on *Back to Reality*, reflecting her role in shooting the pre-filmed material.

The new, glossier series also gained a new, glossier visual identity. Dewynters produced a new serifed version of the **Red Dwarf** insignia, and this was retained for all the remaining BBC shows and the first two batches of Dave shows, with the old blocky logo not returning until Series XI. The Grant Naylor logo was reinvented in the same way, and Chris Barrie's forehead H was also changed to include serifs.

So, despite all of the production problems, **Red Dwarf** was on a high. Ratings were up. During the broadcast of this series, a **Red Dwarf** magazine was launched, rebranded *Red Dwarf Smegazine* from issue 3 onwards. The first **Red Dwarf**-specific fan convention, 'Dimension Jump', took place in Northampton in July 1992. And there had been interest in an American remake, which had been one driver behind pushing the visual spectacle of these episodes, portions of which were cut into a 'sizzle reel' for the networks to look at. With Chris Barrie committed to *The Brittas Empire*, Craig Charles in heavy demand for television work of all kinds and now the possibility of this

US series in the offing, many people wondered if we had seen the last of **Red Dwarf** on UK TV.

That wasn't something bothering Rob Grant and Doug Naylor as they boarded business class flights to Los Angeles to talk to NBC/Universal about remaking their show on the other side of the Atlantic. In the event, this was an unproductive and bruising experience (see Apocrypha in *Volume II* for all the gory details) and the British writers rapidly returned to the UK to discover that the BBC *would* like another series of **Red Dwarf**. In fact, they wanted it as soon as possible.

Impressions of Series V

Written by Rob Grant and Doug Naylor. Designed by Mel Bibby. Costumes by Howard Burden. Produced by Hilary Bevan Jones. Associate Producer: Julian Scott. Directed by Juliet May and 'Grant Naylor'. Starring: Craig Charles, Chris Barrie, Danny John-Jules, Robert Llewellyn, Hattie Hayridge.

S05E01 Holoship ★★★★☆

TX: 20 February 1992 on BBC2. Ratings: 5.63m (1st for the week). Featuring: Jane Horrocks, Matthew Marsh, Don Warrington, Simon Day, Jane Montgomery, Lucy Briers.

My memory of these episodes is foggy, but I put this one on, kind of remembering it was the one nobody liked. Maybe because my expectations were set low, I actually had a pretty good time with it. We begin with the crew (on *Starbug*, for some unexplained reason) all watching the same film, which is a good way of establishing their characters. The movie, alas, seems like yet another rip-off of *Casablanca* and Rimmer is unmoved by the lead character's sacrifice at the end. Elsewhere, Holly's hair is back to regulation length (apparently, the production team received a letter during Series IV claiming that it was 'too long for a computer', whatever that might mean) and Kryten's new mask gives him bee-sting lips, which I don't think suit him.

Before long, we make contact with the holoship of the title, and there's a long, not particularly funny exposition scene with Rimmer and Jane Horrocks's Nirvanah Crane, where what laughs there are come from that Grant/Naylor seaside postcard attitude to sex. But there's a subtlety to both the writing and the acting of Rimmer here that we haven't seen before. Rimmer's joy at being able to touch and interact with the holoship is delightful, and of course, he gets his end away and manages not to be a complete git in the process ('Geronimo'). I can believe it when Crane says that inside him there's someone nice trying to get out, someone who deserves a chance to grow – and I don't think that would have worked for me even as recently as the end of the last series.

The big laughs this episode come from Lister not taking any of Don Warrington's smeg, and royally sending him up when he smarms his way around *Starbug*. With comparatively little for anyone but Rimmer this episode, it's nice to have a little self-contained showcase for Craig Charles. Less successful is Chris Barrie's madly over-the-top insufferable nerd. Nothing 'Professor Rimmer' says is anything more than gibberish and taking both tests simultaneously is butter upon bacon (as is the absurd number of questions on the test), although Barrie flings himself at the material with tremendous gusto. But the biggest problem – as the writers themselves admit – is that the ending doesn't have the tragic power it ought to.

Partly this is due to the fact that the setup is laborious, requiring a one-in-one-out rule for no particular reason, pitting Rimmer against Crane – again for no particular reason – and then requiring Crane to withdraw from the challenge, even if that means her death, because in twenty-four hours she's come to value the potential good in Rimmer more than her own existence. You probably could make all that work, but in twenty-nine minutes, with three other regular characters to service (four if you count Holly, but c'mon) it's a big ask. Also, as well handled as a lot of the relationship stuff is, I don't know how many people turn on this show for this kind of story, and it sits oddly with the sex jokes, space mayhem and comedy robots.

The titles have gained a widescreen effect and there's that new serifed logo. Episode names now have a slight 3D effect as they roll past.

The one with: Him out of *Rising Damp* and her out of *Absolutely Fabulous*.

That Rimmer's a solid guy: He's sitting on what looks like a flight case and later leans on the back of a sofa. The office chair he sits in spins around when he hops out of it. Binks is careful to step out of Kryten's way as he explores *Starbug*. Lister claims to have a holo-whip on board, which Binks is fearful of. The holoship passes right through *Starbug*. They audition other dead crewmembers (including Lucy Briers, daughter of Richard) and Rimmer returns while they're doing it. Who's sustaining all these holograms? How can holograms suffer a hormonal imbalance?

There's a time and a place: Rimmer refers to Nicholas Ray's 1961 film *King of Kings: The Story of Jesus*. Comparisons are made to Albert Camus and Albert Einstein. Rimmer asserts that St Francis of Assisi's motto was 'Never give a sucker an even break', which was the title of a 1941 W.C. Fields film (although the phrase may have predated that). Domestic science teachers are intellectually inferior. The holoship is equipped with Commodore Pet or Apple II style computers, which would have already been fifteen years out of date when this first aired.

Influences, references and rip-offs: This is another riff on *Casablanca*.

Best gag: Lister's sarcastic takedown of Binks is very funny, and 'people I met' is absolute gold.

Worst visual effect: The lovely model shot of *Red Dwarf* over the closing titles has been replaced with anonymous stars and blue blobs.

Continuity is for smegheads: *Starbug* has no defensive shields and no laser canons. Lister is in his mid-twenties. Rimmer has been in effective command of *Red Dwarf* for four years. Rimmer's father had four strokes.

S05E02 The Inquisitor ★★★★☆

TX: 27 February 1992 on BBC2. Ratings: 5.44m (5th for the week). Featuring: Jack Docherty, Jake Abraham.

This is another of those episodes with an idea so good at the centre of it that it almost makes up for some slack execution elsewhere. The notion of a rogue Simulant erasing the worthless from history is excellent **Red Dwarf** style shenanigans (and recalls Douglas Adams's Wowbagger the Infinitely Prolonged, who was insulting every living being in the universe in alphabetical order). The twist that everyone is their own judge is quite magnificent, with the Kryten exchange being my favourite, even if there are no jokes in it. In fact, I admire Rob and Doug for not feeling that they needed to end the scene on a gag.

Starting with the Inquisitor erasing someone shows that same confidence that we saw in *Dimension Jump* and when we catch up with the gang, again, we're on *Starbug* initially, although we do make it back to *Red Dwarf* eventually. It's Kryten and Lister who are targeted for erasure – the Cat and Rimmer having exceeded the low standards they set for themselves. But Kryten from the future comes to rescue them, killing himself in the process. That's the delicious thing about alternate universes, hidden dimensions and regular cast doppelgangers – you can kill everyone off and it doesn't feel like a cheat when you hit the reset button. Or not much of a cheat, anyway.

And for all the behind-the-scenes chaos and confusion, this looks great, with terrific lighting and some fine handheld camerawork as the inevitable chase through the corridors of *Red Dwarf* begins. The Inquisitor's mask is a brilliantly scary design, it's lots of fun watching old Rimmer and Cat come to terms with what are, to them, strangers, and it's nice to see Jake Abraham (who I remember from Channel 4's amazing *GBH*) as an alternative Lister (alternative Kryten gets rather short shrift). However, I can't help thinking – compared to the alt-Lister from *Back to Reality* who takes over playing the game after our guys leave – this Lister is, well, pretty similar to the worthless one which the Inquisitor needed to dispose of, which rather makes his whole judge-yourself-and-be-erased-from-history procedure a bit pointless. I mean, I guess he is nuts, but even so…

When it comes to the final showdown, though, the real problems start. Whatever is supposed to be happening with Lister, that rope and his lighter is vastly unclear. It looks as if Lister drops the lighter and then *another Lister* uses it to set fire to the rope, in a different location, which I don't think was the intention. This, sadly, bears all the hallmarks of being shot in a hurry and/or by someone who didn't know what they were doing, and then it's had to be patched together in the edit without enough footage. But Lister's whole feint with saving the Inquisitor's life is pointless anyway. All he actually needs is for the Simulant to try to use the booby-trapped gauntlet. Lister is fooling us, the audience, not his enemy.

And then other niggling questions start bugging me. Why does *Red Dwarf* have handprint-operated doors all of a sudden? Why does Kryten figure out what his last words meant, and then forget that he's figured that out when the time comes to say them? What happens to all the other erased people once the Inquisitor is erased? Just how much further damage to the timelines has Lister done? For an episode with such a striking idea at its core, this ends up feeling like a bit of a mess. It's kind of the opposite of *Holoship*, where all the right pieces are present, but I don't feel any of the things I'm supposed to.

The one with: Everyone judging themselves.

That Rimmer's a solid guy: No issues, except the usual cowardice.

There's a time and a place: Kryten is familiar with Virgil's *Iliad*, but confuses it with the *Aeneid*. Lister is reading the comic book version. It's the only thing he's ever read that doesn't have lift-up flaps. His days are largely taken up with *What Bike* magazine and Sugar Puff sandwiches. He hasn't painted the ceiling of the Sistine Chapel. Rimmer sarcastically compares him to twentieth-century historian A.J.P. Taylor. Cat suggests he look himself up in 'Who's Nobody' (instead of *Who's Who*). Rimmer used to pledge donations to charity telethons using someone else's credit card. He compares Lister and Kryten to Sidney Poitier and Tony Curtis in the 1958 film *The Defiant Ones*. Kryten refers inaccurately to suicidal lemmings. The Cat hates to say it, but Trans Am wheel arch nostrils is right.

Influences, references and rip-offs: The works of Harlan Ellison in general and *The Terminator* in particular are obvious influences. There are also hints of Marvel's *The Punisher* and *2000 AD*'s Judge Dredd. Wondering what would have happened if you weren't there once again recalls *It's a Wonderful Life*.

Guns that kill the one who fires them are commonplace – examples include the Matt Helm film *The Silencers*, 'The Girl Who Was Death' in *The Prisoner* and *Superman II* (kind of) when the takes-your-powers-away box turns out to give Supes his powers back and takes the bad guys' powers away instead.

Best gag: 'Why did no one mention this before?'

Worst visual effect: The Inquisitor's time woo-woo is cool, and more impressively 3D than we're used to. His laser beams are terribly crap, though.

Continuity is for smegheads: Lister takes his coffee double caffeinated, quadruple sugar. Rimmer's father was a half-crazed military failure, and his mother was a bitch queen from hell. Lister's access code is 000-169 instead of RD-52169 as it was in *Future Echoes*. Reference is made to Rimmer putting 'BSC' after his name, and his stint with the Samaritans (but Lister mis-remembers how many people died as a result). Kryten's right foot jiggles when he's lying. Thomas Allman doesn't appear to go through the judging yourself process – the Inquisitor takes one look at him and erases him on sight. 'Our' Rimmer wears his green Series IV uniform. In the new timeline, he's in his red Series V uniform. Does that mean that *Holoship* takes place in a different timeline?

S05E03 Terrorform ★★★☆☆

TX: 5 March 1992 on BBC2. Ratings: 5.48m (2nd for the week).
Featuring: Sara Stockbridge, Francine Walker.

Never ones to stand still, Rob and Doug start this one with a fresh take on what it means to be Kryten – he's smashed to bits, and has to hack off parts of himself in order to survive. There are some nifty (pre-filmed) physical effects here and some good fast-moving gags in the text displayed on the screen, as well as in the dialogue – Kryten's loss of short-term memory is the source of some excellent comedy. All this, and the sequence with Lister too afraid to speak, is just warming us up for the trip through Rimmer's subconscious – definitely a place you don't want to be.

So, this does continue the theme of *Better than Life*, or – in a different way – *Meltdown*, where Rimmer's mere presence causes everything to go to hell. And for the other three, it's another example of: *the boys visit a wacky planet*, rather than *our heroes' own flaws get them into trouble*. But the combination works well. Compare this to say, *Backwards*. This might be three generic guys on a trip through a nightmare landscape, but the nightmare landscape is all about who Rimmer is. So, while this might be another one-joke story, it's a much richer, funnier joke.

What doesn't quite come off is the ending. The premise is great: only making Rimmer feel loved will save *Starbug*. But somehow it all seems to happen too quickly and easily. And then there's a huge pitched battle taking place on the Psy-moon, but our characters are nowhere near it, so it seems a little bit pointless. There are loads of good ideas here, but the execution is lacking. What I do appreciate is the sheer scale of this one, and the detail. We're a long way from Series I where paradise was a generic (rainy) beach and a nice meal.

The one with: Freshly oiled Rimmer.

That Rimmer's a solid guy: On a Psy-moon, Rimmer is in real physical danger.

There's a time and a place: Kryten's memory chips are affected by magnetic fields, like floppy discs in the 1990s, but unlike the solid-state storage more commonplace today. A cover version of 'Copacabana' is played to soothe Kryten. The recording on the original broadcast was by James Last, but this couldn't be licensed for subsequent use, and so it was replaced by a more generic version. Cat suggests buying a potion from Gandalf the master wizard when he thinks Lister is playing a text adventure game, and he refers to Junior Birdmen, the 1930s Hearst-sponsored organisation for American kids with an interest in aviation.

Influences, references and rip-offs: The Kryten's eye view of the situation recalls RoboCop coming online for the first time (as well as the 'heads-up display' in *The Terminator*). The disembodied hand recalls Thing from *The Addams Family* and having to hack off your own hand to survive recalls *Evil Dead II*. Being menaced by monsters from the id is a lift from the seminal 1956 science fiction film *Forbidden Planet*. Lister slides out from underneath Kryten like a car mechanic. Quicksand was used by many writers of adventure stories from Bram Stoker and H.P. Lovecraft to Quentin Tarantino and the recent *Star Wars* sequels. Rimmer's positive emotions are characters from Alexandre Dumas's 1844 novel *The Three Musketeers*.

Best gag: 'Please don't interrupt, sir, I'm only halfway through my list.'

Worst visual effect: Rimmer's right; those are rather unconvincing red eyes. Also, *Starbug* in the swamp looks a bit *Thunderbirds*.

Continuity is for smegheads: Lister isn't fond of tarantulas. According to *Better than Life*, neither is Rimmer. Sawing Kryten in two will invalidate the Diva-Droid guarantee. His alert conditions include mauve, magenta, taupe, marigold and heliotrope, and his heads-up display implies he was created in the year 2340. The Space Corps anthem has twenty-three stanzas. *Starbug* has caterpillar tracks. When an incorporeal hologram, Rimmer panics at the first hint of danger. Now he can actually be hurt, he has no conception of the danger he's in, keeps cracking gags, and asks to be taken to the 'British embassy'. Anticipating sexual congress, Rimmer wants a four-cheese pizza with extra olives waiting for him.

S05E04 Quarantine ★★★★★

TX: 12 March 1992 on BBC2. Ratings: 5.54m (4th for the week). Featuring: Maggie Steed.

Once again, we're on *Starbug*. There's some nice material early on, when Cat refuses to accept Rimmer's order to 'Launch scouter', and makes a big show of cheerfully obeying Kryten's request to do the same thing. This leads to a power struggle, which in turn leads to Rimmer gaining a holographic copy of all of the Space Corps directives. This will have big implications for the rest of this episode, as well as giving rise to a running gag that fairly quickly outstays its welcome.

Running away from Dr Lanstrom is all pretty much par for the course, but the sequence that follows is one of the very strongest in the history of the show, escalating through different phases without ever sacrificing character beats, losing focus or forgetting to be funny. Because petty, small-minded Rimmer is doing everything by the book, he's keeping the others in quarantine for an eye-watering twelve weeks. Because they're in a sitcom about people who hate each other but who have to live together, it's only a matter of days before social cohesion starts to break down.

Because Rimmer spoke to Lanstrom on the radio, he became infected with the holo-virus himself (the reveal of him in the red gingham dress is a jaw-dropping *coup de théâtre*) and then becomes a real physical threat to the crew. And because her research was into positive viruses, Lister can luck his way out of trouble. The luck virus is a particularly brilliant idea in a very strong episode that would have been four-stars plus even without it. Yes, there are echoes of the Infinite Improbability Drive from *The Hitchhiker's Guide to the Galaxy*, but the luck virus is easier to understand, has a more important plot function and is funnier.

I was fairly sure this was going to be four and a half stars – it's always been one of my favourites – but on rewatching, I genuinely can't find a thing wrong with it (unless you count the fact that Holly is MIA). And isn't that what five out of five means?

The one with: Mr Flibble.

That Rimmer's a solid guy: Once again, *Red Dwarf* can only support one hologram. Kryten says that they will have to commandeer Rimmer's remote projection unit to rescue Dr Lanstrom, but this is never seen to happen. All they do is send Rimmer's hologram physically back to *Red Dwarf*. Why? What purpose does that serve? Being infected with a holo-virus changes the physical properties of a hologram and gives it magic hex powers.

There's a time and a place: Lister thinks they're a real Mickey Mouse operation. Cat doesn't even think they're Betty Boop. He calls Kryten 'Frankenstein' and Kryten has to tell him that's the name of the creator, not the monster. Dr Lanstrom quotes nineteenth-century philosopher Arthur Schopenhauer. Twentieth-century DJs may have been infected with the joy virus. Kryten's assessment of the psy-scanner sounds like *Which* magazine. Kryten wonders if Lister expects to see a Turner seascape or a Shakespearean sonnet in his hanky. To entertain the others, Rimmer offers the work of Reggie Dixon, famed organist at Blackpool's Tower Ballroom. He is not a timeshare villa in the Algarve.

Influences, references and rip-offs: To suggest Rimmer's altered mental state, Chris Barrie sounds like he's impersonating Donald Pleasance. Trapping Cat, Kryten and Lister in the quarantine chamber is another version of stuck-in-a-lift, or indeed two-people-who-hate-each-other-forced-to-live-together.

Best gag: 'I can't let you out. The king of the potato people won't let me.'

Worst visual effect: Hex vision looks dreadful.

Continuity is for smegheads: Sprouts make Lister chuck. I'm sure somebody somewhere has made a list of all of the Space Corps directives and their numbers, but I do not propose to duplicate that effort here. Don't call Kryten 'tetchy'.

S05E05 Demons & Angels ★★☆☆☆

TX: 19 March 1992 on BBC2. Ratings: 6.04m (2nd for the week).

The stakes are very high in this one: *Red Dwarf* has been destroyed, and only by assembling components from two opposing copies can the guys ever hope to get her back. The problem is that on each ship, there are four people who want to kill them and four people who are no help at all. Exploring a version of the ship where everyone and everything is perfect and another version where everyone and everything is ghastly sounds like it should be tailor-made **Red Dwarf** fun. But it doesn't quite come off, and the high stakes end up working against the comedy.

We visit the 'high' ship first of all, but rather than each of the five inhabitants being the best possible versions of themselves in a unique way, they're all similarly ineffectual, peace-loving hippies. Not only does this seem like a missed opportunity, it feels mean (in the same way that the much later episode *Timewave* feels mean). On the 'low' ship, although there's some great costume and make-up work, and the cast are having a ball, the script isn't really servicing them with any good jokes. Instead, this is all about the physical jeopardy they're in. Craig Charles is very impressive as the remote-controlled Lister, but it's a premise that feels like it was left over from another story. I could also do without the homosexual anxiety gags from Low Rimmer.

It's not clear who shot which bits, but the split-screen work feels effortless and the illusion of multiple versions of the same character, whether achieved through video effects, doubles or simple editing, is masterfully maintained. But once the solution is identified, there's nowhere interesting for the story to go, and although there's a satisfying build to a climax, it feels like a lot of running and shouting to not get anywhere. Also, why doesn't Low Lister disappear with Low *Red Dwarf*?

The one with: Remote controlled homicidal Lister.

That Rimmer's a solid guy: Rimmer is turned to minimum power to triple his run time, but it doesn't particularly affect him. On both alternative versions of the ship, he can be sustained along with the other hologram Rimmer. This despite that they have an hour before the ships vanish, and tripling his run time would only give him twelve minutes. He makes kung fu gestures and noises, but will be unable to hit anything. It's not at all clear how hologram Low Rimmer will 'have' Lister, with or without the holo-whip he wields, which appears to be able to inflict pain on corporeal beings (whereas the implication in *Holoship* was that this was a device that a living person could use to hurt a hologram). Low Rimmer leans on a supply cabinet and is often seen shoulder to shoulder with his shipmates.

There's a time and a place: Lister has never had an edible Pot Noodle. The dreadful food on the Low *Red Dwarf* is typified by cinema hotdogs. Lister thinks these guys are two lettuces short of an allotment.

Influences, references and rip-offs: Captain Kirk is split into an aggressive, libidinous incarnation and a kinder but milquetoast specimen in the *Star Trek* episode 'The Enemy Within'. Revealing a darker version of yourself recalls Robert Louis Stevenson's 1886 gothic novel *Strange Case of Dr Jekyll and Mr Hyde*. There's also an echo of the 'angel' and 'devil' personas that I referred to when discussing *Confidence and Paranoia*.

Best gag: 'Rude alert! Rude alert! An electrical fire has knocked out my voice recognition unicycle! Many Wurlitzers are missing from my database! Abandon shop! This is not a daffodil. Repeat: this is not a daffodil!'

Worst visual effect: Lister rolling out of the way of Evil Lister's bazookoid is pretty unconvincing.

Continuity is for smegheads: Lister experiments with the last strawberry in the universe. The triplicator is an adapted matter paddle. Lister runs through some of the highlights of the last several years, including giving birth to twins (off-screen), visiting a parallel universe, and playing pool with planets (even though that timeline should no longer exist). For the second time in three episodes, Lister faces his fear of tarantulas.

S05E06   Back to Reality ★★★★★

TX: 26 March 1992 on BBC2. Ratings: 6.54m (2nd for the week).
Featuring: Timothy Spall, Lenny von Dohlen, Marie McCarthy.

This is everyone's favourite, and while I am for sure giving it the full five stars, and I do absolutely love it, I think that *Dimension Jump* just edges it, having slightly more to say. But this is one hell of a big swing and it's pulled off exceptionally well. The early scenes manage to build up the tension without sacrificing laugh lines, but one of the great strengths of this episode is that there are no gags-for-the-sake-of-gags. When the story naturally becomes funny, it's really funny. When it isn't – when it's just weird, or disorienting, or chilling, or shocking – then it's far too good to need to be funny, and the last thing I'd want is to undercut the tension with a one-liner about folk singing or Pot Noodles.

It is also faultlessly constructed, with the abilities of the despair squid clearly set up, its powers seemingly demonstrated as the crew start bursting into tears for no reason – and then suddenly, terrifyingly, it starts pursuing *Starbug* until… game over. It's a remarkable moment in a remarkable episode. Once Timothy Spall's wonderfully dismissive 'Andy' enters and the team starts reflecting back on some of their adventures, we suddenly see the past five years in a whole new light. ('It's a blatant clue! Blatant!') Lister sneaks a peak at another team playing the same game, and having a blast. Smeg.

When they start discovering who they are and where they are, everyone's alter egos are brilliantly worked out, and this fascist world is sketched in with amazing economy. 'Voter Colonel' is the perfect title, suggesting in two words a pitch-black world of double-talk, state control, and misery. Then, the other shoe drops at the perfect time – just before we might start to question what's really happening, but also just before the very expensive car chase begins. As our central foursome really does come back to reality, they seem genuinely shaken. And so they should be. This is a truly incredible half hour of television, doing far more with the format than I'd ever believed was possible.

The one with: Duane Dibbley.

That Rimmer's a solid guy: For much of this episode, Rimmer believes himself to be non-hologram Billy Doyle. It's not clear how he succumbed to the hallucinogen or why the mood stabiliser was effective on him. He happily sits on flight cases with the other three, and appears to be pressing his head against Cat's and Lister's.

There's a time and a place: Cat says this is 'like Saturday night at the Wailing Wall'. Rimmer thinks a skeleton looks like Norman Bates's mum (from Alfred Hitchcock's 1960 film *Psycho*). Duane Dibbley's belongings include white socks, plastic sandals, an Airtex vest and a key to the Salvation Army hostel. (As with 'skutters', some apparently authoritative sources give this surname as 'Dibley' but the spelling with a double-b is more common.)

Influences, references and rip-offs: Several episodes of *Star Trek* and its spin-offs include the crew exploring a base or ship littered with corpses. Sometimes this even includes the detail that everyone died by their own hand. Many, many instances exist of 'it was all a dream' from *The Wizard of Oz* being Dorothy's dream, to the ninth season of *Dallas* being Pamela Ewing's dream, to the whole of *Newhart* (1982–90) being a dream experienced by the lead character of *The Bob Newhart Show* (1972–8), to the devastating end of Terry Gilliam's *Brazil* – itself influenced by George Orwell's novel *1984*, to which this episode also owes a significant debt.

Best gag: 'You were playing the *prat* version of Rimmer for all that time? For *four years*!?'

Worst visual effect: This all looks pretty great.

Continuity is for smegheads: In this fantasy, 'Red Dwarf' is a Total Immersion Video game, as seen in *Better than Life*. Four years have passed since the game started (and it presumably starts with *The End*). Rimmer feels despair because his brother had the same upbringing as him and is much more successful, but this is also true of the real Rimmer, who has three very successful brothers, so it isn't clear why it affects him so deeply. Kryten refers to the squid ink as secreted from a 'piscine source', but squid aren't fish, they're invertebrate marine molluscs. Last appearance of Hattie Hayridge.

Series VI

The Making of Series VI

Once more, Rob and Doug had been thinking about switching things up. They both felt they'd run out of ideas for Holly – Kryten was much funnier and just as able to deliver exposition, as well as being a character they could place in real jeopardy. Now they were going to ditch the *Red Dwarf* ship as well, and make *Starbug* the characters' home base for Series VI, which would tell the story of the quest to find their missing mining vessel.

That would mean no onboard computer, and no Hattie Hayridge. Wanting to break the news personally, Rob and Doug asked her to come and see them in the Grant Naylor Productions office. Anticipating perhaps a bigger role, or to be asked if she had any ideas about how Holly would develop, when she saw how nervous the writers were, she jokingly asked if she was being given the sack – only to be told that, yes, that was essentially what was happening. Hayridge doesn't appear in any other episodes of the show, but seems to look back on her time with the series very fondly, and has appeared on many convention panels to talk about her association with **Red Dwarf**.

Rob and Doug meanwhile were quickly facing a crisis. They had discussed taking over the director's role permanently, but now word came from the BBC that, despite the fact that the writers had been in Hollywood for most of the year, the new series needed to be ready for transmission in the spring of 1993. That meant that they had about half the usual amount of time to write the scripts, and they would likely still be finishing them when production started. A new producer, Justin Judd, took over and Andy de Emmony came in as director.

De Emmony was someone that Rob and Doug knew from *Spitting Image*, where he'd tackled plenty of practical effects, video effects, last-minute script changes and, of course, puppets. He was a fan of the show, and when he heard that a director was needed, he made an aggressive pitch for the job. Unlike Juliet May, he bonded very quickly with the main cast, who seized on his South African-sounding surname and tortured him mercilessly every day he was on set for being an Apartheid-supporter. Andy de Emmony was born in Leicester. Regardless of his pedigree, he earned the trust of the actors and writers, due to his unflappable enthusiasm, and he delivered a very tight set of episodes, on time and on budget.

However, as feared, production began with only three completed scripts, meaning that advanced planning was very difficult. Crewmembers quickly learned that Rob and Doug would often tip off set designer Mel Bibby about what locations they had in mind for future episodes, so that he at least could start work early – resulting in him often being pressured to reveal what he knew to other heads of department. Meanwhile, Howard Burden was reinventing the look of some of the characters. Chris Barrie's red Rimmer tunic now gained a quilted effect, which Barrie disliked – normally he only cared about whether or not the costume he was given was comfortable, but this one he thought made him look like an eiderdown.

Gaining comfort was Robert Llewellyn, whose new Kryten suit was much more flexible and actually allowed him to sit down while wearing it – an innovation he had been waiting for for three years. It was also given flashing lights on the shoulders, which worked once, during the initial fitting, but never functioned again and were never seen doing anything on camera. Robert Llewellyn speculated that Craig Charles might have touched them, or breathed on them, or looked in their direction. Charles had a remarkable ability to damage props, to the point where the art department defined a working prop as one that Craig Charles hadn't handled yet.

Also adding to the visual spectacle was a pitch that Grant Naylor received from a start-up called SVC Television. The computer graphics revolution was coming, although *Toy Story* was still a couple of years away. But the technology needed to create broadcast quality video effects was now far more affordable than it had ever been before. Two fans of the show, Terry Hylton and Karl Mooney, had set up their own company to create what we'd now call CGI and had offered their services. Their contributions are seen throughout the series – compare some of the glows and lasers this year to the flashing eyes in *Quarantine*, for example – and they make quite a difference to the overall level of visual polish.

First to be recorded and transmitted was *Psirens*. Finally, Rob and Doug were listening to Craig Charles, who still hadn't done more than hold hands with future Kochanski in *Stasis Leak*. Here he gets a full-on snog, but the girl of his dreams rapidly turns into an animatronic monster dripping with KY jelly. Happy now, Craig?

This show also features some more high-profile guest stars. Jenny Agutter joined the crew for a single day's location filming, and C.P. Grogan makes her final appearance as Kochanski, alongside *EastEnders* star Anita Dobson, resplendent in sci-fi black leathers. Dobson's appearance had come about as a result of the need to find a guitar double for Lister. The team approached Anita Dobson's husband, Brian May of rock band Queen, to do the honours. He wasn't available, but when his wife found out which show they were talking about, she asked if there was a part for her – which, as it happened, there was. In the end, the guitar licks were provided by Phil Manzanera from Roxy Music, who crouched behind Craig Charles, and thrust his arms through Lister's sleeves. This cunning illusion, also used for the banjo scene in the 1972 film *Deliverance*, worked brilliantly and Craig Charles was delighted with the result. (The end credits read: featuring the hands of Phil Manzanera.)

The narrative justification for this was the need to tell which was the real Lister and which was the imposter. Once again, a new director was faced with a complicated split screen on his first day in the studio, but Andy de Emmony not only rose to the challenge, he used a new device that allowed for a much more subtle and flexible blending of shots. True, the camera still had to be locked-off (i.e. stationary) but now the split could curve around different shapes instead of having to be a single straight line.

One location used for this episode was Bankside Power Station in Southwark. By the time the **Red Dwarf** team arrived, this was no longer in use, having closed down in 1981, but it was used as a location for a number of different TV shows and movies including the 1995 *Judge Dredd* and Ian McKellan's film version of *Richard III*. Not long after **Red Dwarf** visited, it was largely demolished and the site was reinvented as the art gallery Tate Modern.

Next to go before the cameras was *Legion*, in which Rimmer is given a 'hard light' upgrade, which means he can now feel and touch things (he also gets a blue costume to replace his red one). For more of my thoughts on this, see the review of the episode and the **That Rimmer's a solid guy** section. For the titular villain, Stephen Fry was approached, but the part went to Nigel Williams, who quickly learned that being a guest star on **Red Dwarf** frequently means having to suffer for your art. There hadn't been time before the location filming for a proper costume fitting, and when the wardrobe assistants tried to fasten the back of his suit, the zip broke. As a tight fit was needed to get the proper effect, the actor had to be sewn in and wasn't able to take it off until the end of a long, cold night shoot.

The scenes being shot included some ambitious material for the physical and video effects teams. Rob and Doug's script specified anti-matter chopsticks and the art department had supplied suitably crazy-looking battery-powered contraptions that could twirl around on cue – until they handed them to Craig Charles and then the ends fell off on cue. Meanwhile, the food items that were supposedly being controlled by these devices were being marionetted on fine fishing wire, which wouldn't show up on camera, before being flung at Chris Barrie. And finally, for the reveal of Legion's composite face, all four of the regular cast members had to be individually filmed on location with their heads held immobile in a brace, in order to provide matching elements that could be combined later by the video effects team.

The long night culminated in a slapstick scene inspired by Rik Mayall and Adrian Edmondson's flat share sitcom *Bottom*, which had started on BBC2 in 1991. Chris Barrie recalls that he wished more time had been left to experiment, plan and rehearse what could have been a really intricate and creative sequence but was instead a bit of a last-minute scramble to get the needed shots in the short time left.

In the planning for Series VI, the idea of doing a **Red Dwarf** Western kept coming up, but – remembering what had happened when they blithely wrote 'a beach in paradise' into the scripts for Series II – Rob and Doug wanted to make sure they weren't writing anything that the BBC couldn't realise. That created a Catch 22 because the BBC weren't going to send location scouts out looking for places to film a script that hadn't yet been written. To circumvent this problem, the writers claimed to have a Western script ready to go and outlined the sorts of locations that would likely be needed, secure in the knowledge that they could drop that idea in favour of something else more practical if the search came up empty.

But in fact, it transpired that a recreated old west town was readily available in a Kent village near Sevenoaks. Laredo Western Town in Fawkham was founded in 1971 as a tourist attraction with houses, stores and other buildings all in the typical American Wild West style, *circa* 1865, and populated by actors in period costumes. Still with no actual script, Rob and Doug and a small **Red Dwarf** crew visited the site to make sure it had what they needed, and the owner asked them to describe the events in their story. 'Yes, Doug, tell them about the first scene,' grinned Rob Grant, and Doug made up some nonsense about a gunfight. 'Now tell them about the scene in the saloon,' Rob continued, and again Doug gallantly kept up the pretence. By this method, they devised many of the set pieces that would end up on screen, and they left confident that they could write a story to fit this setting – which became *Gunmen of the Apocalypse*, the third episode of Series VI.

As it turned out, they only had access to the Laredo for one day and the final script made extensive use of not just the surroundings but also the livestock – the Dwarfers make an entrance on horseback. Danny John-Jules had ridden horses before, and Craig Charles seemingly knows no fear. But Chris Barrie had barely ever met a horse, let alone been in control of one, and he was very nervous. Craig Charles couldn't stop himself from slapping Chris Barrie's horse on the rear, whereupon it – and the other two – all galloped off at speed, leaving a terrified Barrie desperately trying to find the brake or the off-switch. Craig Charles still seems to find this very funny – Chris Barrie less so.

The heavy workload was a big test for Andy de Emmony, who storyboarded everything meticulously, and tried to limit camera setups so he could get half a dozen miscellaneous shots from different parts of the episode one after the other, bang-bang-bang, without having to move the camera and reset the lights. In this efficient but frantic fashion, they got everything they needed before the sun went down. The rest of the episode was filmed at Shepperton in the usual way.

Meanwhile, back in London, no less a person than Janet Street-Porter, working in the upper echelons of the BBC, was reviewing the script and immediately insisted on talking to Charles Armitage of Noel Gay Television. She told him that the pages she'd read were completely stupid, and in any case were absolutely impossible to shoot on **Red Dwarf**'s budget, and she didn't know what the team were playing at, but they needed to abandon this episode and find something else to record instead. 'Actually,' ventured Armitage, 'I don't think it will be totally impossible. They finished filming it yesterday.'

In November 2021, a fire broke out in Laredo and emergency services battled the blaze for twelve hours before getting it under control. By that time, fully a third of the town had been destroyed and the facility was forced to close, launching a crowdfunding campaign to try to raise the capital needed for rebuilding. As of October 2022, they have raised £15,000 and recently held an event to celebrate their fiftieth birthday.

Like *Gunmen of the Apocalypse*, *Emohawk* was one of the scripts that wasn't finished when production began. Peter Wragg, veteran effects designer, remembers an enquiry from the writers wanting to know if the polymorph prop from Series III still existed. The answer was yes, it had been kept, but during four years of indifferent storage in a cupboard, it had started to disintegrate and so in the end, only its 'tongue' is ever seen. Also making return appearances were Duane Dibbley from *Back to Reality* – only a handful of episodes ago – and Ace Rimmer from Series IV's *Dimension Jump*. Rob and Doug had been considering an episode in which the Cat would morph into Duane during moments of stress, but in the end, having the polymorph suck out his cool was a much neater solution.

The location work for this episode covered the gang's adventures in the GELF village. As well as sound stages, Shepperton had an extensive 'backlot' and elements had already been used for past episodes including *Meltdown* and *Terrorform*. As it happened, a collection of primitive huts was already available, left over from an ABC series called *Covington Cross*, which had been set in fourteenth-century England (and which included a guest appearance from one Chloë Annett in the seventh episode).

The guest cast included Ainsley Harriot, now far better known as a TV chef, but then only just beginning to transition away from live comedy and music and into on-air food preparation. Together with his friend Paul Boross, he was one half of The Calypso Twins, who had a hit record in 1990 with their song 'World Party'. Shortly after his appearance on **Red Dwarf**, he became resident chef on *This Morning with Anne and Nick* and subsequently lead presenter on *Can't Cook Won't Cook*. This was a big surprise to Craig Charles, who was more used to seeing him on stage at the Comedy Store. In 1998, the cast of **Red Dwarf** would appear in character in a special edition of Harriot's programme called *Can't Smeg Won't Smeg*.

Once the cast and crew returned to the studio for the recording in front of the audience, Peter Wragg had rigged up the latest in a long line of explosions to add some excitement to a scene on board *Starbug*. This time, the charge was so violent that the cast were pelted with bits of polystyrene. Robert Llewellyn found fragments embedded in the back of his rubber head, Craig Charles suffered bruises on his arms and Danny John-Jules was struck in the face, just below his eye. A hush fell over the studio audience as on-set medics were summoned to attend to the cast's injuries. These were all thankfully very minor, but Wragg was mortified. Like all effects technicians, safety was always top of his list of priorities, and he was appalled to discover that he'd miscalculated on this occasion.

The crew returned to the Shepperton backlot for the location filming for episode five, *Rimmerworld*, where Arnold Rimmer populates an entire planet with clones of himself. Once again, Rob and Doug had specified paradise, and the crew were attempting to recreate that in the Surrey countryside in early March. This time, they were lucky and the driving rain of *Better than Life* didn't follow them. The process of Rimmer clones growing from their cocoons was depicted with the sight of a fully naked Chris Barrie rising into frame. However, as the shot required Rimmer to be face to face with his duplicate, a stand-in was engaged who was happy to be photographed from behind in the altogether, and Barrie's blushes were spared on this occasion. Various other stand-ins played other versions of Rimmer, including the concubines he has to kiss at one point.

The closing scene of the episode featured a future Rimmer who darkly hints that something horrible has happened to Lister, but it is never revealed what. A cut scene showed the entirely intact future Lister emerging from the bathroom, making it clear that this was just a wind-up by future Rimmer, but it was decided that it was stronger without the reveal. This was planned as a direct sequel to *Gunmen*, but it was ultimately moved to fifth in the running order.

By the time *Emohawk* was in the studio, Rob and Doug were very behind. A few script pages for the last episode of the series had been circulated and Andy de Emmony spent half a day early in the week rehearsing the cast and then sent everybody home because there was nothing else to do. Doug Naylor gives Rob Grant a great deal of credit for teaching him an important lesson when in this situation: hold your nerve. If you bang out a sub-standard script and get it to the cast and crew in time, they will no doubt be happy to have been given the pages and will gladly get to work. But all the better, funnier ideas you later come up with will count for nothing, and the poor show that goes on the air will live for ever. If you keep rejecting work you don't believe in, and hang on until the right idea comes along, on the day, everyone will hate you for keeping them waiting, but those passions will cool and the far superior episode you produce is what will be remembered.

To be fair, production on the aptly named *Out of Time* pushed that credo to its absolute limit. The finished script wasn't available to the cast until the day of the recording. Learning the words and rehearsing the scenes was absolutely impossible. The only solution was to use autocue technology and spend what little prep time was left embedding screens into concealed areas of the set that could dynamically display the actors' lines. Robert Llewellyn even remembers seeing Rob Grant over in one corner of the studio, frantically typing into the autocue machine, adding new dialogue to the end of the scene they were currently shooting.

Clearly, nobody thought this was an ideal way to work, and several cast and the director were worried that the audience – at home or in the studio – would see the screens or notice the actors reading their lines. I think you can tell sometimes that the eyelines are off – if you're looking for it – but on the whole it's fairly seamless, and the shoot was very quick and easy, leading some people to suggest – half jokingly, half not – that they should scrap all of this tedious line-learning and rehearsing and just stick everything up on cue cards and hidden screens from this point onwards.

Nobody was more annoyed by the late delivery of the script than Craig Charles, for whom word-perfect line memorisation had become an article of faith. When he read the first half of the episode, he is alleged to have been heard asking, 'Is it me, or is this script absolutely terrible?' When word of this got back to the writers, they got their revenge. First, the next draft was titled 'RIP Dave Lister', which they hoped would get the actor suitably concerned about his future employment prospects. Then, they included a scene featuring yet another set of future Dwarfers, in which Chris Barrie is seen as Rimmer with a big false moustache and a pot belly under his now-yellow quilted tunic, Danny John-Jules plays future Cat with a Bobby Charlton comb-over, Robert Llewellyn plays future Kryten in a powder blue suit and a cheap toupée – and Lister is a brain in a jar. Charles was incensed. 'Couldn't I at least be a head in a jar?' he protested. 'Cut a hole in the table and I'll stick me head through.' But a bodyless brain, he remained.

The series was also left on a cliffhanger. The final shot is one of *Starbug* being hit by a laser blast and disintegrating – with a superimposed explosion over existing footage of the *Starbug* model as there wasn't time to build one that they would be happy to blow up, nor time to go back to the effects stage and film it. Once again, Rob and Doug were painting themselves into a corner and – in true **Red Dwarf** style – trusting that their future selves would find a solution. They didn't have to do this. A more traditional ending was written and shot and the transmitted ending seems to have been a late decision, created in the edit. Did they think that going out on an unresolved note would hasten a commission for the seventh series? If so, it didn't work. Or were they reacting to the 1993 edition of fan magazine *Better Than Life* which came out months before Series VI began airing and included full synopses of all six episodes, supplied by people who had attended the taping? Either way, the original ending wasn't seen until the Series VI DVD was released in 2005.

Despite the frantic efforts by the whole team to have the episodes ready for spring 1993, maddeningly, the BBC elected to postpone showing them until the autumn. This had the unfortunate effect of having the series begin broadcasting six full months after publication of the Penguin book *Primordial Soup: The Least Worst Scripts*, which included the full script for *Psirens*. Meanwhile, more **Red Dwarf** was coming to home video. Series II had been released in March 1992, as Series V was being transmitted, followed by Series IV in October 1992. The long-suppressed Series I was released in July 1993 and Series V in July 1994, following a rerun of the first five series in the spring and summer of 1994. But a seventh series wouldn't emerge until January 1997, and it would bring major changes – all of which will be documented in *Volume II*.

Impressions of Series VI

Written by Rob Grant and Doug Naylor. Designed by Mel Bibby. Costumes by Howard Burden. Produced by Justin Judd. Directed by Andy de Emmony. Starring: Craig Charles, Chris Barrie, Danny John-Jules, Robert Llewellyn.

S06E01 Psirens ★★★★☆

TX: 7 October 1993 on BBC2. Ratings: 5.23m (1st for the week).
Featuring: Jenny Agutter, Anita Dobson, Samantha Robson, Richard Ridings, C.P. Grogan.

Once again, it's all change. The catch-up for new viewers, establishing key facts about Lister's personality and relationship with Rimmer, also serves as a catch-up for old viewers. In the eighteen months that the series has been off the air, the boys have lost the *Dwarf* and have been in suspended animation for 200 years. Kryten, Lister and Rimmer all get good material here, but the Cat is mysteriously missing in action. He presumably was also in suspended animation, but he just shows up once the other two are restored to health and vitality. He does get a new superpower this time round: he's *Starbug*'s designated pilot, with his superior reflexes and 'nasal intuition'. Episode titles now just fade on and off the screen.

The hunt for their old ship provides a new quest to go on – when was the last time anyone said anything about getting back to Earth? – but this too will gradually be forgotten about as the series progresses. Our essentially feckless heroes don't want for much, until they're down to their last few thousand poppadoms, so it's often hard to use their own drives and wants as the springboards for stories.

The chief plot engine here is the presence of 'Psirens' who can look into your mind and become the thing you most desire. Oddly, this isn't used much for gags. What they become isn't terribly surprising or funny, being mainly hot chicks of one kind or another (including Kochanski – hello Clare Grogan!). What is funny and very engaging is the guys' reactions, whether it's Cat obliviously charging out of the airlock, Kryten obediently crushing himself into a small cube, or Lister only ever calling Pete Tranter's sister 'Pete Tranter's sister' (and there are some nifty effects here too as Samantha Robson changes into a slimy animatronic while the camera spins around the two of them). Best moment of the episode – both clever and funny – is the gang blowing fake Lister away when the Psiren pretending to be him mistakenly plays the guitar like the expert musician Lister believes himself to be.

It's Rimmer who comes off worst. Having no corporeal brain, he is of scant interest to the Psirens, and he's such a physical coward – despite being made of light – that he generally arranges to be where they aren't. (Although he seems almost frantic with worry when Lister is trapped outside the ship, which is rather sweet.) So, this is a good strong season opener, rather than an all-time classic; an effective plot device which shines a light on most of our regular cast, but doesn't really give us any new insights. Also, I miss Holly.

This is the beginning of the Space Corps directive running gag, which becomes all too predictable as the series progresses.

The one with: Jenny Agutter.

That Rimmer's a solid guy: While Lister has been in suspended animation, Rimmer's light bee has been literally frozen and needs to be defrosted and then his attributes reloaded – presumably from some computer on board *Starbug* (none of this '*Red Dwarf* can only support one hologram' nonsense today). He needs recharging at intervals and he faints at the sight of blood. He also swivels his chair around and leans on the table.

There's a time and a place: Lister attempts to cut his nails with a desktop pencil sharpener. Kryten prefers partnership whist to sex. Lister believes he can play the guitar like the ghost of Hendrix (but the rest of the crew requires him to practise outside the ship). They encounter a meteor bigger than King Kong's first dump of the day, which has the potential to make them deader than corduroy. Kryten refers to the *Angling Times*. Rimmer wants Lister to 'tune into sanity FM' and see what's as plain as a Bulgarian pin-up. Cat is familiar with duty-free shopping. *Starbug* has crashed more times than a ZX81 and has no weapons to speak of.

Influences, references and rip-offs: Clearly this is a riff on the Greek myth of the Sirens whose enchanting songs would lure sailors to their deaths. Captain Tau's name (as well as being a Greek letter) comes from the American pilot – speaking of which…

Best gag: 'Whoever heard of a wormskin rug?' is a great line, which Rob and Doug pilfered from their own script for the *Red Dwarf USA* reshoots.

Worst visual effect: Those meteors are very fake looking. We are treated to a spectacular *Starbug* crash, though.

Continuity is for smegheads: Lister has been in suspended animation for 200 years. He eats Corn Flakes with raw onion and Tabasco for breakfast, washed down with cold vindaloo sauce, and the weathergirl from (groovy, funky) Channel 27 is among his fantasies. Kryten is of no interest to the Psirens because his brain is synthetic (whereas in *DNA* he told us that his brain was part organic). The *Starbug* crew are all now in their 'correct' positions: Lister on the left, Cat on the right, Rimmer behind Lister, Kryten behind Cat. Last appearance of C.P. Grogan as Kochanski.

S06E02 Legion ★★★★☆

TX: 14 October 1993 on BBC2. Ratings: 5.53m (3rd for the week).
Featuring: Nigel Williams.

Supplies are low on *Starbug*, which does something to raise the stakes a bit. That's good, because the main problem with this episode is that there isn't much excitement. None of the characters are forced to confront awkward truths about themselves, and the worst that threatens to befall anyone is being made to endure a life of luxurious captivity. That doesn't mean this isn't an enjoyable episode, but it probably needed a bit more conceptual cleverness to overcome the lack of urgency.

More than anything, this feels like the story is pushing our guys through a fairly standard space adventure plot (*Star Trek* with jokes!), but the gag rate is enviously high – even if there's a fine line between recognisable but fresh character beats (Rimmer's bold message of surrender) and running jokes that are wearing out their welcome (all the fashion choices which the Cat thinks things are deader than). This episode includes any number of classic one-liners and it's obvious that Rob and Doug are still having a ball writing these characters. That counts for a lot.

The only guest artist this time is Nigel Williams as Legion. It's fairly clear that the part was written for Stephen Fry, but Williams does a fine job, his avuncular tones shifting subtly from formal welcome to lightly veiled threats. Of course, this is the episode that sees Rimmer's upgrade to hard light. One huge advantage of this to the writers is that now he can happily be pelted with food, whacked over the head and so forth. However, it does mean that from this point on, Rimmer's nature as a holographic computer simulation of a dead man is downplayed, and he essentially becomes just another member of the crew.

This final slapstick scene doesn't have the lunatic energy of *Bottom*, as was hoped, but does have some good **Red Dwarf**-style zingers. And just to prove that they aren't making life easy for themselves, the episode ends with an explosive decompression of *Starbug*. Series VI is sometimes thought of as 'the beginning of the end' but this is very good stuff, with great jokes, a well-paced plot, and a new challenge for the crew. I think I would have liked to see more time given to the dilemma of the gilded cage and less instant agreement that immediate escape was their only option, but that's not a major criticism. For a show on its sixth year and its thirty-second episode, this is very impressive.

The one with: Anti-matter chopsticks.

That Rimmer's a solid guy: Rimmer gets his 'hard light' upgrade, which means he can now physically interact with the world. This version of hologram technology is even more weakly defined than the previous version (why tie yourself down if you don't have to?) but does mean that Chris Barrie can stop worrying about chairs that move when he sits down on them – not that he worried about that much in any case. It also means he is invulnerable, although not impervious to pain, so we can expect his cowardice to remain intact. The change is signified by a change in tunic colour from red to blue.

There's a time and a place: Frequently recycled water tastes like Dutch lager. The nice Liquorice Allsorts have all gone. Tonight's movie is yet another Doug McClure. Lister has forgotten that he already filled in the 'Have you got a good memory?' quiz in his magazine. The Albanian State Washing Machine Company has a technology far in advance of our own – easy to believe looking at the dot matrix printer read-out on *Starbug*. Rimmer compares himself to George S. Patton, famed American general during the Second World War, memorably portrayed by George C. Scott in a 1970 Oscar-winning film. If they can't outrun the missile, they're deader than tank tops. The whole panel is deader than A-line flares with pockets in the knees. Kryten looks like Herman Munster's stuntman. (Herman Munster was the patriarch of the Munster family, played originally by Fred Gwynne in the CBS sitcom *The Munsters*, which ran for seventy episodes and two season in the mid-1960s and has been revived too many times since then. Herman resembled the Universal version of Frankenstein's monster as played by Boris Karloff, with a flat head and electrodes in his neck.) Lister recommends flagging down a black cab and heading for real street. Rimmer's hard light drive is tougher than vindaloo-ed mutton. The name 'Quayle' in the list of geniuses may have been a joke at the expense of famously dim American Vice President Dan Quayle. (The joke at the time was that if anyone assassinated President Bush, the Secret Service had orders to shoot Quayle.) Others on the list include an existentialist philosopher, a rock singer and a TV impressionist.

Influences, references and rip-offs: In the Gospel of Mark, Jesus asks a demon's name and receives the reply: 'My name is Legion, for we are many.' The word may refer to the division of the Roman army comprising 5,500 soldiers. Mistaking a purely functional part of the room for art is a venerable old joke, which I remember occurring in a 1975 episode of *Columbo* ('Playback', starring Oskar Werner) and I don't think it was new then. The gilded cage was a favourite device of *Star Trek* – speaking of which, Kryten's 'Ionian Nerve Grip' is presumably a reference to Mr Spock's Vulcan neck pinch.

Best gag: 'Step up to red alert.' 'Sir, are you absolutely sure? It does mean changing the bulb.' That is a cast-iron copper-bottomed joke.

Worst visual effect: *Starbug*'s arrival on the space station is very impressive. The polystyrene statue that Lister attacks Legion with... less so.

Continuity is for smegheads: Lister measures distance in 'gee-gooks', whatever they may be. Now that Rimmer can touch again, Kryten puts the puncture repair kit on standby (so presumably Rachel was on *Starbug*, rather than *Red Dwarf*). Rimmer's bedroom is furnished with nocturnal boxing gloves (as seen in *Timeslides*). Legion takes Lister's appendix out, even though *Thanks for the Memory* established that he had already had it removed. (Doug Naylor's novel *Last Human* tells us that Lister was born with a double appendix, and has had each of them removed, resulting in two out of his four scars.) Rimmer thinks Legion will get them back to Earth, and it's a long time since that was an explicit goal. He also asserts that they have met thirty-one individuals on their travels. How this number was arrived at is not known (one per episode?), but for a start they would have met at least that many during their time on Backwards Earth. One of these wanted to 'erase them from history' but this is presumably not the Inquisitor, who erased himself from history and therefore from Rimmer's memory. Lister's favourite sandwich is Sugar Puffs (mentioned in *The Inquisitor*) rather than chilli-chutney-fried-egg. Where does Legion get the expertise to make Rimmer's hard light drive? He's a composite of Cat, Kryten, Rimmer and Lister and nothing more. Could Kryten have upgraded Arnie at any time and he just chose not to?

S06E03 Gunmen of the Apocalypse ★★★☆☆

TX: 21 October 1993 on BBC2. Ratings: 5.98m (2nd for the week).
Featuring: Denis Lill, Liz Hickling, Jennifer Calvert, Imogen Bain, Steve Devereaux, Robert Inch, Jeremy Peters, Dinny Powell, Stephen Marcus.

There's a very striking film noir style opening here – although Craig Charles couldn't be less interested in attempting an accent ('I've gorra admit you look pretty good for a corpse'). Kryten has to get Lister out of the artificial reality machine because rogue Simulants are on their trail, and they despise humans, whom they see as the vermin of the universe. Lister's plan to fool them with one of Kryten's eyes on his chin fails, but rather than wipe out the helpless crew, the Simulants upgrade the ship so that pursuing them will be more fun – you know, like you do with vermin. It backfires when *Starbug* gets off a lucky shot and the Simulants just have time to upload a computer virus before their ship explodes.

That's also known as 'going the long way round'. The point of this story is to give *Starbug* a computer virus, and to dramatise the battle to defeat it as a Western, with Kryten as the sozzled sheriff who needs to get his act together. But the long chain of contrivance and coincidence it takes to get us there doesn't give any of the moments time enough to breathe, rarely creates any good comedy, and feels clunky and laborious. Since the 'AR Machine' appears to be new, would it not have been more elegant and streamlined to have that be the source of the virus rather than introduce Simulants, explain why they aren't a threat, explain why they are a threat again, write them out, and finally have them upload a virus while exploding?

Having *Starbug* locked on a collision course with a moon provides some of the urgency that *Legion* lacked, and the dreamscape setting gives the story some of that **Red Dwarf** topspin, but this isn't quite as specific as *Psirens*. Howard Goodall's honky-tonk rendition of the theme tune is lovely, and the location work is very effective (although it's clear that this is a winter's day in the south of England and nowhere near the United States). The four Western personas are great too, with Rimmer's delight at finally being a successful pugilist a particular highlight. There's also something in the fact that the solution to the problem involves giving Kryten his mojo back, but this just sort of happens. Nothing that the boys do causes it (they just feed him raw coffee) and although the dove symbolism is cool, it's reaching for something deeper than it grasps (and then just falls back on hitting Rimmer again).

This wouldn't be so bad if there were more jokes. *Legion* has a much simpler plot, but as jokesmiths, Rob and Doug are really on song there. This has a huge amount of daring and imagination, and – let's be fair – what other BBC sitcom was doing anything like this in 1993, *2Point4 Children*? I also know this is a fan favourite, so I don't expect every reader to agree with this assessment. But we've had tighter stories, funnier dialogue and sharper character exploration than this – including earlier this series – so for me this ends up as only average, albeit with a tremendous amount of ambition on display in the second half.

The one with: Cowboys.

That Rimmer's a solid guy: He's back in the red tunic until he needs to switch to hard light mode. Before he switches, he briefly rests his hand on the dream machine (you can see Chris Barrie realise the mistake and withdraw).

There's a time and a place: Loretta is the sexiest computer 'sprite' Lister has ever seen. (A sprite is a self-contained image of an object or character in a computer game.) Cat doesn't believe those lying cat-and-mouse cartoons. Rimmer (like many people, including Kryten in *The Inquisitor*) thinks that lemmings throw themselves off cliffs, which they definitely don't. Cat has seen Westerns before and knows Spanish. Rimmer makes a veiled reference to eighties British ice dancing champs Torvill and Dean. Lister wonders if the last Western Rimmer saw was 'Butch Accountant and the Yuppie Kid'. (Yuppie was an eighties term for a Young Upwardly mobile Professional.)

Influences, references and rip-offs: Pursuing humans for sport recalls the 1924 short story *The Most Dangerous Game* by Richard Connell, a hugely influential and often-adapted tale of big-game hunters who prefer to stalk people. Among others, the Western plot echoes the classic movies *High Noon* from 1952 with Gary Cooper, and *Rio Bravo* from 1959 with John Wayne. Patrick Stewart caught this episode on PBS and briefly thought the British show was ripping off one of the instalments of *Star Trek: The Next Generation* which he directed, namely 'A Fistful of Datas', where Worf, Troi and Alexander are trapped in a Holodeck simulation of a Western town where everyone looks like Brent Spiner. Kirk, Spock and McCoy were also trapped in a simulated Old West town in the original *Star Trek* episode 'Spectre of the Gun'. The name Dan McGrew possibly comes from a 1907 poem called *The Shooting of Dan McGrew*. Sharing dreams in general recalls Wes Craven's 1984 horror classic *A Nightmare on Elm Street*, and from the same year, *Dreamscape*, starring Dennis Quaid and Max von Sydow. Virtual reality worlds in which famous films are recreated also brings to mind the TV movie *Overdrawn at the Memory Bank*, also from 1984 (big year for movies about dreams), starring Raul Julia and based on the short story by John Varley. In this case, rather than a Western, the movie being re-enacted is – say it with me – *Casablanca*. There are also very vague hints of *Tron* in this episode. The Four Horsemen from the Biblical Book of Revelation put in an appearance.

Best gag: 'To cut a long story short, it's me. Keys?'

Worst visual effect: *Starbug* sailing off into the sunset is gorgeous. The video effects are not quite as convincing.

Continuity is for smegheads: The game Lister is playing isn't specifically identified as a Total Immersion Video game but it functions very like one.

Unlike the Holodeck in *Star Trek: The Next Generation*, this machine seems to be used almost entirely for sex. Rimmer wants to abandon pursuit of *Red Dwarf*. We're in 'Rogue Simulant Country' (space is very crowded 3 million years from Earth). The Simulants are able to teleport onto *Starbug*, which gets an upgrade and now includes laser canons (and a seat-tilt control that doesn't squeak). It has a single one-person escape pod (which escaped last Thursday). A new piece of Western-inspired music, which segues into an instrumental version of 'Fun Fun Fun', accompanies the end credits.

S06E04 Emohawk: Polymorph II ★★☆☆

TX: 28 October 1993 on BBC2. Ratings: 6.28m (1st for the week).
Featuring: Ainsley Harriott, Steven Wickham, Martin Sims, Hugh Quarshie.

The Space Filth have caught up with *Starbug* – 3 million years out from Earth is a *very* busy place. To evade capture, they head for GELF territory, which includes a nifty sequence of the ship flying through an asteroid as the bad guys blast it to bits. Not very funny, but an idea worthy of a big budget movie, and the effects team really pulls it off.

In many ways, that's the biggest problem with this episode. The series which started as two men who hate each other (and their loopy computer), which became weird explorations of the personalities of a bunch of differently awful guys, has now become the wacky space adventures of four wisecracking dudes. Listen, stasis equals death and I'm all for change and growth, but the wacky space adventures aren't as interesting to me as the character-driven stuff, so that means that the cracks have got to be extra wise. What doesn't help is that the series is also now giving in to the temptation to play the hits, recycling the polymorph from *Polymorph*, Ace Rimmer from *Dimension Jump* and Duane Dibbley from *Back to Reality*. True, those are three fabulous episodes but – *pace* Alan Partridge – my favourite episode of **Red Dwarf** is not 'The Best of Red Dwarf'.

There are other oddities too. Cat's destruction of Lister's guitar is weirdly underplayed. Ace about to snap the Cat's neck is genuinely disturbing. In fact, there's a morbid air to him throughout this episode – all of his plans to save the day seem to involve him sacrificing his own life and/or the lives of others. The Ace of *Dimension Jump* was a smarter cookie than that and far more compassionate (a cut line about how murdering Duane Dibbley would be like garrotting Bambi would have helped a little). And there's something a bit crass and H. Rider Haggard-ish about the trip to the GELF village where sophisticated travellers outwit the savage and physically repellent primitive tribes.

The episode ends with another hunt-the-monster sequence, which doesn't add much to those already seen in *Polymorph*, *The Last Day*, *DNA*, *Justice* and *The Inquisitor*. What's potentially new is that Rimmer might choose to stay as Ace. Why this isn't handwaved away with some bogus science fiction explanation isn't clear ('If we don't re-inject your old personality, your holographic chromosomes will decay exponentially, sir, and in two days, you'll be nothing but a drooling vegetable,' etc. etc.). But we have to conclude that at some point, Ace does choose to go back to being that smeghead Rimmer. Why? Also, at one point, the Cat asks, 'Does mouse shit roll?', which is rather more profane than this series usually gets.

The one with: Ace Rimmer, Duane Dibbley and the GELF village.

That Rimmer's a solid guy: In his hard light mode, he can survive throwing himself on a grenade (probably). Once again, he is as vulnerable to polymorph attack as any flesh-and-blood crewmember.

There's a time and a place: Various references to the English Civil War. Cat is familiar with Hawaiian hula-hoop champions. The Space Corps Enforcement announcement makes about as much sense as a Japanese VCR instruction manual. The Eastbourne Zimmer Frame relay team can easily outrun *Starbug* (even after last week's upgrades). Rimmer is concerned about being turned into a beanbag and probed for lost biros. Among the items Lister attempts to bribe the GELF leader with are Swiss watches and Levi jeans. Not even bothering with the 'We're deader than…' part, Cat just says, 'That's it, we're platform shoes, man.' Lister isn't going down to Moss Bros. His armpit is unattractive after twenty games of table tennis. Duane Dibbley looks so geeky he couldn't even get into a science fiction convention. Ace uses cricketing jargon. Kryten's handshake with the GELFs was Robert Llewellyn's idea, which he says he spotted during the Super Bowl.

Influences, references and rip-offs: As noted, this recycles various characters, situations and catch-phrases from earlier episodes of **Red Dwarf**.

Best gag: Danny John-Jules's slapstick in the kitchen is extremely well done.

Worst visual effect: None of them is particularly good at it, but Craig Charles noticeably sways when he's supposed to be frozen to the spot at the end.

Continuity is for smegheads: Instead of the *Red Dwarf* bunkroom for Lister and Rimmer, *Starbug* has sleeping quarters for Lister and the Cat, with both berths on the same level. Lister prioritises a fourth round of toast over a safety drill, suggesting that *Starbug*'s food supplies have been replenished at some point. Kryten thinks they're as guilty as the man behind the grassy knoll (the second Kryten JFK quip before they actually visit Dallas in 1963 in Series VII). Rimmer calls himself 'old iron butt'. Duane Dibbley, who doesn't care about his appearance, and who hates being the Prince of Dorkness, urgently needs to change into something less cool. In *Polymorph*, the creature needed to trigger a specific emotion in order to feed on it, but this version doesn't waste time with that. To restore their former personalities, it is necessary to capture the polymorph, extract DNA strands from it and reinject its victims, whereas in both *Polymorph* and *Can of Worms*, it is sufficient just to kill it. Cat identifies the weapon that Rimmer ejects into space as 'our only gun' but Kryten procures two bazookoids from the engine room. Lister now measures distance in 'klicks' – the military term for kilometres. *Starbug* sustains significant damage including the loss of three fuel tanks, 80 per cent of the manoeuvring thrusters and the damage report machine.

S06E05 Rimmerworld ★★☆☆☆

TX: 4 November 1993 on BBC2. Ratings: 6.19m (2nd for the week).
Featuring: Elizabeth Hickling.

Emohawk is a disappointment because it's assembled from overfamiliar pieces. *Rimmerworld* is a much bigger swing, which has echoes of *Meltdown*, *Me²* and *Terrorform*, but does feel fresh and original in ways that last week's episode didn't. And yet, the overall effect is curiously muted. Maybe that has something to do with the fact that the big comedy idea of the episode has to be pre-filmed because the technical demands are far too great for a live studio day. Maybe it's because this was one of the scripts written in a hurry, and so there are dangling loose ends. Maybe it just needed another 'gag pass'.

Things feel 'off' right from the start. Rimmer is trying to cheat on the eye exam, ho ho, by copying the charts onto his shoes, where it seems obvious to me that they will be harder to read, not easier. None of the stuff about his health seems to fit at all. I mean, his physical reactions to stress suit his character all right, but they completely ignore his hologram status. Maybe Alfred Molina was right!

In order to salvage the supplies and fuel they need, they board the derelict Simulant ship from *Gunmen*. So this is the **Red Dwarf** B-plot-creates-the-A-plot structure – but the B-plot on board the Simulant ship is a lot funnier and more exciting than all of that to-ing and fro-ing in *Gunmen* (which itself becomes the B-plot that created this episode's A-plot). Rimmer sneaking off to the escape pod is very funny, but even this material – probably the highlight of the episode – has weird non-sequiturs. The fuel situation is urgently kept secret from the Cat, but nothing comes of Lister not being truthful. Likewise,

Rimmer is desperate to keep his medical problems to himself, but that secret is never revealed either, so what was the point of him keeping it? When they try to use the teleporter, they turn up last Thursday, but the story carries on exactly as if they hadn't. This feels like it was written in an awful hurry.

The second half sees Rimmer trapped on The Planet of Inexpensive Stock Footage and becoming God, rather like Lister was supposed to in the *Red Dwarf* Total Immersion Video game. The key joke is that Rimmer's ghastly morality would become the standard in this all-Arnie-all-the-time environment, but that turns out to be a less fun idea than it sounds, raising few laughs from either me or the studio audience. And when we catch up with Rimmer again ('Rimmerworld was weeks ago'), 600 years of isolation, torture and fear seems to have left him totally unscathed, which adds to a kind of weightless feeling for the whole episode.

The section on the fragmenting Simulant ship has a nice mix of gags, character moments and sci-fi adventure, which nudges this up to two and a half stars, but the rest is weirdly uncertain with an unwillingness to follow through on many of its ideas – that's still preferable to last week's death-wish Ace business, though.

The one with: All those Rimmers.

That Rimmer's a solid guy: His hologrammatic status appears to still make him vulnerable to genetically predisposed heart, brain and circulatory medical conditions. In order to benefit from exercise, he will need to be in his hard light form. He requires something called a 'hard light remote belt' to go on a field trip. Although Arnie doesn't look quite the same here as he does in *The End* (or *The Promised Land*), this story tells us that holograms don't age. Nor does his light bee need recharging over 600 years.

There's a time and a place: Rimmer's blood pressure is higher than a hippy on the third day of an open-air festival. Lister thinks they have fewer options than a Welsh fish and chip shop. He hopes that the Simulants are rotting in silicon hell along with all the photocopiers. Rimmer isn't the Robinson Crusoe type.

Influences, references and rip-offs: Time dilation is actual science (although wormholes are not, at least not quite). Prior stories involving this phenomenon include the 1985 Orson Scott Card novel *Ender's Game*, and of course the original 1968 *Planet of the Apes*, among countless other examples. Rimmer creating paradise and then having his creations turn on him parallels the Garden of Eden.

Best gag: Over 600 years, Rimmer has worn the worry balls to little more than ball bearings.

Worst visual effect: The exploding Simulant ship is very pretty, but the escape pod and *Starbug* vanishing into the wormhole look more *Top of the Pops* than *Star Trek*.

Continuity is for smegheads: Rimmer's family all died of heart attacks, aneurysms, strokes, brain clots, you name it. Talk of holograms essentially worrying themselves to death prefigures the fate of Howard Rimmer in *Trojan*. Kryten was certain to bring Chinese worry balls from *Red Dwarf* (not that there's any mention of trying to find their old ship this week). The Simulant ship that was shot down in *Gunmen* is spotted and the boys try to raid it for supplies. Cat observes, 'Last time we met, I was wearing the same outfit,' which is accurate, although Cat's description of it having peach trim does not appear to be (but then what do I know about fashion?). It's not clear where hologram Rimmer gets a sample of his own DNA, while stranded on a desolate world. The Simulant ship includes a fully functional teleporter. When it blows up, Kryten continues to make use of it although all he has left is the remote control (which the guards let him keep before locking him up). See *Lemons* in Series X for more of this peculiar understanding of how technology works.

S06E06 Out of Time ★★★★☆

TX: 11 November 1993 on BBC2. Ratings: 6.26m (2nd for the week).

Is it fair to judge an episode by what didn't come after it? Should you downgrade part one of a two-part story because the second part didn't live up to the promise of the first? It can't be denied that the ending of this instalment is a nothingburger. Once again, Rob and Doug gleefully wrote themselves into a corner, as they had done countless times before. If the show had come back for an immediate seventh series, and a genuine part two had been offered up, continuing and developing the story of the two warring crews, then this might be better remembered. As it is, we had to wait four years and when the show came back, it was reformatted, partially de-Rimmered and Robless. An explanation of sorts was forthcoming, but it's so brief that it's all the more frustrating that it, or something like it, wasn't included at the end of this episode. Even more frustrating, something like that ending *was* shot. It was even included on one of the 'Smeg Up' videos, complete with brilliant 'urine recyc' call-back – just not where it belongs, at the end of the actual episode!

But let's park the last sixty seconds or so, because there's lots of very good stuff here – the characters are clearer and funnier than they've been since *Legion* and the plotting is pretty solid too. I love the opening scene in which

Rimmer establishes himself as morale officer, instigates the first in a series of weekly meetings, insults everyone else present, and then leaves, much happier. And when Lister is injured, we get our first real shock of the story – Lister is a droid! You might think this would be worth an entire episode in itself (in some ways, it's a reverse of *DNA* in Series IV) but this is cancelled out with profligate speed, while Lister is still building intricate log cabins out of chocolate fingers. What we actually have is an unreality minefield – and each one is an opportunity to do a new sketch, to mess with the format in a new way.

The only weird bump in the narrative (other than, again, another spectacular comedy idea is discarded after only a handful of minutes) is the need for Cat and Lister go into stasis. Why has this been included? Why not just make the minefield a bit smaller? There's a very nifty cut once the guys find out what secret the mines were here to protect. On the word 'bingo', we suddenly find ourselves on the time ship. But time travel is useless without a faster-than-light drive, as their jaunt to Renaissance deep space proves. Finally, after the D-plot has created the C-plot, has created the B-plot, we arrive at the A-plot. Our future selves have come to visit – and they're all raging smegheads, even the one reduced to a brain in a jar.

Kryten's attitude to Lister is very funny – knowing his fate but unable to either tell him or contain his emotions – and of course, it's great fun seeing elderly versions of the cast. They do make life hard for themselves by having Kryten welcome their future selves, but making it Lister the one who isn't represented, meaning there are four actors, and four people in the scene, but two of them are played by Robert Llewellyn. Given the nightmare conditions under which this was recorded, it's amazing how good it all looks and how on point the actors are. And I love that Rimmer finally grows a spine. 'Better dead than smeg.' Hurrah!

Then it just stops. Rimmer bazookoids what I think is meant to be the time drive. One *Starbug* shoots down the other – that must mean that the ship with people at the controls shot down the one with everybody on board dead, right? True 'If you kill us, you'll cease to exist', but in a story that included everybody spontaneously turning into animals, that could mean anything. It's a grind to a halt rather than a climax, and it doesn't really work as a cliffhanger, because it wasn't shot that way.

Rob Grant despaired at actors who couldn't say the word 'phenomenon', citing Robert Llewellyn as the only one of the main four who reliably could, but – either due to scripting or acting errors – he usually says 'phenomena' when the singular would make more sense.

The one with: Older us-es.

That Rimmer's a solid guy: This time it seems as if holograms can and do age (and gain weight). He still faints at the sight of blood, but it's okay if it's Lister's. He frets about meeting the crew from the future because, 'What if we discover that one of us is dead? Who could handle that?' Has he forgotten that he's dead?

There's a time and a place: 'Mogadon' is a sleeping tablet. The 3000 series droids are made in Taiwan. The unreality pockets are worse than triple-strength catnip. Lister pleads with Kryten: 'Don't Nixon me, man. Tell me the truth.' Rimmer doesn't want to be thicker than a TV weathergirl. Kryten thinks that his past self looks like he's swapped heads with a damaged crash dummy.

Influences, references and rip-offs: Human-looking mechanical creations sneaking off and living lives as people (some not knowing their true natures) recalls *Blade Runner*. Servants becoming masters recalls *The Prince and the Pauper* by Mark Twain and countless other variations on that theme. Other members of the crew seemingly becoming aware of when and how Lister will die is a lift from *Future Echoes*.

Best gag: 'Is he fat?' 'Far from it. He's lost a bit of weight actually.'

Worst visual effect: Invisible *Starbug*. Both when it vanishes around the boys, and when parts of it disappear as it approaches the time ship.

Continuity is for smegheads: On Christmas Day, they were attacked by that pan-dimensional liquid beast from the Mogadon Cluster. 3000 series mechanoids were not popular – humans find exact duplicates disturbing. That makes Hudzen's humanlike appearance in *The Last Day* somewhat baffling. Lister has an 'I love Petersen' tattoo on his inner thigh. Kryten, who adores doing laundry, is delighted to offload the chore onto mechanoid Lister. (It might not make much sense, but the role-reversal dynamic is very funny.) Having a time drive is useless without the ability to move in space as well. If only they had acquired a handheld teleporter in the previous episode. Yet another mention of Hitler, following appearances in *Timeslides* and *Meltdown*. Last television episode of **Red Dwarf** to involve Rob Grant.

Afterword

And that, for now, is where matters rest. There was no more **Red Dwarf** on television for around four years and when it returned there were many changes. But the story doesn't end here, so come back soon for *Volume II* and read about recreating Dallas in 1963, the return of Kochanski, the return of Holly, the return of Rob Grant (sort of), visiting the set of *Coronation Street*, an episode that failed quality control and very nearly couldn't be transmitted, not to mention the continuing adventures of the boys from the *Dwarf* in novel, comic book, computer game and 'mobisode' form.

Thanks very much for reading and see you in the next volume.

Tom Salinsky
London, October 2023

Appendix

Series I–VI Rankings

S05E06	Back to Reality	★★★★★
S04E05	Dimension Jump	★★★★★
S05E04	Quarantine	★★★★★
S03E04	Bodyswap	★★★★½
S03E02	Marooned	★★★★½
S02E05	Queeg	★★★★½
S10E06	The Beginning	★★★★☆
S01E05	Confidence and Paranoia	★★★★☆
S05E02	The Inquisitor	★★★★☆
S02E01	Kryten	★★★★☆
S01E06	Me^2	★★★★☆
S06E06	Out of Time	★★★★☆
S03E03	Polymorph	★★★★☆
S06E01	Psirens	★★★★☆
S04E04	White Hole	★★★★☆
S05E01	Holoship	★★★½☆
S04E03	Justice	★★★½☆
S06E02	Legion	★★★½☆
S02E06	Parallel Universe	★★★½☆
S02E04	Stasis Leak	★★★½☆
S03E05	Timeslides	★★★½☆
S02E02	Better Than Life	★★★☆☆
S04E02	DNA	★★★☆☆
S01E01	The End	★★★☆☆
S06E03	Gunmen of the Apocalypse	★★★☆☆
S03E06	The Last Day	★★★☆☆
S05E03	Terrorform	★★★☆☆
S04E01	Camille	★★½☆☆
S06E05	Rimmerworld	★★½☆☆

S03E01	Backwards	★★☆☆
S01E03	Balance of Power	★★☆☆
S05E05	Demons & Angels	★★☆☆
S06E04	Emohawk: Polymorph II	★★☆☆
S04E06	Meltdown	★★☆☆
S02E03	Thanks for the Memory	★★☆☆
S01E04	Waiting for God	★☆☆☆

Index

NOTE: Titles of episodes are not included in this index when they appear as their own section, only if they are mentioned elsewhere in the text. Contributors are not indexed when they appear at the top of an episode review, only if they are mentioned elsewhere in the text.

16mm film, 1, 7
1984 (1949 novel), 131
2000AD magazine, 124
2001: A Space Odyssey (1968 movie), 21, 55, 92, 102
2Point4 Children (UK TV series), 145
35mm film, 1
35mm slide(s), 84

Abide with Me (song), 109
Abineri, John, 48
Abraham, Jake, 123
Absolutely (UK comedy series), 115
Absolutely Fabulous (UK TV series), 115, 122
Academy Award, 51, 143
accent, 59–60, 79, 94, 109, 145
Ace (nickname for Rimmer), 47
 see also Rimmer, Ace
Acton Hilton (rehearsal rooms), 10–11, 15, 43, 60, 61, 92
Adams, Douglas, 5, 10, 123
Addams Family, The, 126
Admirable Crichton, The (J.M. Barrie play), 46
adventure game, 126
advertising signs (Victorian, enamelled), 61
adverts, 36, 42
Aeneid, 124
Agnew, Mike, 39, 41, 61–2, 66, 81
Agutter, Jenny, 141
Aigburth Arms, The, 107
air traffic control, 103
airlock, 79, 140

Airplane! (1980 movie), 74
Airtex vest, 131
Ajax, 81
Albanian State Washing Machine Company, 143
Algarve, 128
Alien (1978 movie), 1, 6, 15, 21, 25, 32, 34, 92
Alien (franchise), 79
alien(s), 4, 38, 51, 102, 104, 111
 Rimmer obsessed with, 31, 33, 47, 51
Aliens (1986 movie), 79
Allen, Dave, 2
Allman, Thomas, 125
Alphabetti Spaghetti, 79
alternate universe *see* parallel universe
alternative comedy, 2–3, 58
America, 24, 32, 119, 145
Amstrad, 112
Anderson, Gerry, 81
android *see* mechanoid
angel and devil, 34, 129
Angel Studios, 21
Angels (UK TV series), 43
Angling Times, 141
animatronic, 93, 102, 116–17, 133, 141
Annett, Chloë, 136
Antarctica, 76, 107
anti-matter chopsticks, 134, 143
Apartheid, 132
Apartment, The (1960 movie), 75
A-plot vs B-plot, 31, 80, 149, 152
apocalypse, 146
Apocrypha, 15, 23, 44, 120

appendix (Lister's), 144
Apple II (computer), 122
Arden, Mark, 20
Armitage, Charles, 91, 136
Armitage, Richard, 91
Armstrong, Neil, 57
art college, 46
art department, 16, 94, 133, 134
artificial reality (AR) machine, 145
ASCII, 102
Ash, Debbie, 49
Ash, Leslie, 49
Asimov, Isaac, 49, 53
aspect ratio, 26
asteroid, 21, 75, 147
Astra satellite, 112
AT-AT walker, 52
Atkinson, Geoff, 112–13
Atkinson, Rowan, 2
audience, 74
   at home, 2, 5, 6, 9, 19, 23, 31, 33, 37, 39, 42, 73, 124, 138, 140
   see also ratings
   studio, 7, 10, 11, 16, 17, 20, 27, 38–9, 43, 64, 65–7, 81, 93, 94, 95, 98, 116, 117, 118, 119, 137, 138, 150
audition(s), 7–9, 20, 60, 116, 122
Augins, Charles, 42, 44, 54
autocue, 138
Autry, Gene, 46
Avengers, The (UK TV series), 18
Ayckbourn, Alan, 81

Baby Bud, 51
Babycham, 42
Back to Earth (**Red Dwarf** mini-series), x, 110
Back to Reality (**Red Dwarf** episode), 34, 77, 107, 118, 119, 123, 136, 147, 150
Back to the Future (1985 movie), 83
Back to the Future, Part II (1989 movie), 53, 85
backlot, 136, 137
Backwards (**Red Dwarf** episode), 61–2, 63, 64–5, 67, 77–8, 99, 110, 125, 144
Bader, Douglas, 58
Bailey, Pauline, 98
Balance of Power (**Red Dwarf** episode), 18, 27, 35, 38, 50, 54, 81

Ball, Nicholas, 105
Ballad of High Noon, The (song), 55
Ballard, J.G., 74
Ballard, Kaye, 28
Bambi (deer), 147
Banks, Morwenna, 115
Bankside Power Station, 134
Barber, Frances, 78, 118
Barker, Ronnie, 9
Barrie, Chris, 3, 15, 17, 19, 24, 27, 30, 35, 39, 42, 43, 44, 50, 54, 56, 59, 61, 64, 67, 78, 80, 82, 86, 87, 92, 93, 95, 108, 109, 115, 118, 119, 122, 128, 133, 134, 138, 143, 146
   buff physique, 115, 137
   casting, 7–9
   git overload, 94, 96
   relationship with Craig Charles, 9, 96–7
Barrie, J.M., 46
BASIC (programming language), 105
Bates, Norman, 46, 131
Bathurst, Robert, 10, 16, 25, 29
Batman (1989 movie), 85
Batman (US TV series), 111
battering ram, 107
Battle of Copenhagen, 101
bazookoid(s), 78, 88, 93, 130, 149, 152
BBC, 2, 3, 5, 19, 22, 25, 29, 37, 45, 46, 58, 63, 92, 98, 120
BBC Light Entertainment, 6
BBC Manchester, 6–7, 10, 16, 17, 40, 42, 44, 78
BBC North West, 63
BBC Radio, x, 2, 3, 4, 25, 36, 38, 43, 46, 67
BBC Television Centre *see* Television Centre
BBC1, 8
BBC2, 1, 2, 9, 22, 87, 105, 135
beach, 37, 40, 48, 49, 51, 126, 135
Beardsley, Peter, 48, 102
Beatles, The, 57
Beckett, Samuel, 32
Bellini, Barbara, 104
Benny Hill Show, The (UK TV series), 2
Berlin, 113
Bermuda Triangle (song), 32
Berni Inn, 48
Bertish, Suzanne, 43, 56
Best of Red Dwarf, The, 147

Best Pick (podcast), x
Better than Life (**Red Dwarf** episode), 39–40, 51, 62, 64, 82, 98, 102, 125, 126, 137
Better than Life (**Red Dwarf** novel), 85, 91
Bevan Jones, Hilary, 113
Bewitched (US TV series), 113
Bibby, Mel, 63, 95, 98, 133
Bible (Holy), 144, 146, 150
bicycle clip(s), 109
Big Bang Theory, The (US TV series), 10
Big Broadcast of 1938, The (movie), 51
Bill and Ted's Bogus Journey (1991 movie), 152
Billington, David, 62
Binglebat, Myra, 48, 102
Binks, 123
biscuit tin, 48
black box flight recorder, 104
black cab *see* taxi
black card, 31
Blackadder (UK TV series), 7, 10, 20, 66, 113
Blackpool's Tower Ballroom, 128
Blade Runner (1982 movie), 88, 92, 153
Blaine, Rick, 101
Blake's 7 (UK TV series), x, 5
Blankety Blank (UK TV series), 2
Blob, The (1958 movie), 101
blood pressure, 150
blooper(s) *see* Smeg Ups
blow-up girlfriend *see* inflatable sex doll
Blue Danube, The (music), 102
Blue Midget (spaceship), 47, 51, 52, 63, 82
Blyton, Enid, 2
Bob Newhart Show, The (US TV series), 131
Bodysnatcher (unmade **Red Dwarf** episode), 10, 11, 15
Bodyswap (**Red Dwarf** episode), 31, 59, 63, 66, 101
Bogart, Humphrey, 51, 55, 102
Bonaparte, Napoleon, 49, 98, 101
Bond, James *see* James Bond
Bonehead (nickname for Rimmer), 47, 86
Bongo, 97, 108, 109
book(s):
    about **Red Dwarf**, 1

Biblical, 146
burned, 76
by Barbara Cartland, 53
doing things by the, 127
on CD, 55
read by Danny John-Jules, 25
read by Grant Naylor, 4, 38
read by Lister, 46, 47, 55, 124
read by Rimmer, 105
version of **Red Dwarf**, 4, 28, 35, 48, 49, 54, 62, 63, 69, 85, 91, 119, 139, 144, 154
worst ever written, 34, 76
Boomtown Rats, The, 49
Boop, Betty, 128
boot camp, 110, 111
Borg, The, 105
Boross, Paul, 136
bottom (asteroid shaped like), 54
Bottom (stage show), 87
Bottom (UK TV series), 135, 143
Boulevard Theatre, 2
Bowman, Andy, 18, 19, 40
boxing gloves (nocturnal), 144
B-plot *see* A-plot vs B-plot
Brabin, Tracy, 93
Brando, Marlon, 36, 47, 102
Braun, Eva, 113
Brazil (1985 movie), 131
breakfast cereal, 124, 142, 144
Bride of Frankenstein (1935 movie), 103
Bridge on the River Kwai, The (1957 movie), 55
Briers, Lucy, 122
Briers, Richard, 122
bris, 79
British Embassy, 127
British Empire, 46
British Satellite Broadcasting *see* BSB
Brittas Empire, The (UK TV series), 87, 94, 119
Brittas, Gordon, 87
Brooks, Mel, x
Brown, Carol, 81, 82
Bruce, Angela, 43, 56
BSB, 112
Bubble (*Absolutely Fabulous*), 115
budget, 6, 7

of **Red Dwarf**, 11, 21, 37–8, 56, 63, 68, 91, 93, 98, 110, 114, 132, 136
bulb (need to change), 144
Bulgaria, 141
bunk room, 30, 41, 100, 148
Burden, Howard, 63, 64, 68, 98, 118, 133
Burke, Kathy, 60
Burton, Tim, 85
Bush, President H.W., 143
butler, 38, 46, 82
Bye, Ed, 7, 9, 10, 15, 16, 17, 37, 39, 41, 42, 43, 44, 48, 50, 58, 59, 60, 63, 64, 65, 66, 67–8, 69, 75, 85, 93, 94, 95, 96, 108, 113
   absent, 116, 117
   rendered speechless, 37, 91
   vomiting, 95

C5 *see* Sinclair C5
Caine Mutiny, The (novel and movie), 55, 76
calculator(s), 19
Caligula, 98, 111
Callaghan, 'Dirty' Harry, 81, 105
Calypso Twins, The, 136
camera script, 95, 114, 117, 135
camera(s), 28, 85
   motion control, 21
   rehearsal, 38
   television, 39, 40, 95, 106, 110, 114, 134
      limited number of, 42
   see also photography, Polaroid, slideshow
camerawork, 20, 26, 65, 77, 115, 123, 141
   handheld, 65, 75, 77
Cameron, James, 79
Camille (GELF), 93, 101, 102
Camille (play), 78
Camille (**Red Dwarf** episode), 69, 93, 97, 105
camphor wood, 75–6, 81
Can of Worms (**Red Dwarf** episode), 149
cannibalism, 54
Cannon & Ball (UK TV series), 2
Can't Cook Won't Cook (UK TV series), 137
Can't Smeg Won't Smeg (**Red Dwarf** special), 137
Captain Invisible and the See-Thru Kid, 3
Captain Sadness (nickname for Rimmer), 102

Captain Scarlett (UK TV series), 72
Carcass (band), 68
card (black) *see* black card
Card, Orson Scott, 150
cargo bay, 83
Carlisle, 7
Carpenter, John, 1
Carpenters, The, 55
Carrott, Jasper, 2
Carrott's Lib (UK TV series), 3, 7
Carson, Frank, 3
Cartland, Barbara, 53
cartoon, 2, 34, 47, 73, 74, 129, 146
   illustrations, 15
   single panel, 85
Casablanca (1943 movie), 32, 48, 51, 93, 101, 102, 121, 122, 146
cassette tape (micro), 53, 81
cast (plaster), 41, 51
casting *see* audition(s)
cat (pet), 52
   purchased for research purposes, 4
cat (religion) *see* religion (cat)
Cat Priest, 32, 33
Cat, The, x, 7, 9, 25, 26, 31, 34, 40, 41, 43, 45, 47, 48, 53, 54, 55, 57, 61, 66, 71–2, 73, 74, 78, 80, 81, 82, 83, 84, 95, 97, 102, 103, 105, 106, 107, 109, 110, 111, 116, 117, 119, 123, 124, 127, 128, 136, 138, 142, 144, 146, 147, 149, 151, 152
   evolution of, 1, 4, 18
   hungry, 49, 79
   possibly racist, 8
   profane, 148
   underused, 30, 32, 140,
Catwatching (book), 25
CBS, 20, 143
CD *see* compact disc
ceasefire, 97
cereal *see* breakfast cereal
certificate (content warning), 78
certificate (swimming), 36
CGI, 26, 35, 52, 77, 79, 82, 88, 133
Chain Reaction (Diana Ross song), 44
Champion the Wonder Horse, 46
Changeling, The (*Star Trek*), 88
Channel 27, 49, 142
Channel 4 (UK TV channel), 2, 6, 112, 123

chapel (on *Red Dwarf*), 86
Chapman, Graham, 68
Charles, Craig, 8–9, 19, 21, 24, 27, 32, 33, 35, 36, 43, 44, 60, 61–2, 65, 66, 67, 68, 80, 93, 95, 97, 98, 114–15, 118, 119, 122, 129, 134, 145, 148
  ability to destroy props, 133, 134
  acting, 24, 28, 35, 45, 80, 94, 129
  band, 68
  birth of son, 41
  does all his own stunts, 42, 64, 135, 137
  eats his own dog food, 65
  learning lines, 117, 138
  relationship with Chris Barrie, 9, 96–7
Charles, Emile, 68
Charlton, Bobby, 138
Cheers (US TV series), 60
Chen, 18, 24, 25
chess, 54, 55
Chetham's Hospital School, 2
chicken, 23, 26, 47, 79, 88
  Cat would prefer, 49
  Hollister in costume, 52
  Lister turned into, 103
chicken nugget, 47
Chicken Song, The, 3
Chinese worry balls, 151
chocolate fingers, 152
chopsticks (anti-matter) *see* anti-matter chopsticks
choreography, 42, 44
Christie, Agatha, 34, 50
chromakey, 26, 47, 76, 95, 109, 153
cigarette(s), 23, 25, 36, 59
  eaten spontaneously, 115
cinema (on board *Red Dwarf*), 31, 36, 129
Cinzano Bianco, 107
circumcision, 79
Citizen Kane (1941 movie), 36, 84
civil war *see* English Civil War
class (social structure), 4–5, 49, 59, 79
class traitor, 103
Cleese, John, 9
Clement, Dick, 5
Cliché (UK radio series), 2, 25, 46
  see also Son of Cliché
cliffhanger, 34, 43, 62, 138, 152
clipboard, 25

Clive, Lt Col Robert, 46
cloaking device, 74
Cloister the Stupid, 31, 33
clone(s), 137
Close Encounters of the Third Kind (1977 movie), 6
clothes, 15, 19, 29, 32, 40, 42, 44, 51, 63, 64, 65, 72, 73, 76, 79, 100, 119
  see also costume
clue (blatant), 130
Clues (*Star Trek: The Next Generation*), 51
coffee, 125, 145
Coleman, David, 8
Coleman, Noel, 18, 32
Coleridge, Samuel Taylor, 84
Colonel Bogey (song), 55
Columbo (US TV series), 32, 144
comedian, 2–3, 7, 9, 19, 64, 68, 96, 98
comedy (alternative) *see* alternative comedy
Comedy Store (venue), 2, 137
comic book, 110, 124
  Red Dwarf, 154
Comic Strip, The (comedy team), 2
Commodore Pet (computer), 122
Como, Perry, 103
compact disc, 55, 81, 109
compound interest, 85
computer game (**Red Dwarf**), 154
Confidence and Paranoia (**Red Dwarf** episode), 15, 31, 35, 38, 39, 77, 83, 129
Connell, Richard, 146
Connery, Sean, 9, 21
Conservative Party, 113
convention (fan event), 38, 119
convention (**Red Dwarf**), 1
  see also Dimension Jump (convention)
Cooper, Gary, 146
Copacabana (song), 126
copyright, 93
Corn Flakes, 142
Cornes, Lee, 20, 33–4
Coronation Street (UK TV series), 154
costume, 18–19, 42, 59, 60, 61, 63, 64, 68, 72, 93, 98, 100, 116, 117, 119, 125, 133, 134, 143, 151
Counter-Clock World (1967 novel), 74
Covington Cross (UK TV series), 136
Coward, Noël, 98

cowboys, 145
Crane, Frasier, 60
Crane, Nirvanah, 121–2
Crapola Inc, 107
crash test dummy, 153
Craven, Wes, 146
credits (opening/closing), 18, 20–1, 22, 26, 29, 33, 42, 43, 46, 47, 50, 54, 57, 62, 68, 69, 70, 71, 74, 92, 93, 100, 109, 111, 119, 122, 123, 134, 140, 147
crew evaluations, 33
Crusoe, Robinson *see* Robinson Crusoe
CSO *see* chromakey
cue card(s), 66, 138
Curious Case of Benjamin Button, The (1922 short story), 74
currency, 49, 107
curry, 24, 36, 140, 142, 143
curry monster, 103–104, 116
Curtis, Tony, 124
Cushing, Peter, 74
Czechoslovakia, 101

Dad (unmade **Red Dwarf** episode), 62, 68, 86
Dalek(s), 17, 28
Dallas, 85, 154
Dallas (US TV series), 131
dandruff, 103
Dark Star (1974 movie), 1, 3, 15, 25
Dave (UK digital channel), x
Dave Dee, Dozy, Beaky, Mick & Titch, 84–5
Dave Hollins Space Cadet, 3–4, 8, 36
Davro, Bobby, 113
Day of the Daleks (*Doctor Who*), 28
Daz, 53
DC Comics, 103
de Emmony, Andy, 132, 134, 135, 137
de Niro, Robert, 116
Deadly Assassin, The (*Doctor Who*), 49
Dear Dave (**Red Dwarf** episode), 108
death, 1, 3, 7, 8, 24, 25, 27–8, 29, 36, 48, 49, 51, 57, 75, 88, 100, 101, 104, 106, 110, 115, 122, 123, 125, 128, 142, 149, 150, 151, 152, 153
Defiant Ones, The (1958 movie), 124
Deliverance (1972 movie), 134

Demons & Angels (**Red Dwarf** episode), 34, 114, 119
Dent, Arthur, 5
Dent, George, 87
Descartes, René, 103
desert island, 46
Desert Storm *see* Operation Desert Storm
despair squid, 131
Devitt, Matthew, 43, 56
Dewynters, 69, 76, 85, 119
Dibbley, Duane, 119, 131, 136, 147, 148, 149
dice (furry) *see* furry dice
Dick, Philip K., 73
Dick Van Dyke Show, The (US TV series), 113
dictator(s), 30, 86
Die Hard II (1990 movie), 104
Dietz, Howard, 51
Dimension Jump (fan event), 119
Dimension Jump (**Red Dwarf** episode), 77, 96, 98, 99, 100, 123, 130, 136, 147
directives (Space Corps) *see* Space Corps
director, 84
  of 'Androids', 46
  of **Red Dwarf**, 7, 16, 21, 39, 68, 113, 119, 132, 134, 138
    see also Bye, Ed; de Emmony, Andy; May, Juliet
Dirty Dozen, The (1967 movie), 111
Dirty Harry *see* Callaghan, 'Dirty' Harry
disc (hologram) *see* hologram, disc
disc jockey, 88, 128
Disney (animation studio), 34
Disney+ (streaming service), 1
display (heads up) *see* heads-up display
DiStefano, Dona, 16, 42
Diva-Droid International, 88, 126
Dixon of Dock Green (UK TV series), 18
Dixon, Reggie, 128
DJ *see* disc jockey
DNA machine, 102–104
DNA (molecule), 149, 151
DNA (**Red Dwarf** episode), 94, 105, 142, 148, 152
Dobson, Anita, 133
Docherty, Jack, 115–16
Doctor Who (UK TV series), x, 5, 17, 18, 21, 28, 36, 49, 53, 68

dog, 53
dog food, 65, 75
Dog, The, 43, 56
dollarpound(s), 49, 107
Domestos, 81
Donovan, Jason, 46
double, 42, 52, 62, 79, 129, 133–4
Doyle, Billy, 131
draughts (game), 55
dreadlocks, 67, 82
dream(s), 40, 41, 44, 49, 131, 145–6
Dreaming is a Private Thing (short story), 49
Dreamscape (1984 movie), 146
drive plate, 26, 82, 84
droid rot, 94
Drop the Dead Donkey (UK TV series), 87
drugs, 30
dubbing (sound), 1, 26, 31, 47, 59, 65, 67, 68–9, 80, 82, 105, 116
Duke, nickname for Rimmer, 102
Dumas, Alexandre, 126
duty-free, 141
Duvitski, Janine, 60
DVD (**Red Dwarf**), 15, 44, 97, 98, 114, 139

Ealing Studios, 6
Earth (planet), 1, 29, 74, 77, 110, 140, 144, 147
  Backwards, 73, 144
Earthshock (*Doctor Who*), 68
Eastbourne, 107, 148
EastEnders (UK TV series), 21
Easy Rider (1969 movie), 47
Edinburgh, 60, 61
Edinburgh Fringe, 58, 61, 62
editing (of **Red Dwarf**), 17, 44, 64, 65, 68, 72, 86, 91, 115, 116, 117, 119, 124
Edmondson, Adrian, 2, 7, 135
effects *see* CGI, sound effects, special effects, video effects
Einstein, Albert, 98
Electrical, Electronic, Telecommunication and Plumbing Union, 11
Elephant Man, The, 103
Ellison, Harlan, 124
Elton, Ben, 3, 6
Emohawk: Polymorph II (**Red Dwarf** episode), 136, 137, 149

End, The (**Red Dwarf** episode), 8, 17, 31, 44, 52, 54, 62, 106, 150
Ender's Game (1985 novel), 150
Enemy Within, The (*Star Trek*), 129
English Civil War, 148
escape pod, 147, 149, 151
Eskimo, 107
Esperanto (language), 45, 48
Esperanto, SSS, 119
Evil Dead II (1987 movie), 126
Evil Dead, The (1981 movie), 29
Ewing, Pamela, 131
exam(s), 20, 24, 25, 30, 31, 33, 46, 106
eye, 149
exercise (physical), 28, 35, 55, 57, 150
explosion, 20, 34, 83, 86, 117, 137, 138, 145, 151
  see also special effects

Falconberger, Blaize, 84
false perspective, 95, 98
fan (devotee), 6, 16, 20, 21, 113
  of (**Red Dwarf**), xii, 1, 5, 42, 59, 60, 65, 92, 96, 119, 133, 139, 145
  theories by, 59, 84, 96
fan (industrial), 59, 63, 96
fan club(s) (**Red Dwarf**), 1, 99
fan convention *see* convention (fan event)
fascism, 30, 86, 110, 130
fashion, 109, 142, 143, 151
fatherhood, 43, 56, 62, 95
Fawkham, 135
Fawlty Towers (UK TV series), x, 87
Female Eunuch, The (book), 57
Ferguson, Craig, 20, 33–4
Fiddler on the Roof (musical), 85
Fields, W.C., 122
fighter pilot, 4, 58, 97, 108
Fiji, 24, 26
film(s) *see* movie(s)
film (16mm) *see* 16mm film
film (35mm) *see* 35mm film
film can, 48
Filofax, 1, 28
Filthy, Rich and Catflap (UK TV series), 7
firing squad, 110
fish and chip shop (Welsh), 150
Fistful of Datas, A (*Star Trek: The Next Generation*), 146

Fitzgerald, Ella, 51
Fitzgerald, F. Scott, 49, 74
Five Go Mad in Dorset (*The Comic Strip Presents…*), 2
Five O'Clock Club, The (UK TV series), 105
flares (trousers), 3, 143
flashback, 18, 30, 52, 108
Flea in Her Ear, A (play), 58
Fletcher, Norman Stanley, 5
Flibble, Mr, 117, 127
Flintstones, The (US TV series), 73
floor manager, 2, 16, 41, 42, 66, 81, 115
  see also Agnew, Mike; DiStefano, Dona
Flowers for Algernon (novel), 107
flu (gastric), 95
Fly Me to the Moon (song), 28
folk song, 130
food, 29, 32, 35, 45, 50, 65, 75, 76, 79, 81, 82, 108, 126, 129, 134, 136, 142, 148
Football, It's a Funny Old Game (fictional book), 34
Footlights (Cambridge), 10
Forbidden Planet (1956 movie), 126
forehead H, 15, 72, 74, 95, 119
Foster, Jodie, 81
Four Horsemen of the Apocalypse, 146
Fowler, Michelle, 21
Francis, of Assisi, 122
Frankenstein (1818 novel), 25, 128
Frankenstein (cat), 25, 83
Frankenstein's monster, 105, 143
Freaky Friday (1976 movie), 81
free will, 95
Freemasons, 109
French windows, 6
French, Dawn, 2, 3
Friday the 13th (film series), 49
fridge logic, 82, 84
From Here to Eternity (1953 movie), 51
Frost, Mark, 118
Frost, Steve, 20
fruit machine, 103
Fry, Stephen, 134, 142
Full Metal Jacket (1987 movie), 111
Full Wax, The (UK TV series), 113
Fun, Fun, Fun (song) *see* theme music
funeral, 24, 26
furry dice, 109

Fushal, 32
Future Echoes (**Red Dwarf** episode), 19, 20, 33, 41, 47, 49, 57, 62, 74, 82, 106, 125, 153

Gaffney, Simon, 86, 109
gallows, 110
Galton, Ray, 3, 9
gambling, 85
game, 39, 48, 54, 55, 111, 118, 123, 126, 130, 131, 146, 150
  see also adventure game, chess, computer game, draughts, Risk, Total Immersion Video Game
game-hunter(s), 146
Gamesmaster (UK TV series), 95
Gandalf, 126
Gandhi, Mohandas, 98
Ganymede and Titan (song) *see* Lunar City 7
Ganymede Holiday Inn, 41
Garbage World, 91
Garden of Eden, 150
gauntlet, 124
GBH (UK TV serial), 123
gee-gooks (supposed measurement of distance), 144
Geldof, Bob, 49
GELF(s), 69, 77, 93, 101, 102, 106, 136, 147, 148
German(s), 25
Gershwin, George, 51
ghost, 25, 141
GI Joe (doll), 88
Gibson, William, 49
Giftie, The (UK TV play), 36
gilded cage, 143, 144
Gilliam, Terry, 131
Gilman, Charlotte Perkins, 57
gingham, 127
Girl Who Was Death, The (*The Prisoner*), 125
Girls on Top (UK TV series), 7
Glasgow, 60
glove puppet *see* puppet
God, 103, 150
golf, 76, 86
Gone with the Wind (1939 movie), 53
Good Life, The (UK TV series), 5

Goodall, Howard, 20, 26, 43–4, 55, 68, 69, 93, 145
Goodbye to Love (song), 55
Goodyear blimp, 81
Google (better not to), 98
Göring, Hermann, 30
grade (picture), 26, 49
Grammer, Kelsey, 60
Granada (UK media company), 112
Grand Canyon, 107
Grant Naylor (pseudonym), 62, 119
Grant Naylor (writing team), 1, 2–3, 5, 7, 8, 10, 11, 15, 16, 19, 20, 27, 31, 34, 38, 41, 42–3, 48, 54, 58, 60, 62, 64, 66, 69, 72, 79, 83, 85, 94, 97, 101, 108, 113, 114, 116, 118, 120, 122, 123, 125, 132, 135, 136, 137, 142, 145
   as directors, 117, 119
   as editors, 91, 116, 117, 119
   as producers, 91, 133
     painted into corner, 138, 151
     plagiarising selves, 46, 141
Grant Naylor Productions, 69–70, 91, 132
Grant, Jo, 28
Grant, Rob, 16, 24, 32, 66, 68–9, 97, 119, 135, 138, 152, 153, 154
   as director, 118
   continuity, 92
   late scripts, 137–8
   see also Grant Naylor (writing team)
grassy knoll, 148
Great British Bake Off, The (UK TV series), 30
Great Gatsby, The (1925 novel), 49
Greek mythology, 141
Greenwood, Kali, 109
Greer, Germaine, 57
Gregory's Girl (1981 movie), 17
Grogan, C.P., 17, 31, 41–2, 54, 93, 133, 140, 142
groinal socket *see* socket (groinal)
guitar, 69, 86, 133–4
   Lister's, 32, 75, 76, 141, 147
Gulf War, 4
Gulliver's Travels (1726 novel), 32
Gunmen of the Apocalypse (**Red Dwarf** episode), 135–6, 137, 149
Guns of Navarone, The (1961 movie), 110

Guthrie, Thomas Anstey, 81
Gwenlan, Gareth, 5–6, 46

H (forehead) *see* forehead H
Hab (fictional computer), 3
Haggard, H. Rider, 147
haggises (irradiated), 30
hairdresser, 28
HAL 9000, 55
Halloween (1978 movie), 1
hallucinations (solid), 33
Hammer, Mike, 3
Hammond organ, 109, 128
Hammy the Hamster, 101–102
handheld cameras *see* camerawork
handprint, 124
handshake, 109, 148
hangover, 51, 61, 119
Happy Families (UK TV series), 6
hard light, 134, 142, 143, 144
   remote belt, 150
Hardy, Robert, 55
Hardy, Thomas, 55
Harriot, Ainsley, 136–7
Harris, Barbara, 81
Harrods (department store), 74
Hauer, Rutger, 86
Hawks, Tony, 16, 19, 48, 72, 98, 113
   as The Fabulous Tony, 64
Hayridge, Hattie, 27, 43, 56, 60, 69, 72, 74, 86, 93, 97, 105, 106, 108, 131, 132
   underused, 36, 78, 115
   heads-up display, 88, 126
Hearst, William Randolph, 126
Hefner, Hugh, 49
Heil Honey I'm Home (abandoned UK TV series), 113–14
Hell's Angels, 28
Helm, Matt, 125
Henry, Lenny, 2, 3
Here We Go (song), 26
Herland (1915 novel), 57
Hess, Rudolph, 105
High Noon (1952 movie), 146
Hill, Eric, 46
Hilly (computer), 43, 60
hippy, 129, 150
Hitchcock, Alfred, 46, 81, 131

Hitchhiker's Guide to the Galaxy, The, x, 5, 10, 27, 62, 85, 127
Hitler, Adolf, 85, 98, 110, 111, 113, 153
Hoare, John, 11
Hoffman, Dustin, 84
Holden, Thicky, 84
Hollins, Dave *see* Dave Hollins, Space Cadet
Hollister, Captain, 4, 8, 9, 18, 51, 52, 53, 84
Holly (computer), 4, 9, 25, 26, 27, 28, 29, 32, 33, 34, 35, 40, 42, 43, 47, 53, 54, 55, 60–1, 69, 72, 73, 76, 77, 80, 81, 82, 83, 88, 96, 108, 109, 141, 147
   hair length, 100, 121
   IQ, 28, 106
   new material, 26, 35
   underused, 78, 122, 127
   video effect, 26, 47, 72
Hollymobile, 40
Holmes, Sherlock *see* Sherlock Holmes
holocage, 50
Holodeck (*Star Trek: The Next Generation*), 146, 147
hologram, 17, 27, 28, 39, 58, 73, 93, 115
   abilities, 29, 30, 32, 34, 55, 57, 81, 101, 107, 149, 153
   Alfred Molina's concerns, 9
   disc, 31, 81
   hard light, 134, 142, 143, 144, 146, 148, 150
   Kochanski, 10, 15, 31
   newsreader, 49
   power needed to sustain, 34, 36, 53, 122, 128, 129, 141
   Rimmer resurrected as, 1, 27, 46, 48, 83–4
   visual signifier, 15, 24, 26
   vulnerabilities, 24, 126–7, 129, 150, 151
hologram simulation suite, 51
Holoshop (**Red Dwarf** episode), 115, 124, 125
holo-virus, 128
holo-whip, 129
home video *see* DVD, VHS
homophobia, 108, 129
Hope, Bob, 51
Horrocks, Jane, 115, 121
horse(s), 24, 46, 135, 146

hostage, 80
hotdog, 129
Howard, Bart, 28
Hudzen-10 (mechanoid), 68–9, 86, 88, 153
Hugo, Victor, 32
Huis Clos (play), 30, 75
hunt-the-monster, 103, 116, 148
Hylton, Terry, 133
hypochondria, 41

I Love Lucy (US TV series), 113
I, Lovett (UK TV series), 60
If I Were a Rich Man (song), 85
Iliad, 124
impression(s), 7–8, 42, 54–5, 67, 80, 128
India, 46
Indian food *see* curry
Indian restaurant, 36
Infinite Improbability Drive, 127
Infinity Welcomes Careful Drivers (**Red Dwarf** novel), 4, 28, 62, 69, 85, 91
inflatable sex doll, 55, 86, 106, 144
in-flight magazine, 109
Inland Revenue, 49
Inquisitor, The, 116, 123–5, 144
Inquisitor, The (**Red Dwarf** episode), 115–16, 144, 146, 148
internet, 69
Ionian Nerve Grip, 144
iPhone, 1
IQ, 28, 53, 107
Iron Duke (codename for Rimmer), 111
Ishtar (1987 movie), 84, 86
It's A Wonderful Life (1946 movie), 83, 85, 124
Izzard, Eddie, 98

Jackson, Michael (singer), 76, 88
Jackson, Paul, 2–3, 5–9, 10–12, 17, 20, 37, 38–9, 41, 42, 44, 58, 60, 62–3, 91, 96, 113–14
   absent, 116, 117
   taking over as director, 95–6
Jackson, T. Leslie, 2
Jacuzzi, 59
Jaguar (E-type), 40
James Bond, 109
Janine (Rimmer's sister-in-law), 102

Index

Jaws (1974 movie), 104
Jazz FM (UK radio station), 103
Jeeves and Wooster (stories), 104
Jesus, 144
Joeys, The, 58
John-Jules, Danny, 9, 25, 32, 34, 42, 44, 57, 61, 69, 93, 95–6, 97, 118, 119, 135, 137, 138, 148
Jongleurs, 16
Judd, Justin, 132
Judge Dredd (*2000AD* character), 124
Judge Dredd (1995 movie), 134
Julia, Raul, 146
Junior Birdmen, 126
Junior Encyclopaedia of Space, 74
Jupiter Mining Corporation, 45, 51
Justice (**Red Dwarf** episode), 55, 95, 148
Justice Complex, 95
Justice World, 104

Kafka, Franz, 105
Karloff, Boris, 143
Keaton, Michael, 85
Keegan, Kevin, 34
Kendall, Felicity, 54
Kennedy, Gordon, 68, 86, 105, 115
Kennedy, John F., 149
Kenny Everett Video Show, The (UK TV series), 95
Kenobi, Obi-Wan, 4
Kent, 135
Kerr, Deborah, 51
Keyes, Daniel, 107
Kick Up the Eighties, A (UK TV series), 2
Kilborn, Craig, 20
Kind Hearts and Coronets (1949 movie), 6
King Kong (1933 movie), 141
King of Kings: The Story of Jesus (1961 movie), 122
king of the potato people, 128
kippers, 108
Kirk, Captain (from **Red Dwarf** novel), 4
Kirk, Captain James T., 88, 129, 146
kiss, 43, 51, 88, 93
klick (measurement of distance), 149
Kochanski, Kristine, 23, 41, 52, 53, 81, 84, 92, 93, 133, 140, 142, 154
  hologram, 10, 15, 29, 31, 83
  original casting, 10
  relationship with Lister, 30, 104
Kryten (mechanoid), x, 23, 38, 39, 46, 47, 58, 61, 69, 71, 72, 74, 77–8, 80, 81, 84, 85, 86, 87, 88, 92–3, 96, 101, 102, 105, 107, 110, 114, 116, 117, 121, 122, 123, 124, 128, 131, 132, 133, 138, 140, 142, 144, 145, 149, 151, 152, 153
  ability to lie, 100, 125
  brain, 104, 126, 142
  spare heads, 94, 103
  transformed into human, 94, 103
Kryten (**Red Dwarf** episode), 39, 51, 57, 62, 71, 86
Kubrick, Stanley, 21, 55
kung fu, 129
Kuwait, 4

La Forge, Geordi, 33
La Frenais, Ian, 5
lager, 44, 69, 104, 143
Lancaster, Burt, 51
Lance Bland News Hound, 3
Land that Time Forgot, The (1974 movie), 73
landfill, 41
Lanstrom, Dr, 127–8
Laredo Western Town, 135–6
Last Day, The (**Red Dwarf** episode), 68, 100, 102, 105, 148, 153
Last Human (**Red Dwarf** novel), 144
Last, James, 110, 126
Late Late Show, The (US TV series), 20
laugh track, 10, 39, 65, 67, 81, 118, 150
Laughton, Charles, 55
Laurel and Hardy, 107
Laurel, Stan, 98
Laurie, Hugh, 7
Lazlo, Victor, 101
Leach, Robin, 84
leaflet campaign (major, and I do mean major), 78
Legend of Xanadu, The (song), 84
Legion (character), 142, 144
Legion (**Red Dwarf** episode), 134, 145, 151
Leicester, 132
lemming(s), 124, 146
Lemmon, Jack, 75
Lemons (**Red Dwarf** episode), 151

Lenahan, John, 19, 96
Letter to Brezhnev (1985 movie), 8
Levi jeans, 148
Lewis, C.S., 85
Liaisons Dangereuses, Les (play), 7
lie (falsehood), 88, 100, 101, 125
Lifestyles of the Rich and Famous (US TV series), 84
lift (elevator), 16, 53, 128
light bee, 111, 141, 150
Light Entertainment, 46
light speed, 28
lighting, 39, 63, 67, 95, 123, 136
Lincoln, Abraham, 98
lipstick, 43
Liquorice Allsorts, 143
Lister, David, x, 1, 4, 7, 17, 19, 24, 26, 27, 29, 30, 31, 35, 40, 41, 43, 47, 51, 53, 54, 55, 61, 62, 65, 66, 68, 72, 73, 74, 75, 76, 78, 79, 80, 81, 82, 83, 84, 88, 93, 95, 97, 103, 106, 107, 109, 110, 111, 117, 121, 123, 124, 125, 128, 129, 131, 137, 138, 141, 142, 143, 144, 145, 146, 148, 149, 150, 152, 153
   costume, 45, 100, 118
   descendants, 28, 57, 130
   doubled, 52, 129, 133–4
   fear of tarantulas, 116, 126, 130
   musical prowess, 69, 83, 85–6, 134
   painting the ship, 26, 21
   promotion, 10, 18
   reading, 46, 47, 76, 124
   reduced to one foot tall, 95, 104
   relationship with Kochanski, 10, 15, 23, 30, 53, 92, 93, 104, 133
   relationship with Rimmer, 23, 27, 30, 50, 140
Lister, Deb, 56
Live Aid, 49
Liverpool, 8, 61, 64, 68
Liverpool University, 2
Llewellyn, Robert, 38, 46, 58, 59, 60, 62, 64, 65, 68, 69, 71, 74, 77, 86, 87, 96, 97, 103, 109, 133, 138, 148, 152
   long speeches, 65–6, 78, 108
   make-up, 47, 59, 61, 78, 92–3, 94, 95, 100, 121
Lloyd, Christopher, 8

Lloyd, John, 2, 5, 7, 22, 69
location filming, 6, 37–8, 39–40, 41, 42, 48, 49, 50, 59, 61, 64, 95, 98, 133, 134, 135, 136, 137, 145
logo (**Red Dwarf**), 69–70, 76, 85, 119, 122
Lolita (1955 novel), 76
London, 2, 7, 9, 16, 18, 19, 22, 44, 60, 61, 69, 72, 118, 136
lookalikes, 110
Looney Tunes, 34
Loretta (sprite), 146
Lovecraft, H.P., 126
Lovett, Norman, 9, 17, 25, 36, 40, 42, 54, 60–1, 74
luck virus, 127
Lumley, Joanna, 115
Lunar City 7 (song), 29, 36
Lund, Ilsa, 101
Lynch, David, 118

Mackintosh, Cameron, 105
magazine, 25, 55, 84, 86, 109, 119, 124, 128, 141, 143
Mahler, Gustav, 21
make-up, 15, 18, 24, 29, 63, 67, 118, 129
   Holly, 43, 96
   Kryten, 59, 61, 92–3, 94, 95
Malden, Karl, 102
Mammon: Robot Born of Woman (Fringe show), 58
Man from UNCLE, The (US TV series), 111
Man without a Face, The (*Sapphire & Steel*), 85
Manchester, 1, 2, 7, 8, 11, 15, 17, 18, 19, 22, 41, 43, 58, 60, 61, 65, 92
Manilow, Barry, 32
Manning, Bernard, 3
Manzanera, Phil (hands of), 134
Marigolds, 54
Mark (disciple), 144
Mark, Clayton, 98
Marksman, The (UK TV series), 45
Marooned (**Red Dwarf** episode), 29, 59, 63, 65, 77, 78, 79
Marshall, Rocky, 78
Marvel comics, 124
Marx Brothers, x

mask (costume), 116, 123
mask (prosthetic), 38, 47, 78, 92–3, 94, 100, 121
Mason *see* Freemasons, 109
Matrix, The (1999 movie), 49
Matrix, The (*Doctor Who*), 49
matter paddle, 110, 111, 130
May, Brian, 133
May, Elaine, 84
May, Juliet, 113–17, 119, 132
Mayall, Rik, 2, 3, 7, 135
Mayor of Warsaw, 34
McClure, Doug, 73, 143
McCoy, Dr Leonard 'Bones', 146
McDonald, Mac, 9, 18, 25, 41, 54
McDonald's (restaurant chain), 47
McGrew, Dan, 146
McGruder, Yvonne, 34, 49, 76
McIntyre, George, 17, 24, 53
McKellan, Ian, 134
McNugget *see* chicken nugget
McQueen, Steve, 101
Me and My Girl (musical), 91
Me² (**Red Dwarf** episode), 15, 18, 20, 62, 80, 149
mechanoid(s), 38, 39, 46, 58–9, 68–9, 77, 85, 87, 88, 93, 94, 100–101, 102, 105, 109, 152, 153
  see also Kryten, Hudzen-10
Meddings, Derek, 21
Melissa V (spaceship), 4
Mellie, 97, 108
Meltdown (**Red Dwarf** episode), 97, 98, 125, 136, 138, 149, 153
Memories Are Made of This (song), 103
memory, 15, 16, 18, 22, 30, 50–1, 76, 84, 107, 125, 126, 143, 144
Mendelssohn, Felix, 30
merchandise, 44
Merton, Paul, 53
Mickey Mouse, 128
microcassette *see* cassette tape (micro)
Midland Hotel, 41
milk (dog's), 45
military grey *see* ocean grey
Miller, Glenn, 103
Milne, Gareth, 64
Minogue, Kyle, 46

Miranda, Carmen, 57
Mirror Universe (*Star Trek*), 57
Mitchell, Bill, 78
Mitchell, Pete 'Maverick', 109
mobile phone(s), 1
mobisode, 154
model (miniature), 21, 26, 38, 63, 74, 81, 117, 123, 126, 138, 142, 146
Mogadon, 153
Molina, Alfred, 8–9, 73, 149
money, 76
Moneypenny, Miss, 97
Monroe, Marilyn, 49, 54, 84, 88, 98, 111
monster, 66, 77–9, 93–4, 116, 148
  curry, 103, 104
Montague, Paul, 15, 20
Monty Python, 10, 51, 68, 74
moon, 57, 126, 145
Mooney, Karl, 133
moral choice, 75
More, Kenneth, 46
Morecambe & Wise Show, The (UK TV series), 2
Morris, Desmond, 25
Morris Minor's Marvellous Motors (UK TV series), 113
Moss Bros., 28, 148
Most Dangerous Game, The (1924 short story), 146
motion control, 21
motorbike, 110
Motörhead, 30
movie(s), 1, 6, 8, 15, 18, 21, 28, 38, 61, 85, 92, 112, 114, 134, 147
  referenced in script, 34, 36, 47, 49, 51, 53, 55, 57, 73, 74, 76, 81, 84, 85, 88, 93, 101, 104, 109, 111, 122, 124, 125, 126, 131, 143, 145, 146
  watched by characters, 48, 49, 78, 121, 143
Mozart, Wolfgang Amadeus, 30
Mr Bean (UK TV series), 20
Mr Fat Bastard 2044, 51
Munsters, The (US TV series), 143
Murder on the Orient Express (1934 novel), 34
Murdoch, Rupert, 73, 112
Murphy, Eddie, 6

music, 20–1, 26, 29, 30, 31, 33, 36, 43–4, 46, 49, 52, 55, 57, 68, 69, 71, 82, 84, 88, 93, 109, 112, 133–4, 136, 141, 145, 147
 see also guitar, song, theme music
musical, 44, 76, 85, 91, 105
Mutiny on the Bounty (novel and movie), 55
mutton, 143
My Life in Football (2018 book), 34
mythology, Greek see Greek mythology

naff, 5
Napoleon see Bonaparte, Napoleon
Narnia, 85
Naylor, Doug, 4, 7, 29, 39, 44, 51, 56, 61, 98, 114, 135, 144
 artificial leg, 4, 59
 continuity, 92
 editor, 119
 taught important lesson by Rob Grant, 137–8
 see also Grant Naylor (writing team)
Nazi, 30, 85, 110, 113
Nearer My God to Thee (song), 109
Neighbours (Australian soap opera), 46
Neil (*The Young Ones*), 66
Netflix (streaming service), 26, 92
nepotism see rule one of show business
Never Give a Sucker an Even Break (1941 movie), 122
New Yorker, The (magazine), 85
Newcastle Brown Ale, 76
Newhart (US TV series), 131
newsreader, holographic, 49
Newton-John, Olivia, 53, 85
Nielsen, Brigitte, 88
Nightingale, Florence, 105
Nightmare on Elm Street, A (1984 movie), 146
Nixon, Richard M., 153
No Way Out (play) see Huis Clos
Noel Gay Television, 91, 136
Nomad (*Star Trek*), 88
Norweb, 55
Nostromo (spaceship), 21
Not the Nine O'Clock News (UK TV series), 2, 20, 113
Nova 5 (spaceship), 38, 46, 47, 50, 103

novel (**Red Dwarf**), 4, 28, 35, 48, 49, 62, 63, 69, 91, 119, 144, 154
 see also book
NOW TV (UK streaming service), 26
nugget see chicken nugget
Nuremberg rally, 85
Nutkin see Squirrel Nutkin

Oates, Captain Lawrence, 107
O'Bannon, Dan, 1
observation dome, 41, 49, 52
ocean grey see military grey
Odor Eaters, 51
Officer and a Gentleman, An (1982 movie), 111
Old Iron Butt (nickname for Rimmer), 149
Old Vic (theatre), 58
Olivier Award, 78, 81
Olivier, Laurence, 76
Om (song), 68
On the Waterfront (1954 movie), 36
Operation Desert Storm, 97
Operation Valkyrie, 85
organ (pipe), 21
Orwell, George, 131
Oscar see Academy Award
Osmond family, 79
Osmond, Jimmy, 51
O'Sullivan, Richard, 36
Ouroboros (**Red Dwarf** episode), 57
Out of Time (**Red Dwarf** episode), 138
Outland (1981 movie), 21
Overdrawn at the Memory Bank (TV movie), 146
Oxbridge, 7
Oxford Road Show, The (UK TV series), 113
Oxford Road studio, 10–11, 67, 92
oxygen (tank), 104

painting, 15, 16, 21, 26, 41, 48, 52, 63, 81, 85, 112, 117, 124
 see also make-up
paper (in the future), 25, 48
paradise, 82, 126, 135, 137
parallel universe, 43, 56, 57, 108, 109, 123, 125, 130

Parallel Universe (**Red Dwarf** episode), 27, 41, 43–4, 62
Paris Studio, 67
parrot(s), 105
Parrot's (bar), 101
Partridge, Alan, 147
Pascoe, Judy, 93
Patton (1970 movie), 143
Patton, General George S., 111, 143
Paul Jackson Productions, 5
Paul, Les, 75
Paxo, 53
PBS, 51, 146
Pearson, 112
Pember, Ron, 48
penal colony, 104
Pennell, Andrea, 92, 96, 118
Perrier (award), 58
Perrier (water), 49
Pete Tranter's sister, 140–1
Petersen, Olaf, 18, 24, 29, 41, 52, 54, 84, 153
photocopier(s), 102, 150
photography, 17–18, 25, 29, 53, 67–8, 82–5, 86, 94, 103, 105
Pigg, Alexandra, 9, 17
pilot, 81, 140
  see also fighter pilot
pilot (episode), 4, 10, 23, 27, 141
pilot (script), 3, 7
Pinewood Studios, 92
Pinky and Perky, 49
pizza, 76, 127
Planer, Nigel, 2, 7, 66
Planet of the Apes (1968 movie), 53, 150
play (theatre), x, 7, 10, 30, 32, 46, 53, 57, 58, 62, 65, 76, 78, 81
Playback (*Columbo*), 144
Playboy (magazine), 49
Pleasance, Donald, 128
pod, 31, 33, 86, 88, 104, 106, 147, 149, 151
podcast(s), x, 1
Points of View (UK TV series), 5
Poitier, Sidney, 124
Polari, 5
Polaroid, 28, 29, 84
  double, 94, 103
poll (of **Red Dwarf** fans), 119

Pollock, Jackson, 88
polymorph (prop), 78, 104, 136
polymorph (creature), 77–9, 116, 147–9
Polymorph (**Red Dwarf** episode), 34, 65, 103, 104, 107, 147, 148, 149
Pomphrey, John, 67
pool (cue sport), 88, 106, 130
pool (swimming), 40
Popeye (cartoon character), 103
pork pie jelly, 65
Porridge (UK TV series), 3, 5, 30, 105
post, 49
Pot Noodle, 76, 129, 130
Potter, Beatrix, 103
POV (abbreviation), 114
practical joke, 55, 80, 137
pregnancy, 43, 56, 62
prerecording, 16, 20, 38, 61, 64, 116, 149
Presley, Elvis, 98, 111
press launch, 44
pretzel logic, 52, 67, 82
Primordial Soup: The Least Worst Scripts (book), 139
Prince and the Pauper, The (1881 novel), 153
printer (dot matrix), 143
prison, 104, 105
Prisoner, The (UK TV series), 125
producer(s), 1, 2–3, 7, 15, 17, 39, 60, 62, 63, 105, 113, 114, 116, 117, 132
Promised Land, The (**Red Dwarf** episode), x, 60, 63, 150
Psirens (creatures), 140–1
Psirens (**Red Dwarf** episode), 133
Psycho (1960 movie), 46, 131
Psy-moon, 126
P.T. *see* exercise (physical)
pub, 9, 16, 24, 43, 65, 84, 88
Pugwash (UK TV series), 18
pun, 101
punishment detail, 52
puppet(s), 2, 18, 49, 105, 116, 117, 132
  see also animatronic
Pussycat Willum, 105

Quaid, Dennis, 146
quality control, 154
Quantel, 103

quarantine, 33, 34, 127
Quarantine (**Red Dwarf** episode), 107, 117, 119, 133
Quayle, Dan, 143–4
Queeg (**Red Dwarf** episode), 39, 42, 51, 57, 75, 76, 79, 107
Queeg 500 (fictional computer), 42, 80
Queen (band), 133
Question of Sport, A (UK TV series), 6
quicksand, 126

Rachel (sex doll) *see* inflatable sex doll
racism, 8, 97
radio (communications), 76, 115, 127
  see also BBC radio
radio control *see* remote control
Radio Times, 25, 69
Random Quest (short story), 36
ratings (viewers), 2, 6, 22, 44, 62, 69, 87, 91, 119
Ray, Nicholas, 122
Raymond, Teasie Weasie, 28
Reagan, Ronald, 8
Reaper, Jim, 86
Rebel Without a Cause (1955 movie), 47
red alert, 144
Red Dwarf (spaceship), 4, 39, 46, 56, 63, 71, 76, 77, 87, 102, 104, 115, 117, 123, 128, 147, 148
  CGI version, 26, 77
  model, 21, 80, 117, 123
Red Dwarf Remastered, xi, 24, 71, 78
Red Dwarf Smegazine, 119
Red Dwarf USA, 23, 27, 119–20, 141
Red Queen's Race, 53
Rediffusion, 105
rehearsal, 10–11, 15, 37, 38, 43, 61, 92, 138
religion, 31–2, 87–8
  cat, 10, 47, 86, 87
remastered *see Red Dwarf Remastered*
remote control, 18, 129, 151
Renaissance, 152
repeat (of **Red Dwarf** episodes), 37, 92, 98, 139
Restaurant at the End of the Universe, The, 85
Revenger's Comedies, The (play), 81
Reynolds, Charles, 98

Rhatigan, Suzanne, 93
Rhyl, North Wales, 40
Rhys Jones, Griff, 2
Richard III (1995 movie), 134
Richard III (play), 57, 76
Richard, Cliff, 76, 77
Richardson, Peter, 2
Rickman, Alan, 7–8
Ridsdale-Scott, Peter, 7, 10, 11–12, 22, 42, 44, 58, 67
Rigsby, Rupert, 87
Rimmer, Ace, 69, 96, 97, 108, 119, 136, 147–8
  real life version of, 4
  with death wish, 150
Rimmer, Arlene, 56
Rimmer, Arnold, x, 4, 10, 18, 19, 24, 27, 32, 33, 34, 35, 40, 43, 45, 46, 56, 61, 65, 66, 72, 74, 75, 78, 80, 81, 82, 83, 84, 87, 88, 101, 103, 104, 105, 107, 108, 110, 111, 115, 121, 122, 124, 126, 128, 129, 131, 133, 138, 142, 144, 145, 147, 148, 149, 150, 152
  casting, 7, 9, 20
  costume, 118
  death, 25, 36, 51, 151
  doofus, 31, 33, 45, 48, 75, 80
  duplicate, 35, 52, 137
  father, 28, 48, 49, 77, 123, 125
  hologram, 1, 9, 15, 25, 26, 29, 30, 34, 111, 134, 141, 142, 144, 149, 151
  middle name, 36, 49
  mother, 65, 79, 109, 125
  nickname, 47, 51, 86, 102, 149
  relationship with Lister, 23, 27, 30, 50, 140, 141
  sex life, 33, 34, 49, 50, 51, 55, 76, 86, 106, 121, 127, 144
Rimmer, Frank, 49, 79, 86, 88
Rimmer, Howard, 79, 151
Rimmer, John, 79
Rimmerworld (**Red Dwarf** episode), 137, 150
ring modulator, 17
Rio Bravo (1959 movie), 146
Ripley's Believe it or Not (US TV series), 105
Rising Damp (UK TV series), 87, 115, 122

Risk (board game), 111
Roadrunner (cartoon character), 76
Robeson, Paul, 107
Robinson Crusoe (1719 novel), 150
RoboCop (1987 movie), 59, 68, 104, 126
robot(s), 4, 18, 38, 58, 59, 60, 71, 88, 111, 122
   see also mechanoid(s), skutter(s), waxdroid(s)
Robson, Samantha, 141
Rock Follies (UK TV series), 43
Rocket (camera operator), 115
rogue Simulant *see* Simulant(s)
Rolls-Royce, 81
Roman(s), 144
Ross, David, 38, 46, 47, 58, 59, 78, 96
Ross, Diana, 43
Ross, Shirley, 51
Rossiter, Leonard, 9
Rowland, Tiny, 73
Roxy Music (band), 134
Royal Academy of Dramatic Art, 5, 7
Royal Air Force, 4
Royal Mail, 49
Royal Shakespeare Company, 7, 78
royalties, 68
Rozhenko, Alexander (*Star Trek*), 146
rule one of show business, 91, 93
rules (self-imposed), 4, 18, 31, 38, 72
Run for Your Wife (play), 53
running gag, 141, 142
running order (of **Red Dwarf** episodes), 19, 27, 41, 51, 72, 96, 97–8, 100, 115, 118, 137
Russell, Jenna, 21

safety drill, 148
Salvation Army, 131
Samaritans, 87, 125
sandwich(es):
   bacon with mustard, 29
   chilli chutney fried egg, 50, 81
   Sugar Puffs, 124, 144
Sapphire & Steel (UK TV series), 85
Sartre, Jean-Paul, 30, 75
Satellite Show, The (UK TV series), 63
satellite television, 112–13
satire, 32

Saturday Live (UK TV series), 3, 8, 9, 53
Saunders, Jennifer, 2, 3, 6
Sayle, Alexei, 2
scar(s), 144
school, boarding, 15, 45
Schopenhauer, Arthur, 128
science, 20, 38, 49, 150
science fiction, 1, 3–6, 7, 18, 20, 21, 29, 33–4, 35, 38, 56, 58, 61, 77, 92, 104, 110, 114, 126, 148
Scott Fitzgerald (spaceship), 49
Scott, George C., 143
Scott, Robert Falcon, 76
scouter, 127
scouts *see* Space Scouts
script(s) (**Red Dwarf**), 1, 10, 12, 20, 23, 37, 54, 59, 60, 64, 66, 73, 86, 87, 94, 95, 98, 110, 114, 115, 116, 118, 129, 132, 133, 134, 136, 141, 149, 152
   draft, 4–9, 25, 56, 62, 135
   late, 68, 132, 137–8
   published in advance of transmission, 139
   rewrites, 18, 43, 132
   see also camera script
Scrubs (US TV series), 80
Second World War, 15, 58, 110
Secret Service, 143
See You Later, Alligator (song), 26
Seinfeld (US TV series), 10
Seksmisja (1984 movie), 57
Selby, 18
self-destruct, 80, 82
Sensational Reverse Brothers, 73
Serling, Rod, 85
set design, 39, 41, 45, 63–4, 92, 95, 100, 133
   grey, 15–16, 19, 23–4
   including studio structure, 20, 39
sets (stored privately), 11
Sevenoaks, 135
sex (intercourse), 5, 24, 49, 50, 51, 55, 76, 78, 83, 86, 106, 108, 121, 122, 127, 141, 144, 147
sexism, 50, 56
Shah, Eddie, 73
Shake and Vac, 51
Shakespeare, William, 32, 57, 76, 128

Shakespeare, Wilma, 57
Shapiro, Helen, 28
She's Out of My Life (song), 76
Shelley, Mary, 25
Sherlock Holmes, 43
Shepperton Studios, 92, 96, 136, 137
sheriff, 145
Shields, Brooke, 49
shoes (with souls), 54
shoetrees, 51
Shooting of Dan McGrew, The (poem), 146
shotgun (sawn-off), 88
shower, 30
silicon heaven, 87, 88
silicon hell, 150
Silver, Long John, 105
Simpson, Alan, 3, 9
Simulant(s), 105, 106, 123–4, 145, 149, 150, 151
   rogue, 147
Sinatra, Frank, 28
Sinclair C5, 19–20
Sinclair, Clive, 19
Sinclair ZX81, 53, 141
Sindy (toy), 76
Sirens (mythical creatures), 141
Sistine Chapel, 124
sitcom, 1, 2, 3, 6, 10, 37, 42, 65, 79–80, 113, 115, 127, 143
   British vs American, 24
sketch (broken comedy), 2, 3, 46, 58, 113, 152
Skipper (nickname for Lister), 109
Skipper (**Red Dwarf** episode), 33
Skippy the Bush Kangaroo (Australian TV series), 109
skutter(s), 18, 25, 26, 30, 49, 54, 56, 57, 80, 131
Sky TV, 112–13
slapstick, 105, 135, 143, 145, 148
Slattery, Tony, 47
slide rule (speaking), 25
slide show, 86, 105
   see also 35mm slide(s)
smeg, 121, 130
   better dead than, 152
   word coined, 5, 6
Smeg and the Heads, 68

Smeg Ups, 117, 151
smegazine *see Red Dwarf Smegazine*
smeghead, 5, 52, 148, 152
Smith, Arthur, 64
Smith, Mel, 2
smoking *see* cigarette
Smurfs, The, 56
snake, 79
soap flakes, 59, 63, 64
socket (groinal), 79
solid hallucinations *see* hallucinations (solid)
Someone to Watch Over Me (song), 51
Son of Cliché (UK radio series), 3, 25, 36, 43
song, 3, 20, 21, 26, 28, 29, 43–4, 51, 55, 68, 83, 85, 87, 91, 103, 109, 136, 141
   see also music, theme song
Sons of Gordon Gekko, The (band), 68
sound effects, 26, 80, 82
   see also dubbing
soup:
   chicken, 26
   gazpacho, 35
   primordial, 139
South Africa, 132
Southwark, 134
space, 1, 3, 20, 21, 23, 26, 33, 41, 49, 58, 74, 77, 86, 100, 102, 104, 106, 122, 123, 142, 147, 149, 152
Space Adventure (tourist attraction), 44
space bike, 47
Space Corps, 79, 83, 126, 127, 128, 141, 148
space heroes, 96
space mumps, 104
space pneumonia, 33
Space Scouts, 54
spaceship, 16, 21, 26, 29, 58, 75, 114
   invisible, 73, 74
   with sofa and French windows, 6
spacesuit, 21, 41
Spain, 103
Spall, Timothy, 118, 130
Spam, 25
Spanish Detective, The, 3
Spanners, 97, 109
Sparkes, John, 116

special effects, 18, 20, 21, 34, 42, 132, 137, 151
Spector, Phil, 20
Spectre of the Gun (*Star Trek*), 146
speed of light *see* light speed
speed run, 10
spelling mistake, 29, 47, 54
Spiner, Brent, 146
Spitting Image (UK TV series), 2, 3, 5, 7, 15, 17, 37, 113, 132
split-screen, 29, 36, 93, 108, 114, 117, 129, 134, 152
Spock, Mr (*Star Trek*), 78, 81, 144, 146
Spot the Dog (book series), 46
Spotlight (directory of actors), 17
sprite (computer), 146
sprouts, 128
Squarial, 112
Squirrel Nutkin, 103
St Elsewhere (US TV series), 101
stand-in, 62, 137
stand-up comedy *see* comedian
Star Cops (UK TV series), x
Star Trek (US TV series), 6, 55, 57, 81, 88, 102, 129, 131, 144, 146, 151
  with jokes, x, 3, 142
Star Trek IV: The Voyage Home (1986 movie), 73
Star Trek: The Next Generation (US TV series), 33, 51, 73, 101–102, 105, 115, 146, 147
Star Wars (1977 movie), 21, 73
Star Wars (media franchise), 4, 52, 126
Starbug (spaceship), 63, 72, 73, 74, 75, 77, 80, 96, 97, 106, 109, 121, 122, 123, 126, 127, 130, 132, 138, 140, 142, 143, 144, 146, 147, 148, 152
Starr, Ringo, 57
stasis, 12, 24, 25, 29, 33, 47, 152
Stasis Leak (**Red Dwarf** episode), 41, 51, 82, 84, 107, 133
Steel, Mark, 68
Steer, Bill, 68
Steptoe and Son (UK TV series), xii, 3, 5, 23
Steptoe in space, xii, 3, 23, 58, 77
Stevenson, Robert Louis, 105, 129
Stewart, Patrick, 146
stock footage, 111, 150

Stoker, Bram, 126
Stop Thief (*The Brittas Empire*), 87
Strange Case of Dr Jekyll and Mr Hyde (1886 novel), 129
Strauss, Johann, 102
strawberry, 130
Street-Porter, Janet, 136
strike, 11, 17, 21
stroke(s), 123, 151
structure (plot), 3, 50, 66, 79–80, 102, 149
  see also A-plot vs B-plot
studio, 10–11, 16, 17, 18, 19, 20, 21, 28, 39, 42, 44, 67, 77, 92, 95, 114, 134, 137, 138, 149
  see also audience, Oxford Road, Shepperton
stunt(s), 42, 64, 74, 143
submarine, 15
Sudden Impact (1983 movie), 81
Sugar Puffs, 124
Sunbury Pump House, 95
Super Bowl, 74, 148
Superman II (1980 movie), 125
Surrey, 92, 137
SVC Television, 133
Swamp Thing (comics character), 103
swearing, 4–5, 62, 148

Tales of the Riverbank (UK TV series), 101–102
Talkie Toaster, 19, 27, 96, 106
Taming of the Shrew, The (play), 57
tank top(s), 143
tapas, 103
Tarantino, Quentin, 126
tarantula(s), 126, 130
TARDIS, 21
Tate Modern, 134
tattoo, 153
Tau, Captain, 4
tax *see* Inland Revenue, 49
taxi, 98, 143
Taxi (US TV series), 8
Taylor, A.J.P., 124
telegraph poles, 109
teleporter, 111, 147, 150, 151
TelePrompTer *see* autocue
telescope, 51

telethon, 124
Television Centre, 92
Tension Sheet, 84
Terminator, The (1984 movie), 87, 88, 105, 124, 126
Terra Nova (expedition), 107
Terrorform (**Red Dwarf** episode), 116, 117, 136, 149
Terry and June (UK TV series), 2
Tess of the D'Urbervilles (1891 novel), 55
tetchy, 128
Tetteh-Lartey, Alex, 98
text adventure *see* adventure game
Thanks for the Memory (**Red Dwarf** episode), 41, 51, 76, 81, 144
The Silencers (1966 movie), 125
theme song (**Red Dwarf**), 20–1, 69, 71, 145, 147
 Hammond organ version, 109
 sung by 'Elvis', 111
 see also music, song
Thing (*The Addams Family*), 126
Thing from Another World, The (1951 movie), 76, 79
Third Man, The (1949 movie), 92
This is Your Life (UK TV series), 2
This Morning with Anne and Nick (UK TV series), 136
Three Doctors, The (*Doctor Who*), 36
Three Musketeers, The (1844 novel), 126
Three of a Kind (UK TV series), 2, 5
Thunderbirds (UK TV series), 126
Tiger (nickname), 51
Tikka to Ride (**Red Dwarf** episode), 83, 85, 106
TikTok, 1
time dilation, 150
Time of Passage (1964 short story), 74
time travel, 27, 28, 41, 53, 67–8, 72, 82, 84, 85, 116
Timeslides (**Red Dwarf** episode), 144, 153
timetable (revision), 30
Timewave (**Red Dwarf** episode), 129
tin soldiers, 76
Titanic, RMS, 109
title sequence *see* credits (opening/closing)
toaster *see* Talkie Toaster
Today (newspaper), 73

Todhunter, 4, 10
Tongue Tied (song), 43–4, 57
Top Gun (1986 movie), 109
Top of the Pops (UK TV series), 44, 151
Top Secret! (1984 movie), 74
Torvill and Dean, 146
Total Immersion Video Game, 39, 48, 118, 131, 146–7, 150
Toussaint, Lorraine, 4
Toy Story (1994 movie), 133
traffic cone, 88
traffic warden (small, off-duty, Czechoslovakian), 101
train, 7, 18, 22, 44
transmission order *see* running order
transphobia, 108
transportation, 4, 7, 18, 19, 22, 40, 41, 44, 47, 61, 66, 72, 73, 98, 110, 120, 131, 143
transvestite, 30
Tranter, Pete, 140
 see also Pete Tranter's sister
Treasure Island (1882 novel), 105
Trial, The (1925 novel), 105
triplicator, 130
Triumph of the Will (1935 movie), 85
Troi, Deanna (*Star Trek: The Next Generation*), 146
Tron (1982 movie), 146
Tucker, Mike, 116
tuna, 65
Twain, Mark, 153
Tweety Pie, 110
Twilight Zone, The (US TV series), 85
Twin Peaks (US TV series), 118
two men who hate each other, 33, 77, 101, 127, 128, 147
Two Ronnies, The (UK TV series), 2, 57, 113

Ullman, Tracey, 2, 5
Uncle Rob (boring), 94
United Nations, 97
United States *see* America
University of Southern California, 1
Unspeakable One, The, 116
Ustinov, Peter, 81

vacuum, 20

Index

Valentine's Day, 97
van Dohlen, Lenny, 118
Varley, John, 146
VCR, Japanese, 148
Verhoeven, Paul, 104
VHS, 36, 40, 44, 69, 73, 114
   Red Dwarf episodes released on, 78, 91, 98, 99
Vice Versa (novel/movie), 81
video effects, 26, 29, 36, 47, 49, 55, 57, 68, 72, 78, 85, 86, 93, 94–5, 106, 107, 125, 129, 132, 134, 141, 151, 153
   on Holly, 17, 26
video game, 51, 52
   see also adventure game, Total Immersion Video Game
Vimto, 88
vindaloo, 142, 143
Virgil (Roman poet), 124
Virgin (media company), 112
virtual reality, 146
virus:
   computer, 145
   fictional, 20, 33, 62, 95, 127–8
   real, 95
Vocoder, 69
Volkswagen, 76
von Stauffenberg, Claus, 83
von Sydow, Max, 146
Voter Colonel, 130
Voyage of the Dawn Treader, The (1952 novel), 85
Vulcan Neck Pinch, 144

Wailing Wall, 131
Waiting for God (**Red Dwarf** episode), 15, 18, 27, 35, 36, 45, 47, 50, 80, 87, 106
Waiting for Godot (play), 32
Walker, Jeffrey, 68
Wall of Sound, 20
Walt Disney *see* Disney (animation studio)
war, 4, 15, 32, 58, 110, 143, 148
Ward, Burt, 111
warm-up (comedian), 16, 19, 20, 64, 98
Warner Bros., 93
Warrington, Don, 115, 121
watch (wrist), 53, 148
Wax, Ruby, 7, 39, 68, 86, 113

waxdroid(s), 77, 110
Wayne, John, 30, 31, 32, 146
weather, 40, 49, 126, 137
weathergirl, 142, 153
Wells, John, 36
Werner, Oskar, 144
West Side Story (musical), 76
West, Adam, 111
Western (genre), 135–6, 145–7
Westworld (1973 movie), 110, 111
What a guy, 36
What Bike magazine, 124
What's My Line (UK TV series), 2
Where No Man Has Gone Before (*Star Trek*), 102
Which magazine, 128
Whippey, Jem, 65, 69
whisky, 35
white hole (fictional space phenomenon), 91, 106, 107
White Midget (name for spaceship), 63
Whitehouse, Mary, 113
Who's Who, 124
wig, 96, 118
Wild One, The (1953 movie), 47
Wilder, Billy, 75
Williams, Hugh, 7
Williams, Lia, 81
Williams, Mark, 24, 41, 54
Williams, Nigel, 134, 142
Williams, Sabra, 41
Wilton, Nick, 3
wine bar, 103
Winnie-the-Pooh, 110
Wizard of Oz, The (1939 movie), 57, 131
Wizard of Oz, The (book series), 36, 49
Wodehouse, P.G., 104
Wogan (UK TV series), 8, 113
Wooster, Bertie, 104
Worf (*Star Trek: The Next Generation*), 146
World Party (song), 136
wormskin rug, 141
worry balls *see* Chinese worry balls
Wouk, Herman, 55, 76
Wow Show, The, 20
Wragg, Peter, 21, 41, 59, 63, 93, 116, 136, 137

Wrinkles (UK radio series), 2, 38
Wyndham, John, 36
Xanadu, 84, 86
Xenomorph, 79

Yates, Lise, 41, 50
Yes Minister (UK TV series), 5
Yom Kippur, 113

Young Ones, The (UK TV series), 2, 3, 7, 20, 66
YouTube, 1
yo-yo, 32
Yuppie, 1, 146

Z Cars (UK TV series), 18
ZX81 *see* Sinclair ZX81

Dear Reader,

We hope you have enjoyed this book, but why not share your views on social media? You can also follow our pages to see more about our other products: facebook.com/penandswordbooks or follow us on Twitter @penswordbooks

You can also view our products at www.pen-and-sword.co.uk (UK and ROW) or www.penandswordbooks.com (North America).

To keep up to date with our latest releases and online catalogues, please sign up to our newsletter at: www.pen-and-sword.co.uk/newsletter

If you would like a printed catalogue with our latest books, then please email: enquiries@pen-and-sword.co.uk or telephone: 01226 734555 (UK and ROW) or email: Uspen-and-sword@casematepublishers.com or telephone: (610) 853-9131 (North America).

We respect your privacy and we will only use personal information to send you information about our products.

Thank you!